M000223510

DITCHING IMPOSTER SYNDROME

HOW TO FINALLY FEEL GOOD ENOUGH AND
BECOME THE LEADER YOU WERE BORN TO BE

CLARE JOSA

Dedication:
For everyone who has ever lost sleep, worrying that someone might find
out they're not good enough.

If that's you, believe me: you are!

And by the end of this book, I hope you'll believe it, too.
x Clare

© Clare Josa, 2019

Published by Beyond Alchemy Publishing, UK.

Book's Website: www.DitchingImposterSyndrome.com

A CIP catalogue record for this title is available from the British Library.

Paperback ISBN 978-1908854964

Also available in hardback, eBook and audio book.

For bulk orders, please visit www.clarejosa.com/contact-clare/

The right of Clare Josa to be identified as the Author of the Work has been asserted by her, in accordance with the Copyright, Designs and Patent Act 1988.

All rights reserved. No part of this publication may be reproduced, stored in a retrieval system, or transmitted, in any form or by any means, without the prior written permission of the Author.

Cover design by Jacquie O'Neill: www.jacquieoneill.com

Printed and bound in Great Britain by Clays Ltd, Elcograf S.p.A.

Limit of liability:

The advice in this book is intended for educational purposes only, and is only for personal use. This book is not a substitute for professional, individual advice, especially if you are suffering from symptoms of clinical anxiety or depression. Please consult your chosen medical professional if you have any questions about whether working on Imposter Syndrome is appropriate for you.
Just as the Author and Publisher would not claim the credit for the successes you create, as a result of reading this book, so they do not accept responsibility or liability for the effects of your actions. If you are in doubt as to the suitability of the concepts in this book for your individual situation, always consult your chosen professional, first.   ·

Every effort has been made to ensure all information in this book is correct. Any unintended errors will be corrected in the next edition.

Opening Note:
The techniques in this book are intended for personal use only and reading the book does not qualify you to use these techniques with clients. To become a certified Imposter Syndrome Coach™, either in your own coaching business or as an internal corporate coach, please visit the link in the Readers' Resource Vault to apply for the certification programme. This is also where you will find a directory of approved, certified coaches, if you want one-to-one support. (www.DitchingImposterSyndrome.com/vault/)

Permissions:
You have my total permission to write in this book, to scribble notes, to use your highlighter pen, to jot down ideas, to make it your Imposter Syndrome ditching workbook – as long as it didn't come from a library or was borrowed from your bestie.

You also have my permission to try everything on for size and only to keep that which resonates for you – each of us is on a unique journey. All I ask is that you *genuinely* try everything out, rather than dismiss things because they contradict how you have assumed life works; after all, you're not going to ditch Imposter Syndrome if you subconsciously cling to the old ways of doing and thinking about things.

Also by Clare Josa

Non-Fiction
Dare To Dream Bigger
The Little Book Of Daily Sunshine
52 Mindful Moments
A Year Full Of Gratitude
28 Day Meditation Challenge

Novels
You Take Yourself With You
First, Tell No Lies

Who Am I To Have Imposter Syndrome?

The Silent Epidemic

*I don't know how I got to be where I am, but
I hope no one finds me out.
Everyone else has got their stuff sorted. I'm
the only one who feels like this.*

I was the biggest fraud in the world.

The only person on the planet who knew I was faking it – winging it – achieving success by pure luck – was me. I couldn't believe I had pulled the wool over everyone's eyes. I hadn't intended to. They actually thought I was good at my job. They even promoted me to Senior Engineer. Five years ahead of schedule.

The stress of keeping up appearances was making me die inside. I was terrified I would finally slip up and show them I wasn't as good as they thought I was; that my luck would break.

So I worked 14-hour days and did the work of three people, hoping that might buy me some goodwill slack, once the truth inevitably came out.

Then, one day as I walked back from the coffee machine with a friend who was the only other female engineer in the factory, I plucked up the courage to ask her a question that had been keeping me awake at night for months.

I was terrified she would judge me; but I knew I had to talk to someone. I couldn't keep pretending things were ok. My heart was racing, my mouth had gone dry and I held my breath as I waited for her to answer my question:

"Do you ever worry that they'll *find you out* and realise that you don't *belong* here? That you're not up to the job?"

She stopped walking, looked me in the eyes, and I saw the scared expression on her face:

"You, too?" she whispered.

It was only years later that I discovered this feeling had a name: Imposter Syndrome, and that it was responsible for stress, anxiety, performance issues and career-trashing across the world. By that point, Imposter Syndrome had contributed to me leaving my much-loved engineering career to become the Head of Market Research for one of the world's most disruptive corporations - a role where I never once felt Imposter Syndrome, for reasons we'll cover later.

Each person who struggles with Imposter Syndrome has a story with a variation on that theme. Maybe it was the promotion we now regret not going for, because we didn't think we were sufficiently qualified, even though our appraisals told us we were. Maybe it was being overlooked for a dream opportunity, because we had spent decades attributing our outward success to luck or timing or 'the team', rather than letting our talents shine. Maybe it was the time we had a brilliant idea, but didn't speak up in the meeting, leaving someone else to suggest one that was a pale comparison to ours, with them getting the praise and the credit.

If you have ever found yourself lying awake at 3 a.m. worrying about being 'found out', feeling like a fraud, wondering how you got to the position you're in, in your career or business, feeling secretly terrified that they will realise that you 'don't belong', and that everyone else knows more than you, then this book is for you.

The five-step Imposter Syndrome Ditching process you'll learn will guide you through practical inspiration and proven strategies for connecting with your *true* inner confidence and reaching your full potential, without 'pretending' or 'pushing on through'. I have developed and refined these techniques over the past decade-and-a-half of running my business and helping thousands of people, just like you, to tame their Inner Critic, ditch Imposter Syndrome and make the difference they are *really* here to make in the world.

We're going to be blending the best bits from the worlds of performance psychology and demystified neuroscience, so you understand why Imposter Syndrome keeps you stuck and how to turn around the negative thinking that can trigger it. This is combined with ancient wisdom from the worlds of yoga and meditation (I teach both) to give you insights that create breakthroughs in minutes, not months. My engineering background, specialising in Lean Manufacturing and Six Sigma, combined with my fifteen years as an NLP Trainer, means that the work I'm going to share with you is fluff-free and easy to learn.

In addition, I'm going to share what I have learned from leading the landmark 2019 Imposter Syndrome Research Study on how Imposter

Syndrome affects people's wellbeing, their performance, what triggers it, and how to clear it. As you'll discover, Imposter Syndrome goes beyond the realms of self-doubt or lack confidence. It's about how we see ourselves, at a 'who am I?' level, relative to what we want to achieve.

It's not something you can 'think' your way out of and it takes more than 'mindset' to sort it. Having a 'positive mental attitude' helps but it can be a sticky plaster[1] – a coping strategy that risks amplifying Imposter Syndrome, as we'll cover in due course.

This book will guide you through how to spot the warning signs and give you practical strategies to set yourself free from Imposter Syndrome – without pretending, white-washing or trying to succeed, *despite* it.

To get the most from our time together, please read this book in the order it is written. Each step builds on work from the previous step. You'll gain the most from this if you read the book with an open mind – I'm going to be challenging some common preconceptions that keep people stuck in the Imposter Syndrome cycle. And take the time to try each technique on for size – I guide you through how – rather than skimming over them. It's in experiencing those processes that you'll get the biggest benefits.

There are bonus resources in the 'Readers' Vault', which you can find here: www.DitchingImposterSyndrome.com/vault/

It's worth popping over there and registering for access now, so that you can easily download the addition support resources at the key points where they are mentioned in the book.

Ditching Imposter Syndrome will help you both at the 'emergency quick fix' level and the 'ditch it forever' level. Both of these are important, because there are times when you need to know how to press 'pause' in a hurry, and others when you need to do the deeper behind-the-scenes work to set yourself free.

By the end of our time together, you'll know how to deeply connect with your *true* inner confidence, without feeling like a fraud or subconsciously self-sabotaging your success. If those secret 3 a.m. self-talk gremlins rear their ugly heads, you'll know exactly how to handle them. And you'll have taken practical steps towards becoming the leader you were born to be, letting your inner light shine. It's time to set yourself free – to ditch Imposter Syndrome.

---

[1] 'Band Aid' for my American friends! I'm a Brit and you'll see UK spelling and terminology in here. Plus you'll see we talk about 'imposter' rather than 'impostor'. That's not a typo. Both spellings are correct, but 'imposter' is more common in the UK, where I live, so that's the one we'll be using. I hope that's ok with you.

What The Experts Say

*"Research is formalised curiosity. It is
poking and prying with a purpose."*
Zora Neale Hurston

Imposter Syndrome: What Is It?

The term Imposter Phenomenon was coined by two American psychologists: Dr Pauline Clance and Dr Suzanne Imes, back in 1978. They described it as: 'an internal experience of intellectual phoniness that those who feel fraudulence and worthlessness have in spite of outstanding academic or professional accomplishment'.

In 1985, Joan Harvey and Cynthia Katz conducted research on Imposter Syndrome, which they termed the Imposter Phenomenon. They described it as: 'a psychological pattern rooted in intense, concealed feelings of fraudulence when faced with achievement tasks'.

And the Cambridge English Dictionary tells us that it is: 'the feeling that your achievements are not real or that you do not deserve praise or success'.

But none of these definitions really helps us with the "Oh, yes! That's me!" lightbulb we need, to recognise that Imposter Syndrome might be affecting us and to start turning it around.

Sheryl Sandberg, Chief Operating Officer of Facebook, describes it as: 'capable people being plagued by self-doubt'.

More recently, Michelle Obama has described it as:

*"The question I ask myself - 'am I good
enough?' - that haunts us, because the
messages that are sent from the time we
are little is: maybe you are not, don't reach
too high, don't talk too loud."*

These are descriptions that more of us can identify with, taking out the academic jargon.

In their 1985 book on their research (*If I'm So Successful, Why Do I Feel Like a Fake? The Impostor Phenomenon*) Harvey and Katz proposed that all three of the following primary conditions must be met for the Imposter Phenomenon to be confirmed:

1. the belief that you got where you are by fooling other people
2. the fear of being exposed as an imposter – a fraud
3. the inability to attribute your achievements to internal qualities such as your abilities or intelligence

However, my former corporate career, my fifteen years of running a business, my work with thousands of students and clients on this topic, combined with the 2019 Imposter Syndrome Research Study have shown me that this is not the case: any one of these aspects is sufficient for the behaviours and self-talk associated with Imposter Syndrome to kick in.

Here's how I define Imposter Syndrome:

Imposter Syndrome happens when there is a mismatch between who you see yourself as currently being, and who you think you need to be to achieve or create a goal, despite the evidence that you're more than capable.

This is effectively the 'Imposter Syndrome Gap'. Imposter Syndrome is a subconscious, identity-level issue – hence the "who am I, to...?" question that runs so frequently in our self-talk when Imposter Syndrome strikes.

What do I mean about imposter syndrome being an 'identity-level' issue? Think for a moment about the kinds of words we use when we're talking to ourselves about Imposter Syndrome:

Who am I to do that?
What if they find me out?
What if they realise I am a fraud?
What if they spot that I don't belong here?

So much of our Imposter Syndrome self-talk vocabulary is about who we **are**, not what we **do**.

And when we're talking to ourselves like that, it's about how we see ourselves, as a person, not our thoughts or feelings or actions or mindset. Imposter Syndrome isn't a 'mind-trap' or 'mindset' issue. It's about *who* we see ourselves as *being* – an identity-level issue.

The fears and limiting beliefs that support Imposter Syndrome are often illogical, irrational and evidence-free. These trigger behaviour that can lead to self-sabotage, competition-avoidance, anxiety, depression and worse, yet we keep ignoring it.

Those most likely to struggle with Imposter Syndrome look outwardly successful, but you wouldn't want to be listening to their inner dialogue, as they lie awake at night, worrying about being found out as 'faking it'.

How Many People Are Struggling With Imposter Syndrome?

The 2019 Imposter Syndrome Research Study made it clear that Imposter Syndrome is a well-concealed blight on people's lives. The respondents were self-selecting, but contained a wide variety of people, including those who didn't have Imposter Syndrome. Two studies have been carried out in recent years to assess the percentage of the total population that struggles with Imposter Syndrome and the results were 62% and 70%, so it's fair to estimate that two thirds of those around us have struggled with it, to some degree.

According to this data and my research study, this would indicate that about one third of both men and women are struggling with Imposter Syndrome on a *daily* or *regular* basis – enough for it to have a measurable impact on their performance and mental health. A further quarter of people find it sometimes gets in their way. Yet their cries for help and understanding were going unheeded.

I decided to run this research study because it was getting tedious hearing high-level decision-makers in organisations tell me they didn't think Imposter Syndrome was an issue; that if someone in their organisation had it, they would ask for help; that it wasn't affecting their teams or their business. My fifteen years of working in this field and my corporate years before that meant I knew this wasn't true.

I looked for studies to back up my instincts and couldn't find them. Nearly everything we knew about Imposter Syndrome came from small-scale studies with low sample sizes or from surface-level opinion polls.

I decided to create the research study to provide the data we so desperately needed. I put on my former Head of Market Research hat and designed a study that combined depth interviews, focus-group-style discussions and a specially designed questionnaire, completed by respondents across industries and in companies from one-man-bands to FTSE-100. I'll be sharing key findings with you over the course of this book and you can read the White Paper from the research in your Readers' Resource Vault[2].

The main – and most shocking – conclusion of this research is that a huge proportion of people are struggling in silence with Imposter Syndrome – both men and women – and that it is affecting their performance, their mental and emotional health, their relationships and even their career. Many people I talk to either haven't heard of Imposter Syndrome or think it's just a trendy new form of self-doubt for the 'snowflake generation'. This couldn't be further from the truth. Imposter Syndrome is a silent epidemic that we ignore at our peril.

What Imposter Syndrome Isn't:

It isn't a clinical condition, which is what the term 'syndrome' would normally imply, which is why some use the phrase 'The Imposter Phenomenon' instead. A psychiatrist isn't going to diagnose you with it. A doctor won't give you time off work for it. That doesn't mean it doesn't feel real for you, if you have it.

It's about more than 'self-doubt', as we'll soon discuss. Some of the most confident and competent people I have ever met have been kept awake every night by Imposter Syndrome. They just had very good coping strategies, which is why no one was noticing. But I want more for you than 'coping' and having to put up with this.

Imposter Syndrome isn't a predictor of performance, as sometimes claimed in articles, because those without it often out-perform those with it, for reasons we'll discuss in the next section.

And it is not a useful way of keeping your ego in check. People often tell me they don't want to let go of 'my Imposter Syndrome' (turning it into a possession, which is a really bad idea), because it keeps them from bragging. This is a particular concern for Brits, where it is culturally less

---

[2] Readers' Resource Vault:
www.DitchingImposterSyndrome.com/vault/

acceptable to shout about your achievements than, say, in the USA. But it's rubbish to claim that Imposter Syndrome is the antidote to or a preventative against being 'big-headed'. Humility, compassion and a sensibly-sized ego will keep you humble. Denial of your competence – your achievements – and discounting praise is not humility. It's Imposter Syndrome.

And running that pattern makes it much more likely you won't have achievements to brag about.

Imposter Syndrome is never useful or necessary.

In fact, when someone tries to cling to Imposter Syndrome, it's usually a warning sign that there is a hidden fear running under the surface that needs to be dealt with, because they are subconsciously choosing to sabotage their success.

In the business world, we're comfortable talking about confidence or self-doubt and perhaps even having training or coaching to help with it. Being sent on time management or presentation skills training is a routine part of team development. And as you rise through the ranks, leadership and people management training slot into your schedule. But:

The one last taboo is Imposter Syndrome. It's the final frontier of the personal performance journey.

No one wants to talk about it. And because no one else does, we fall for the myth that it's just us with the problem – and everyone else has their sh*t together. We convince ourselves that we are the only one who is lying awake in the dark of the night, fretting that 'they' might find us out, pushing ourselves to work even harder to prevent the one mistake that might make them spot we're a fraud.

Imposter Syndrome can be invisible. Yet it trashes careers and businesses every day.

We don't realise that every boardroom has a generous helping of well-concealed Imposter Syndrome or that the staff canteen would be nearly empty if everyone who had once struggled with Imposter Syndrome didn't show up.

Those struggling with Imposter Syndrome are often seen by others as successful high-achievers. And because they tend to work hard and be perfectionists (more on this later), their bosses see them as coping fine. It's only when Imposter Syndrome becomes 'maladaptive' that problems start to become obvious to the outside world.

And there's another incentive for bosses not to want to talk about this: so many of them are struggling with it, too. Having open conversations about the fear of being found out as not belonging is a Pandora's box that few have the courage to open.

People are scared to admit that Imposter Syndrome exists – and that's not just in the corporate world.

In fifteen years of running my business, it's only in the last eighteen months that I have seen entrepreneurs start to admit how much they struggle with Imposter Syndrome. Podcast interviews on Imposter Syndrome will often see a spike in downloads, because people are finally getting out into the open a topic that they have been hating having to deny for so long.

When we keep it secret and struggle in silence with Imposter Syndrome, we add shame to the pain.

Often, simply having the courage to start to talk with your colleagues and leaders about Imposter Syndrome can be immensely healing, as you realise at least half of the people you are working with are feeling the same way as you do. It doesn't matter how confident they might seem, their 3 a.m. self-talk is just like yours. The relief that brings is incredible, as I found when I opened up to my friend, at the start of this book.

When leaders deny people the opportunity to have this conversation, they are reinforcing the guilt and shame that Imposter Syndrome can create. Ignoring the costs to individuals and businesses, which we will come to on page 50, is damaging for everyone. It's the same crazy logic I hear from CEOs who don't want to invest in staff development, in case their staff then leave.

Those in our teams who struggle with Imposter Syndrome try to hide it, sometimes hiding mistakes or even blaming others for them, to protect themselves from their 'mind-story fears'.

'Mind-Story' Vs 'Legitimate' Fears

I call the thoughts that are about a genuine danger our 'legitimate fears'. A legitimate fear is walking along a cliff edge on a windy day.

I call fear-thoughts that are created by going over past events or possible future events are 'mind-story fears'. A mind-story fear is worrying about whether you'll mess up that presentation next week. Your body can't tell the difference between these two types of fear and obliges by setting off the mind-body-emotion stress cycle required for survival. You'll learn how to tame your mind-story fears in Step Two.

We live in a society that demands authenticity, yet we fight to hide our vulnerability, for fear of being judged – or fired or shunned or rejected. We only show our confident, strong side, living in secret terror that we are where we are because of some one-off fluke or timing or luck – or because 'they will realise they made a mistake' in choosing us.

Nobody knows how isolated we feel, as we assume that we really are the only person going through this; after all, how could 'real' successful people possibly experience this?

We fret, worry, stress, and replay self-talk stories about every tiny piece of evidence that proves we're not up to the job; that our boss and clients are misguided in thinking we're doing well.

Can you imagine a working environment where people feel free to talk openly, without fear of judgement, about Imposter Syndrome? Where we could be honest about how it makes us feel? Where we could feel safe to be who we really are?

Until we move towards that place, Imposter Syndrome will continue to cost businesses billions each year in high-return risks their teams don't take, performance issues from anxiety and fear, and brilliant team members who subconsciously turn into micro-managing bullies or even leave the company, because they secretly feel like a fraud.

We need to have the courage to speak up and to trust that we will be heard. The wave of relief that would spread through a business as people finally get to be honest about the challenges they are facing could be transformational.

Your Inner Critic On Steroids

My regular readers, students and clients know I'm always talking about taming your Inner Critic. It's that voice in your head that tells you all the bad stuff about who you are and what you can achieve.

It poops on your parade and squishes your most exciting dreams. It talks us out of golden opportunities that we later regret turning down. It tells us we're not good enough to reach for our goals. It keeps us awake in the middle of the night, worrying and stressing.

But your Inner Critic has got your best interests at heart.

Yes, I'm ducking behind this book right now to avoid the rotten tomatoes that could be lobbed my way for saying that. Your Inner Critic's biggest job is to protect you. I know it might not feel that way when your heart is singing the song of something exciting and that voice in your head is ranting about why it's the wrong thing to do; drowning out the part of you that wants to encourage you. Deep down, that mind-chatter is because part of you is secretly scared.

The actions we take depend on which inner voice wins.

One of your Inner Critic's mantras is that small is safe and growth is scary. It keeps check that you're not taking risks it might not approve of, or sticking your head above that parapet. And because 'safety' tends to get prioritised by the brain over 'success', the Inner Critic tends to win.

Surely It's Just A Trendy Form Of Self-Doubt?

I hear this in comments on social media posts, regularly. I did some informal research on Linked In recently and found that nearly everyone who responded believed they had Imposter Syndrome *because* they had negative self-talk and struggled with self-doubt. When I was doing the depth interviews for the 2019 Imposter Syndrome Study, I found similar results.

The thing is that self-doubt does not necessarily mean you are running Imposter Syndrome – they are two different beasts. Whilst self-doubt can be a symptom of Imposter Syndrome, you can have an unhealthy dose of self-doubt without fearing you'll be found out as a fraud. And a normally confident person can become paralysed by the fear of being found out as a fake – that they don't belong in the role they're in – if Imposter Syndrome strikes.

When it comes to Imposter Syndrome, you're no longer just looking at thoughts and actions – but at who you fundamentally believe you *are* and your existential fears. So your Inner Critic cranks things up to work with you to prevent an identity-level crisis.

*Imposter Syndrome is more than self-doubt in a spiky suit. It's not about your beliefs about what you can or can't **do**. It's driven by who you think you **are**.*

That's why Imposter Syndrome wakes you up at 3 a.m. like no 'simple' worry ever could.

Self-doubt usually parties with your thoughts and beliefs about what you can *do*, with your inner dialogue telling you (thoughts) that you're not good enough at something (belief about a capability). When it's running at these levels, then cognitive approaches such as CBT (Cognitive Behavioural Therapy) can have some positive effect. Working with your mindset can help. Mindfulness can help. But they're all about helping with the *symptoms*, rather than clearing the root causes.

But Imposter Syndrome doesn't hang out there. It's lurking in the depths of 'who *am* I?', not 'what can I *do*?' self-talk discussions. At that deeper level, cognitive and mindset strategies don't touch the sides, because they're busy with your thinking mind, which is the surface level symptom of what's really driving the show. We'll cover this in detail when we get to the Imposter Syndrome Iceberg in the next section.

Self-doubt is about your skills and capabilities. Imposter Syndrome is about your sense of identity.

All of this is good news for people with self-doubt, because handling the surface level thoughts and beliefs that trigger us doubting ourselves can produce fast and effective results with your confidence. That's why in this book we will start with taming your Inner Critic (that negative self-talk) and ditching your limiting beliefs, as the foundations for your Imposter Syndrome journey. So if you've just realised you're dealing with self-doubt, not Imposter Syndrome, please keep reading!

For some, Imposter Syndrome can become a 'badge of honour', as they subconsciously justify its self-sabotage behaviours. When you combine this with the myths and fears that Imposter Syndrome is hard to shift or something we're stuck with, mistakenly picking up the Imposter Syndrome label helps no one.

So if you're realising that you *don't* have Imposter Syndrome, after all, and it's 'just' a case of self-doubt and needing to crank up your confidence, please celebrate! Steps Two and Three will really help you. But if you're realised you *do* struggle with Imposter Syndrome and that what you're running is about more than self-doubt and confidence, please throw a party right now, because you're in the perfect place to get this sorted.

Let's get started by finding out where it came from!

Where Did It Come From?

The Evolutionary View Of Imposter Syndrome

---

*"It's no use going back to yesterday,
because I was a different person then."
Alice In Wonderland ~Lewis Carroll*

There's more to Imposter Syndrome than a few moments of feeling bad or the occasional sleepless night.

Most people follow the well-intentioned advice of ignoring it, throwing in a few positive affirmations, then feeling the fear and pushing on through to do it anyway. But this can lead to anything from reduced performance to becoming a terrible boss to damaging a business, trashing productivity, self-sabotage and even mental and physical health issues.

How do things get that bad?

When Imposter Syndrome strikes, we think thoughts that come from a place of fear, which trigger the body's Sympathetic Nervous System – our fight-flight-freeze response – preparing us to defend ourselves from an external threat. The body gets us ready to battle the perceived threat, to run from it or to hide from it. The body's defence mechanisms fire off the stress hormones we need to increase our heart rate, forget about digesting that last chocolate bar, and run, if that's the decision the primal part of the brain makes.

The issue is that the body can't tell the difference between genuine threats and imaginary threats. It gets fired up on adrenalin and cortisol (stress hormones) whether our thoughts are about the sabre-toothed tiger that's prowling outside our hut or the mind-stories we're telling ourselves, worrying about the awful things that might happen if we are *finally* found out to be a fraud.

Imposter Syndrome triggers the part of the brain that wants to protect us from shame, embarrassment and rejection, just as much as it wants to keep us from being munched for lunch by a long-extinct enemy.

And those hormones that flood through the body cause other biochemical reactions, which are the triggers for our emotions, which feed our thoughts, which affect our bodies...

All of this happens at a subconscious level and is governed by the Autonomic Nervous System, which is responsible for processes we can't consciously control, like keeping the heart beating and hair growing. So if we have an Imposter Syndrome trigger, such as a big presentation to do, our stress response will be subconscious – automatic.

The fight-flight-freeze stress response is designed for emergencies when we might need to run faster than we've ever sprinted before, so the body – helpfully – diverts blood flow from non-essential processes (at least, they're not essential to running). It winds down processes like digestion, cellular-level renewal, clearing the body of toxins and all the other things that our Autonomic Nervous System (ANS) is responsible for. When we're relaxed and happy, the ANS keeps these processes ticking over happily.

Instead, the body cranks up our heart rate, perspiration, and blood flow to key muscle groups, so we're ready to run in an instant. It even shifts the balance of blood flow in the brain to focus on the primal part that is brilliant at figuring out how to stay alive. It knows we'll need to rely on our animal instincts to know what to do, so it diverts blood flow away from the pre-frontal cortex, which is responsible for processing data, drawing conclusions, and rational and creative thinking. The body knows that kind of thinking would be likely to slow down our decisions and would risk us meeting a sticky end.

When we run Imposter Syndrome-driven mind-story fears as the favourite radio station in our heads, humming away in the background without us even noticing, we're constantly triggering those stress responses, at low levels, running on adrenalin. We end up living in a state of chronic, low-level stress, which the body wasn't designed for. This leads to fatigue, inability to concentrate and other health issues.

That's why, if we get a shock or genuinely need our fight-flight-freeze response, most of us feel utterly exhausted and empty afterwards. It takes a lot of energy to maintain that high-alert state for more than a few minutes.

This cycle is meant to come back to equilibrium if our cortisol levels become too high. But when our stress becomes a chronic part of our daily lives, many of us become unconsciously addicted to the adrenalin and cortisol that accompany the body's Sympathetic Nervous System kicking off. This need for adrenalin to keep us going through the day can lead to adrenal fatigue, digestive issues, difficulty concentrating, exhaustion, irritability and stress-related illness.

Whereas the tiger might wander on past, distracted by a yummy looking antelope sprinting through the trees, allowing the body to stand down its panic stations, our mind-stories don't allow us to do that.

We go round the stress-thought merry-go-round, *what-if*-ing, analysing, second-guessing, imagining, constantly feeding those mind-story fears and maintaining that heightened fight-flight-freeze response for hours, days or even months, instead of minutes.

The long-term mind-story fears train us to worry more and to feel generally less confident (we're constantly mentally rehearsing our worst-case scenarios).

Hypervigilance – being in a constant state of high alert – can trigger anxiety and exhaustion. Our bodies are designed to handle this stress response for an hour or two and then to return back to balance – relaxed, but alert – to replenish our energy levels and go back to useful stuff like digestion and cellular-level healing. With chronic, long-term stress, they rarely get the chance to do this.

The chronic stress state means we regularly have less blood flow to the frontal cortex in the brain, because the body is prioritising the primal part that houses our animal instinct for survival. This – coupled with exhaustion – is why it can be hard to concentrate when we're worrying about being 'found out'. This leads to reduced performance and, ironically, increases the risk of *actually* being found out as not being good enough. So we try harder and trigger our inner perfectionism, to overcome our now well-founded fear that we may be revealed as having made mistakes.

It's easy to see how this behaviour can lead to poor productivity, burnout (see page 60), loss of confidence, anxiety and even depression.

It can also lead to us becoming a terrible boss (as we'll explore on page 36) and can lead to volatile behaviour that damages our relationships. In that section we'll also talk about how it leads to addictions, as a form of escapism, and how it can stall our professional and personal development.

All of these issues are made worse, more quickly, by pushing on through, *despite* Imposter Syndrome, effectively pretending it's not there, yet with it still triggering the Sympathetic Nervous System's stress response, without us realising. If we ignore the early warning signs, it has direct health costs for us as individuals, but it costs employers, too, which is why we need to open up the conversation and break the Imposter Syndrome taboo.

Where Did All Those Red Cars Come From?

The world is full of cars of many different colours – mainly silver – but if you buy a red car, suddenly there are red cars everywhere. As you sit behind the wheel of your shiny, red vehicle, it's as though someone went out with a paint can overnight and brightened up the colour balance on the roads, as yet another red car pulls up next to you at the lights.

You had no idea they were so common.

That's a part of your brain at work called the Reticular Activating System. Along with regulating wakefulness, it is responsible for filtering sensory information. You are bombarded with information from the outside (and inside) world. At any given time, your body is aware of the air pressure in your left ear, the blood flow in your right big toe, and the weight of a book in your hands.

But your conscious mind is – normally – wonderfully oblivious to this. Imagine a world where you had to squeeze all of that information through the queue in your thinking mind, which can only process about three pieces of information at a time.

Your Reticular Activating System (we'll call it RAS) filters out almost all of the information, flagging up only the essentials that are important to your conscious mind. The air pressure in your left ear only pops into your thinking mind when you're on an aeroplane that's coming in to land and you need to swallow or wiggle your jaw to equalise it. You're only aware of the blood flow in your right foot's big toe when you've been sitting weirdly for too long and it gets pins and needles. You only become aware of the weight of this book as you hold it one-handed and try to turn the page, whilst reaching for your mug for a quick sip.

How does your RAS decide what's important to you? Well, 'keep-me-safe' information gets straight through, unfiltered. Aside from that, it prioritises information you have told it is important to you. And one of the ways it does that is through your thought habits.

If you think a thought once, it passes on through – like the cuddly bear or food processor on the conveyor belt of the old Generation Game TV show or like fluffy clouds in a blue summer sky. If you *engage* with that thought, though, telling yourself a story about it, it can trigger chemical reactions in your body, which create emotions, which feed the thought and the emotions and those chemicals and so the cycle continues, until we either decide to move on to the next topic or we get distracted.

If you do that only once, those neural pathways that get created when your synapses fire don't do much. It's like walking through a field of waist-height grass once. Within a few hours, there will be no sign of your path as the grass springs back up.

But if you walk that path every day, multiple times a day, wearing heavy boots, after rain, and stomp with gusto, over time a path will appear. Do it often enough and the path becomes a permanent shortcut. Similarly, if you think a thought often enough, firing off intense emotions and diving into the drama of the story, it's like the muddy boots in that field. Adding in strong emotions to a thought creates a motorway in the neural pathways of your brain, changing your neurology, that becomes an autopilot response to a particular trigger.

So if you spend a lot of mind-story time, energy and emotions thinking about how you're bad at presenting (you're not – but I don't need you to believe me, yet), you'll have autopilot neural pathways like motorways in your brain, lurking in the background, ready to take traffic as soon as someone asks you to present... poised like a panther stalking its prey, with your Imposter Syndrome self-talk ready to kick off the fight-flight-freeze response in your body at the merest hint of the word 'presentation'.

And in such situations, your RAS is on standby to filter in all available evidence to support the belief that you're no good at presenting. So if your boss or client compliments you on your presentation, you will brush off the praise, waiting for the single 'but' that your RAS will send through with a fanfare of in-your-head trumpets to remind you that you were right – you *are* bad at it.

Why is this so important with Imposter Syndrome?

It's one of the reasons why external validation and feedback doesn't fix it. It doesn't matter how often we are told that we are doing a great job, if our RAS is set to filter through evidence to support the belief that we're a fake, that's what will get through. Your repeated Imposter Syndrome self-talk has trained your RAS to spot the sensory information that supports your secret fears.

The rest of this book is all about how to clear this, by the way, so please don't start beating yourself up.

Alas, there's more. These negative self-talk habits, which are training your RAS and setting up the autopilot motorways, also trigger emotions. Emotions are biochemical reactions in your body. There's evidence now that the body gets addicted to these chemical reactions, developing a tolerance of them, meaning we need to trigger stronger emotions to meet that need (more in the Readers' Resource Vault: www.DitchingImposterSyndrome.com/vault/)

The biochemical addictions that can be set up during a bout of Imposter Syndrome stay with you as autopilot habits, even once the phase has passed – unless you clear them out (and that's what you'll be doing in Step Two).

But for now, I'd like to invite you to play a game with me.

Which Came First: The Self-Talk Or The Fear?

There's an exercise I'd like you to try out.

Exercise: The Mind-Body Link

You'll need to be somewhere where you can move from sitting to standing without bumping into fellow commuters or crashing a car. So if you're reading this on a train or listening while you're driving, just imagine this for now and try it out properly later.

Start by saying to yourself – out loud if that's an option – the phrase "I am tired and weak." Put some effort into it. Give all of your attention to "I am tired and weak." Say it at least ten times.

Now try to stand up. Notice how that felt in your body.

As you're standing, give your body a shake to let go of that feeling.

Sit down again.

Now say to yourself, "I am powerful and strong!"

Give all of your attention to saying the words out loud. Let "I am powerful and strong" fill every cell in your body, expanding from the top of your head to the tips of your toes.

Say it at least ten times.

Now stand up.

What difference did you notice?

When I play with this in workshops, the 'tired and weak' round has people *heaving* themselves out of their chairs, often using their hands to push themselves up to standing. Every fibre of their being is screaming how tired they are. Then, when we swap to 'powerful and strong', the room is full of beaming faces as people almost leap across the room.

Your body feels every thought you think.
And it obeys, without questioning.

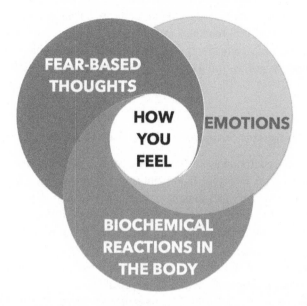

If you are feeding that mind-story about being tired or stupid or not good enough or a fraud, it will fire off the biochemical reactions to support that command, especially if it is preceded by "I am". (More on that on page 241). These biochemical reactions set off what we experience as emotions and the physical sensations they create in our bodies. And these feed the thoughts.

Most of us have mind-chatter running throughout our waking day, even if we're not consciously listening to it. It's like a radio station running in the background – always there, but we're not tuning in to what is being said; at least, not consciously.

But, given that your body hears every thought you think, if you are thinking happy thoughts, it fires off the biochemical reactions for 'happy', whether or not you're consciously paying attention to those thoughts. If you're thinking anxious thoughts, it does 'anxious'. You get the idea.

Sometimes it's only once we become aware of the emotion via the physical sensations in our bodies that we notice the thoughts. Sometimes our awareness of the thoughts comes first. So you might notice a tightness in your jaw and a heaviness in your stomach and then become aware of a fear-thought story going on in your head. Or you might have a fear-thought that suddenly sends ice-cold shivers through your body.

Which of these came first doesn't really matter, though it has kept centuries of philosophers in employment. What's important is to understand that your mind, body and emotions are linked. A thought can trigger those biochemical reactions in your body which create emotions which cause the body to respond with tension or relaxation, all of which feeds the thought stories. You'll learn how to press 'pause' on this in Step Two.

Why Does Imposter Syndrome Make Your Mind Go Blank?

When a fear-based thought-biochemical-response-emotions cycle kicks off, it sends us back into that fight-flight-freeze mode to keep us safe, whatever that means in that moment, calling in the Sympathetic Nervous System. As we discussed on page 21, the fight-flight-freeze response prioritises blood flow to the primal part of your brain that is on the look-out for perceived danger. It isn't so fussed about the frontal cortex area that analyses data and comes up with brilliant strategic ideas. Your body's fight-flight-freeze response is wired to keep you alive.

That is why when you're sitting in a meeting with, say, a client and they ask you a question that hits one of your autopilot triggers for Imposter Syndrome, your mind goes blank. The trigger hit your *'but if I give the wrong answer, they'll find me out'* autopilot, dragging you into your fight-flight-freeze response and doing that blood flow shift that turns your 'look how great I am at my job' bit of your brain to fog. You desperately want your brain to say something vaguely intelligent about the quarterly sales figures, but instead it's screaming the Imposter Syndrome equivalent of *"No! Look! Tiger! Teeth! Run!"*

This mind-body-emotions link can create fear-based cycles that restrict our behaviours. If our mind, body or emotions tell us something is scary, we're much less likely to do it, even if that 'scary' is only a mind-story fear.

The difficulty we have in concentrating on conceptual tasks when we're feeling stressed (low-level fear causing the Sympathetic Nervous System to divert blood flow to the primal part of the brain) means we develop a coping mechanism of working extra hard, pushing ourselves to perform, fighting our emotions, and being afraid of mistakes – so-called maladaptive perfectionism triggered by the 'fight' response (more on that in a moment!)

When we're drowning in overwhelm and secretly addicted to

'busyness', we're dancing around the task that is our red rag trigger for feeling like a fraud, dipping into it when we have to, but basically running away – the 'flight' response.

And when we effectively pretend the task isn't there and ignore it until we no longer have the choice, we're stuck in paralysis – the 'freeze' response – like the proverbial rabbit in headlights.

Which of these options we 'choose' – because it *is* a choice, at a subconscious level – comes down to our thought habits and how we have wired the brain's autopilot programmes to respond.

The brilliant news is that neuroplasticity – our ability to rewire our brains – means we can change this. It's the same process that means we can learn to ride a bike or drive a car or speak a language. If you have ever learned something new, then you can change your neurology, your beliefs, your RAS' filters, your thoughts and your behaviours. And I'll be teaching you how in Step Two.

So Imposter Syndrome is not in your imagination.

The purpose of this book is to guide you through how to ditch it in a way that's healthy and empowering; no more pretending or pushing on through, despite the effects that Imposter Syndrome is having on your emotional state, confidence and performance.

The Imposter Syndrome self-talk cycle reinforces those neural pathway autopilots and the filters in your RAS. It's the equivalent of paving those motorways in your brain with gold. This generates behaviours that include the Four Ps of Imposter Syndrome: Perfectionism, Procrastination, Paralysis and People-pleasing.

The Four Ps Of Imposter Syndrome

When going on a journey, it's easier to
follow a map than a photograph.

Imposter Syndrome doesn't come with a label on your forehead (thank Goodness), but there are some key indicators that can give you insights into whether you're running it and how it might be affecting you. The model I'm going to share with you in this section gives us understanding about the only information we have about a person – their behaviours. They can act like a map to help you to understand your Imposter Syndrome journey.

The 2019 Imposter Syndrome Research Study showed that how people talk about Imposter Syndrome falls roughly under the three categories identified by Harvey and Katz in 1985.

1. The belief that we got to where we are by fooling other people
What if they realise they made a mistake in hiring me?

2. The fear of being exposed as a fraud
What if they find me out?
Why if they realise I don't belong?

3. The inability to attribute your achievements to internal qualities
It was just luck / a fluke / timing!
Anyone could do it!

These three main categorisations from Harvey and Katz have formed the basis of many future research studies, but they miss out the most important element of Imposter Syndrome – how it is linked with our sense of self.

Whilst Harvey and Katz proposed that all three of these must be present at the same time for the Imposter Phenomenon to be confirmed, the 2019 Imposter Syndrome Research Study indicates that this is not the case. We feel the effects of Imposter Syndrome as soon as any *one* of these strikes.

There is also a major segment of Imposter Syndrome missing from the Harvey and Katz definitions – and according to the 2019 research respondents, it's a key way that we express and experience Imposter Syndrome:

Who am I to...?

38% of respondents expressed Imposter Syndrome with this identity-level phrasing. When we experience this, we don't feel like we're actively fooling anyone, we don't fear being exposed as a fraud and we haven't achieved anything to which we could refuse to attribute internal qualities. We have turned those fears into a block at the deepest level – who we see ourselves as being.

When someone is struggling with Imposter Syndrome it triggers their stress response, firing off cortisol and adrenaline from the fight-flight-freeze mechanism. This is designed to keep sabre-toothed tigers at bay. But when it comes out to play with Imposter Syndrome, the 2019 Research Study shows it creates one or more of four core behaviours. These are symptoms of Imposter Syndrome that correlate with the subconscious internal stress responses. They can be useful for helping someone – or their boss – to spot when help is needed to address this, before a person self-sabotages.

We don't ever know what is going on inside someone's head. But we can see their external behaviours. The Four Ps of Imposter Syndrome are useful indicators at a behavioural level of what is potentially running below the surface. They are Perfectionism, Procrastination, Paralysis and People-Pleasing. Let's cover each in turn.

Paralysis

Have you ever played 'hide and seek' with a 3-year-old? You know that thing they do where *they* are the one supposed to be hiding, but they stand somewhere obvious, with their hands over their eyes, singing 'you can't see me'?

Imposter Syndrome Paralysis is like that game of hide and seek. By covering our eyes – pretending we can't see the big, scary task we are secretly avoiding, because we're scared it will show the world we're not good enough – we believe we become invisible, too, so Imposter Syndrome won't catch us out. This relates to the 'freeze' response from our fight-flight-freeze options. We become the proverbial 'rabbit in the headlights', unable to move or take action on the task, in an effort to keep ourselves safe.

54% of those I surveyed, for whom Imposter Syndrome played a regular or major role in their life, described the 'who am I, to...?' paralysis as a key way they experience it. They talked about completely avoiding tasks, rather than dancing round the edges, as with procrastination. They described not taking up brilliant opportunities and leaving projects until it was almost too late to complete them. They use the ensuing adrenalin rush as leverage to get them pushing through their fears, despite Imposter Syndrome. Or they would consciously miss the deadline and then find an external circumstance or person to blame.

The 'Paralysis' version of Imposter Syndrome stops us from speaking our mind or sharing our opinions. It gets us turning down the perfect opportunities to shine, whether in the workplace or in the media. It stops us from publishing the book we were dreaming of or launching a high-impact project, because we don't see ourselves as being the kind of person who has 'permission' or who is 'good enough' to do that.

But where does that permission need to come from? The outside world is telling us that we *are* good enough, but we are refusing – or unable (remember the RAS on page 23?) – to hear its message.

When people talk about how Imposter Syndrome affects them, those running the paralysis pattern describe not starting projects that were important to them and ignoring offers that would excite them.

A classic example is the item that falls off your to do list every single day, until it's too late. Not completing projects is a classic Imposter Syndrome Paralysis response.

For Susan, a productivity trainer, this was a pitch for a training project that would have been a dream course for her to run. She was approached by a business she loved and they specifically wanted to work with her. But it would have involved foreign travel, major juggling of childcare and – if she did it wrong – it could have wrecked her relationship with the people working for that firm, many of whom were now personal friends. So she found that pitch slipping off her list each day, with each day's delay making it less likely that she would get the go-ahead.

She was paralysed by Imposter Syndrome in the form of 'who am *I*, to run this programme?' Her common-sense brain knew that was nonsense. The CEO specifically asked to work with her; she had known the leadership team at the firm for six years; she knew their business inside out; she had a good grip on their national cultural differences; and there was the small matter of the fact that she had been running courses on the topic they asked for, for over ten years. But none of that mattered.

It wasn't a conscious thought each day, to delay submitting the proposal. Susan wasn't aware that 'who am I, to...?' was running in the background. Instead, she convinced herself that she was too busy or the timing wasn't right or she didn't want to pull in that many childcare favours.

It was a full month before she caught herself at this pattern and spotted Imposter Syndrome paralysis. We worked together to help her clear it, got the proposal sent off, and rescued the deal. But it was a close-run thing.

So one of the big, bold warning signs of Imposter Syndrome is when something important keeps slipping off your 'to do' list, day after day, and you find yourself secretly justifying it.

Another is when you have that Great Big Scary Goal, but don't get started on it. Each New Year's Eve rolls past with that promise that *this* will be *the* year that... and 365 days later you're sitting there, beating yourself up, because it wasn't.

Even in a corporate environment, this is rife.

Helen was struggling with a member of her team who, on paper, was over-qualified for the role and was, in fact, qualified to do Helen's job. But when he had applied for it, he wasn't given it because he didn't have any experience of managing people. Helen got it, instead. This team member had a weekly meeting with Helen to update her on project progress.

The whole team used the group's internal communication system each morning to share their day's priorities, so Helen felt she had a good handle on what her team member was doing... until the deadline for the database upgrade came – and went – and nothing had happened. Looking back, Helen could see that the team member had never actually lied about the progress of the project, but he had been clever about giving the impression that it was being worked on. Helen was hauled over the coals by her CEO because the project was business critical and she 'should' have known that it wasn't running to schedule. Helen didn't have the courage to tell him it hadn't even been started.

She felt ready to fire this member of her team, as a punishment, but that wasn't an option under employment law. Working together, we were able to help her to see that this non-action – this paralysis and covering of tracks – was a cry for help from the team member, rather than a refusal to accept Helen's authority. And, sure enough, an open and honest, blame-free conversation with the team member showed it was down to Imposter Syndrome paralysis. He didn't know how to carry out the project, but with a PhD he felt he *should* have known. It would have been easy for him to learn how; it was well within his skillset. But the fear of being found out as a fraud paralysed him into non-action, covering his tracks to keep his job.

Paralysis of this nature *can* be down to a genuine lack of skills or experience, or the avoidance-inertia that comes with the fear of stretching comfort zones, but if it's a project you know – deep down – you are capable of, then it's important to check whether Imposter Syndrome has come out to play.

Procrastination

The second P of Imposter Syndrome is Procrastination. It is closely related to paralysis, but with clear differences. It's where we outwardly seem to be working towards a goal, but our actions keep us treading water instead of making progress. It's as though we're dancing around the boundaries of the project, but never quite diving in to do it.

We procrastinate, rather than taking clear and definite action. In *Dare to Dream Bigger* I talk about this 'busyness' as filling our time with stuff that creates burnout, not breakthroughs. It's about the difference between 'inspired actions' and one of my favourite German words: *Kleinkram* – trivial details – the stuff that fills time and steals energy but doesn't really make any progress.

"Never mistake motion for action." Ernest Hemingway

We convince ourselves these small actions have to be performed; that we can't move forward without them. But they lead to us drowning in our 'to do' lists and never making tangible progress. We are subconsciously using 'busyness' to hide the fact that we're not taking *real* action because that could lead to us being 'found out'.

In the entrepreneurial world, a great example of this is the rabbit hole of social media. We go online with a clear purpose and, three hours later, we have watched two webinars, listened to a new podcast, signed up for the latest must-have download, commented on twenty social media statuses and the morning has gone. We allow ourselves to get distracted, in order to subconsciously avoid taking the actions we are scared of. This 'busyness' is one of the biggest killers of productivity in UK industry and one of the biggest reasons why managers and entrepreneurs can end up with burnout and breakdowns. But classic time management training won't fix it, because it's not a skill-level problem.[3]

Procrastination relates to the 'flight' in the fight-flight-freeze response. We are moving, keeping ourselves stuck in 'busyness', but not making progress towards the goal, effectively running from it.

Another form of Imposter Syndrome procrastination is not completing projects. If you don't finish something, it can't go public, so you can't be found out as a fake.

In the business world, an unfinished project can't generate revenue. If you're on a mission to make a difference, an idea doesn't help change the world until it is launched. Not finishing projects means never having to be accountable for their success or failure. It means no one gets the chance to 'spot you're not good enough'.

Corporate environments make this 'procrastination' symptom of Imposter Syndrome more difficult to get away with, because employees usually have clearly defined objectives and their performance reviews measure their progress against them. Someone not delivering on their objectives by not completing projects will normally be spotted – and hopefully helped.

This can lead to people feeling they have 'push on through' Imposter Syndrome. But bottling up the emotions that go with those 3 a.m. inner conversations can trigger chronic stress and anxiety and can even lead to depression. Forcing yourself to keep going, despite feeling like a fraud, creates a severe internal conflict that can lead to more generalised performance issues. Irritability and stress symptoms can affect working relationships, too.

In an entrepreneurial environment, this form of Imposter Syndrome procrastination has a special name: 'Shiny Object Syndrome' (SOS). It might manifest itself as someone always chasing the next shiny, exciting tech solution or social media platform. It might show as someone pouring their energy into an exciting new project, only to leave it hanging to chase the next idea they have – and the next one, convincing themselves that each shiny new idea is better than the last.

If you want to run your own business, the absence of a CEO and a board to report to means you need to be ruthless with your time management and self-discipline. The more Imposter Syndrome grows, the easier it is to dive into those distractions and to leave behind you a trail of unfinished, brilliant ideas that will never generate you sales, but which will lead to

---

[3] There's an article on this in the Readers' Resource Vault.
www.DitchingImposterSyndrome.com/vault/

exhaustion and burnout. Shiny Object Syndrome is like a genuine SOS from a deep part of your psyche, trying to protect you by making it impossible to finish and launch anything important.

When I teach time management and productivity, I find that it is only a small minority of people who genuinely need help with prioritising and structuring their time. For nearly everyone else, if they're overwhelmed and stressed, addicted to 'busyness', Olympic-level procrastinators and divas of distraction (there's a lot of drama in it), their issues are not down to time management; they're due to below-the-surface hidden anxieties and fears about performance. Imposter Syndrome is the single biggest trigger I have seen for this in over twenty years of teaching it. Deal with those underlying fears, and the time management and productivity techniques will work. Ignore that inner dialogue, though, and we'll find a way to subconsciously self-sabotage our results.

Perfectionism

Moving on to the third P: Perfectionism. There are people who indicate that – at an identity level – they *are* perfectionists, in every area of life. They're the mums who won't do the school run without immaculate hair and clothes, with a pristine car and a house that could feature in the local county magazine with zero notice of the photographer's visit. And then there are those who *behave* like perfectionists, as a stress response in certain areas of their life.

If someone is running the stress-response of perfectionism, it shows because – for example – their work ethic may revolve around perfectionism, but their shoes might be dirty. It applies in some contexts, but not others.

Imposter Syndrome is a key trigger for what psychologists call 'maladaptive perfectionism', where someone raises their internal standards to impossibly high levels, in an effort not to be 'found out' as lacking. They become terrified of making mistakes and may go to great lengths to hide them or even to point the blame at others. Yet if they *do* succeed, they write it off as a fluke or luck or a team effort. Or they might convince themselves that if they found it easy, then anyone would. They struggle to 'own' their role in the success.

Personally, I don't believe that 'perfectionism' is ever positive, so it is always maladaptive – a warning sign. Yes, attention to detail and getting things right is important. But needing everything to be perfect is an impossible and unhealthy standard to set and can lead to anxiety and mental health issues.

Perfectionism relates to the 'fight' in the fight-flight-freeze response: we are using our mega-high-standards as a way to go to war with the task. "If I'm going to do this, I'm going to *slay* those goals today!" It turns people into workaholics.

This is one of the most common symptoms of Imposter Syndrome in a corporate environment, especially for someone who was previously brilliant and then got promoted, only to turn into a micro-managing, nit-picking, bullying boss from hell – totally out of character. The previously healthy dose of good attention to detail and sensibly high standards that used to mean they would make sure clients were sent work without mistakes in it becomes control-freak level DEFCON 1. It can trash a formerly happy team's performance and can lead to stress-related mental health issues for both the manager and the team members.

In the self-employed world, a classic example of Imposter Syndrome based perfectionism is the constant signing up for courses.

"When I'm qualified in X, I will finally feel ready to take on that new client / raise my fees / get the PR visibility I want."

It's incredibly common for everyone from yoga teachers to software start-up bosses to keep taking 'just one more course'; the subconscious driver being that this will (they hope) *finally* be the qualification that means they *finally* feel *good enough*.

But this type of perfectionism is not about self-doubt, which covers our skills and capabilities, as we've already discussed. If it were, then taking that course would lead to an increase in self-belief and self-worth and the person would then change their behaviour. They don't. It becomes an expensive fear-based treadmill where you collect courses that cost thousands, often never even studying them, hoping that you no longer feel scared that people will 'find out you don't belong'.

Then we come to the fourth P, which is a bit like number three and a half, because it is a learned behaviour, rather than an involuntary stress response. But once it has been learned, it can become someone's go-to way of expressing Imposter Syndrome, so it belongs firmly in here with the other three Ps.

People-Pleasing

This relates to a relatively new category in the discussion of the Sympathetic Nervous System's fight-flight-freeze response, which is termed 'fawning'. In this a person *fawns* – tries to win favour – in order to feel safe and accepted. I don't personally include this in the primal fight-flight-freeze response because you wouldn't go and stroke a sabre-toothed tiger, to stop it from attacking you.

However, it is now a recognised, learned stress response, especially with Complex PTSD, which can be triggered by Imposter Syndrome, and we talk more about this on page 114. 'Fawning' is rarely discussed, but is a major trigger for overwhelm in a corporate environment and it's a key reason why so many entrepreneurs (especially women) struggle to succeed with their businesses.

In this context it triggers 'people-pleasing' where you take on tasks you don't need to, in an attempt to show you belong and to win favour. It also triggers boundary issues.

There's a strong element of wanting to be liked with this pattern. In a business environment, people might be highly consultative in their decision-making, to try to make sure everyone is happy with their choices. Or they might volunteer for unpopular projects, to show they are helpful.

In the entrepreneurial world, it can lead to over-giving, doing far too much for free, offering discounts without being asked, not charging what you are worth. It can lead to poor boundaries and feeling taken advantage of.

In the 2019 Imposter Syndrome Research Study, 62% of respondents who said they regularly struggled with Imposter Syndrome reported that they had will 'yes' when they wanted to say 'no', which is a classic sign of people-pleasing. 57% of entrepreneurs reported behaviours that fall under 'over-giving' and not valuing their services.

People may be running one of these four Ps or a combination of them. If you have someone in your team who you think might be struggling with Imposter Syndrome, the key is to look for *changes* in their behaviour – like a 'personality transplant'. The Four Ps are behaviours triggered by the stress caused by Imposter Syndrome, in this context, rather than natural traits.

A person might behave, for example, a people-pleaser without having Imposter Syndrome. But if a team member who is usually confident, with clear boundaries, suddenly becomes too collaborative after stepping up to a new challenge, this can be a useful early warning sign.

Now you've had a tour of the four key behaviours that can indicate someone is running Imposter Syndrome, it's time to look at how those behaviours are created. To understand that, we're going to visit the Imposter Syndrome Iceberg.

The Imposter Syndrome Iceberg

"The problems we face cannot be solved with the same level of thinking we were at when we created them." Albert Einstein

I remember, back in my engineering days, being sent on training to 'make' me less impatient. I was in my mid-twenties and loved the work I did. The problem solving that came with Lean Manufacturing and Six Sigma had me cruising on an adrenalin high, even if it meant staying at the factory until 2a.m. to get the production line running again.

But, apparently, I thought too quickly and made massive leaps as I got to grips with the root causes and I didn't wait for others to catch up. Also, I wasn't good at small talk when suppliers phoned me, and apparently that was a problem, too.

These courses had zero effect on my impatient behaviour. Yes, they gave me a crib sheet of small talk options for every time the phone rang. And they taught me how to push down my enthusiasm, to slow down in meetings and be more aware of how others needed me to behave. But these were all sticky plasters that required me to override the behavioural impulses that had already been triggered. They were asking me to bite my tongue; to act a role; to be less 'me'.

I look back now and see that the small talk thing was simply that I preferred to cut straight to the reason for the call (usually what they were going to do to fix the quality issue that was costing the company thousands). I can also now see that impatience was the flip side of my passion and drive to get things done. I've always been the kind of person who has a great idea and then takes massive action to make it happen, rather than waiting around until 'later'.

Having spent the past fifteen years as an NLP Trainer[4], studying how to create behavioural change and performance improvement at a conscious and subconscious level, I now understand why these courses didn't work. And it's what led me to develop the Imposter Syndrome Iceberg model, to help people to understand why we can stay stuck, for decades, with a

---

[4] You can find out more about NLP (Neurolinguistic Programming) in the Readers' Resource Vault: www.DitchingImposterSyndrome.com/vault/

behaviour that is clearly no longer serving us and is making us feel miserable.

Model: The Imposter Syndrome Iceberg

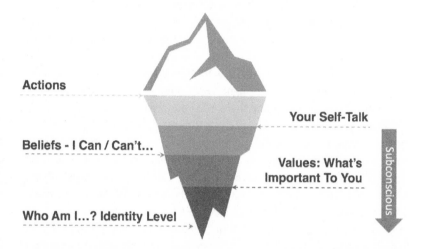

External behaviours – the stuff others can see – are the tip of the iceberg, floating above the surface. And most training tries to 'fix' maladaptive behaviours by teaching people other behaviours to use, instead. So a presentation skills course might teach you how to stand, to feel more confident, and give you a three-step strategy to find something interesting to say, and help you to speak in a certain way, ask questions at key points and tell jokes, without cringing.

All of these are behaviours. And they help. But they're still just plastering over the cracks of the inner dialogue that's screaming at you that you're going to be found out as a fraud and you're not as good at presenting as your peers.

You do the presentation (behaviour), *despite* the fears (self-talk and limiting beliefs) beneath the surface.

Our behaviours are governed by our thoughts. If we think we can do something, we'll be able to do it (within reason; at 5'2" I'm unlikely to become an Olympic high-jumper); if we think we can't, we'll struggle. As Henry Ford famously said: "Whether you think you can or you think you can't, you're right."

These thoughts are at that border between being above and below the surface of the water for the iceberg. Sometimes we are consciously aware of them and sometimes we're not, but they're still running. Usually people can't tell what we're thinking (which is no doubt a relief to most of us, since so much of it is not what we'd want published on the front page of a national paper), but sometimes they can. We've all had the experience of being able to sense whether someone is telling us the truth or not; or whether they *really* mean it when they say they are feeling confident; or if something is wrong and a person needs our help.

Back in my corporate days, a few pioneering training courses tried to get me to *think* differently – to *shift my inner paradigm*, to use the buzzword of those times. They usually didn't work, because you can't simply replace one set of thoughts with another, especially not when you've spent years hard-wiring them into your brain.

As we talked about previously, our thoughts – and what we become aware of from the inside and outside world – are influenced by how we have programmed our brains: both the autopilot neural pathways and Reticular Activating System's filters. And another key programmer of the RAS is what we *believe* to be true about the world and ourselves. If we believe that we live in a friendly universe, then we're more likely to spot the red-car-equivalent to back that up. If we *believe* that our boss is a pain in the backside, then we'll filter in sensory information and pay attention to the experiences that prove that. If we *believe* that we don't belong, that we're going to be found out, we'll be hypervigilant for evidence to back that up, to keep ourselves safe.

So, the first two layers are your behaviours and your thoughts. Then we come to your beliefs: the third layer of the iceberg.

This is one of the hardest things about conducting research: it's hard not to filter out or write off results that disprove your pet theory.

Back when I was a guest lecturer at the University of Bath Business School I was invited to do a PhD on Neurolinguistic Programming. It was a potentially exciting project and I was ready to say yes, until my PhD supervisor explained that I would have to be open to the idea of proving that NLP was useless and ineffective and a waste of time. Having seen the transformations that this 'applied psychology' could create for my clients and having read about people like Milton Erickson and Virginia Satir, two of the therapists who inspired the development of NLP, I knew in my heart that I wasn't open to that potential outcome. I suspected I would be subject to experimental bias, if I did the PhD. So I turned the offer down.

Our beliefs filter the thoughts we become consciously aware of and set the frequency for our inner radio station (more on that in Step Two). Someone who is struggling with anxiety will have an inner radio station featuring wall-to-wall chat shows about things to worry about. Someone who believes that they are great at what they do and are recognised for that will have an inner radio station that plays them a motivational soundtrack for their day. And those thoughts affect the actions we take. Even if you aren't consciously aware of the thoughts you're thinking, they can trigger your Sympathetic Nervous System's stress response on autopilot, causing you to feel the emotional and physiological effects of those thoughts, whether you're aware of them or not, as we've discussed. The strategies you'll learn in Step Two will help you, whether or not those thoughts are conscious or subconscious.

Some of our beliefs are held consciously, but most aren't. So these form the first layer of the iceberg that's hanging around below the surface of the ocean in the unconscious mind.

Beneath our beliefs lies the zone of what's important to us – our values. This is the fourth level and is normally deeply unconscious, unless somebody accidentally stamps on one of our values! These values are often concepts we pick up as young children from our families and society. They govern our choices, usually without us realising.

For example, if family is the most important thing in someone's world, they're less likely to take opportunities at work that require longer periods of travel. And if they feel forced to do so, they're more likely to resent it and to struggle with negative emotions, as a result.

If learning and growing is hugely important to someone, they are more likely to need to regularly move roles or companies, to feed that deep need for personal development, unless their current employer is forward-thinking enough to be able to meet that need. So if you want to keep that kind of person in your team, you need to make sure you provide them with the stretch challenges that they crave.

Values add emotions to beliefs and thoughts, making them more potent.

If we *believe* we can't do something that's really important to us, that sets up a huge stick with which our Inner Critic will beat us. It makes us super-sensitive to evidence that proves the belief. We are running around with a massive inner conflict if we try to achieve something we believe we can't.

For example, if making a good impression and communicating your message clearly are important to you, but you're running a belief that you're rubbish at networking, then it's like pouring petrol on a barbecue for that belief. You're more likely to become hyper-sensitive to feedback (your RAS goes into overdrive), and you increase the likelihood of the Four

Ps of Imposter Syndrome coming out to play. No amount of positive thinking or power posturing is going to prevent the triggering of that autopilot fear cycle.

This is also why the behavioural change training courses I used to get sent on didn't work. They couldn't *shift my inner paradigm* because they weren't engaging with me at the *values* level; they wanted me to recite things like 'shareholder value is key to every decision I make', without helping me to connect with that at a value-level – at an emotional level. They hadn't made 'shareholder value' *important* to me at a level with which I connected emotionally. It was an abstract concept for those of us on the course and none of us really believed it would make much difference to our day-to-day work in a multinational company.

The training was trying to change an external behaviour (adopting a new decision-making process), without helping us to connect with the new values we needed to adopt for that to become *genuinely* important to us. Pretty much everyone who went through that course left with their old decision-making processes intact, simply adding on the *'oh and how can we make this fit with the shareholder value stuff'* tagged on at the end.

And then we get to the deeply subconscious bit – where the *real* decision-maker hangs out. Level five is about your sense of self. I call it the 'identity-level'. Deep below the surface lies the whole 'who am I' malarkey. *What kind of person am I? Who do I see myself as being?*

When a belief and value get tied together in conflict, our inner dialogue starts taking the form of, "Who am *I*, to do that?" or "What kind of person does it make me, if I can't achieve X, despite it being so important to me?" It all boils down to "I'm not good enough."

This adds more lighter fuel to the fire of that inner conflict, because now we're adding conclusions about who we *are* as a person to the limiting belief that we can't do something that's hugely important to us. Our actions – up at the top of the iceberg which are just the symptoms of the fire raging below – end up like Doctor Doolittle's *pushmi-pullyu* animal, yo-yoing between 'full steam ahead' and 'brakes on!' One head is yelling at us that we really want to do whatever it is, because it's so important to us. The other is shrieking like a hysterical banshee about all the reasons why we can't do it – why we're not capable and not the kind of person who could ever achieve that.

This is where the self-sabotage comes in. We get excited about an opportunity, take that inspired action, then pull the plug at the last minute. It might be by not returning *that* call, or discounting our prices before being asked, or not asking for a pay rise that we know we deserve, or saying we're too busy to take up that golden opportunity, or by not speaking up with that brilliant idea, or by giving a speech that doesn't fit with our goals. And most of this is running subconsciously, below the surface.

When your desire to do something is strong enough, it can win out against the banshee-screams of your fears. But that's a painful and difficult way to achieve your dreams – constantly living in fear that your self-doubt will win and having to spend all of that extra energy to overcome it. It takes tremendous willpower and determination to achieve something you believe is impossible for a 'person like you' to create.

And the more important a goal is to you (the value-level layer), the louder the limiting beliefs and identity-level blocks will shout to protect you from potential failure, rejection, death and annihilation – no, I'm not being melodramatic here – all the things you fear. So the more you connect with your passion for what you want to achieve, whilst trying to pretend your blocks and fears aren't there, the more likely everything is to crash and become Imposter Syndrome.

> *Imposter Syndrome is the gap between how you see yourself as **being** and who you think you **need to be**, to achieve that goal.*

When you *see* yourself as being a fraud and question who you *are* to do something, you risk setting up filters in your brain to spot evidence to support that identity-level fear. No amount of external positive reinforcement is going to get past your RAS' filters to change your thoughts and beliefs, when the trigger for them is running at an identity level.

> *When this happens, our internal referencing systems for assessing our performance get out of balance. We end up taking 'constructive criticism' as identity-level feedback.*

This is a classic symptom of Imposter Syndrome. We make the mistake of believing that our *behaviour* is who we *are*, rather than a surface-level effect. And this act of conflating actions with our sense of self makes it much harder to imagine changing our habits.

This is why 'mindset' is not enough to clear Imposter Syndrome.

Clearing out your negative thinking is a great place to start, which is why we tackle that in Step Two. But cognitive-level work only deals with what we can now see are the surface-level effects, rather than the subconscious drivers and root causes. You need to get below the surface, to the bits that are subconsciously running the show, to the beliefs, the values and the identity-level factors that are at the causal level, to create lasting change. You need to shift who you see yourself as *being* to set yourself free from Imposter Syndrome. And that's what we'll be doing in Steps Two, Three and Four.

The Difference Between Your Inner Critic And Imposter Syndrome

I have lost count of the number of people who tell me they have Imposter Syndrome because they have a well-developed Inner Critic. They're actually two separate issues. You can have an over-zealous Inner Critic *without* having Imposter Syndrome.

Your Inner Critic's job is to keep you safe. The deeper down the Imposter Syndrome Iceberg a trigger lies, the harder your Inner Critic's team will work to protect you. So if you're hanging around above the surface of the water, looking at which actions to take, that negative self-talk doesn't have to work so hard to persuade you to play small. But if your triggers start to go deeper, reaching below the conscious surface, then your self-talk has to work harder, because it's not just dealing with a few pesky actions or positive thoughts, it's heading into the beliefs and values territory – what's important to you about life. And if those triggers hit the identity-level realm, it has to get the klaxons out, set off more fireworks than bonfire night, and do everything it can to stand in your way, to keep you safe.

Imposter Syndrome raises the stakes on your Inner Critic's dialogue because 'keeping you safe' becomes a survival issue, at that identity level. The great news is that, although Imposter Syndrome can feel like having your Inner Critic on steroids, there is plenty you can do to tame your inner dialogue, without fighting it or pretending it's not there. And you'll discover how to do that very soon. Knowing how to calm your self-talk sets you free to handle the deeper triggers of Imposter Syndrome, so you don't have to keep riding that roller coaster.

You will start with learning how to tame your Inner Critic, even pressing 'pause' on its ranting. Yes, that is totally doable, when you know how. Then you'll learn how to clear limiting beliefs and stretch comfort zones, without pretending, white-washing or forcing. And then you'll learn techniques to ditch Imposter Syndrome – both emergency quick fixes and longer-term strategies that mean it no longer rules your secret inner world.

Common Triggers

Imposter Syndrome can lie dormant for years until something triggers it to remind you it's there. And it's hard to predict when that might happen, which is why it's important to clear it out, rather than pushing on through 'despite' it. Many of my clients have spent years living in fear that Imposter Syndrome might strike, making career-limiting decisions to avoid that possibility.

> *We need to stop ignoring Imposter Syndrome. By the time we realise it might be a problem, it has usually done damage.*

There are some common triggers that make Imposter Syndrome more likely to come up. But it's important not to use these to create the fear that it might come back, or you'll be into self-fulfilling prophecy territory.

One of the most common triggers is stretching a comfort zone. If we're offered an opportunity to grow, it can feel like being pushed into the deep end of a swimming pool, before we have knew how to swim. We need to learn fast and keep performing at the level that caused us to be offered the opportunity. Stretching comfort zones doesn't need to be scary, as you'll find out in Steps Two and Three.

Another common trigger point is a life-changing, value-changing event. For example, Imposter Syndrome often strikes after becoming a parent, because you get a sense that suddenly your job 'matters' more than it did before – you have to keep it to support your family. It's no longer a game. But at the same time you've got to look after a baby, are probably sleep-deprived and you might worry it will make it harder to work at the level you used to manage.

A traumatic event can also trigger Imposter Syndrome, with PTSD-style flashbacks triggering autopilot responses. You don't have to have been in a war zone to experience trauma. In Step Two you'll cover how any negative experience with strong emotions can hardwire a new autopilot in your brain.

How Criticism Triggers Imposter Syndrome

People often tell me that stretching a comfort zone is the only trigger for Imposter Syndrome, but that's not the case. One of the most common triggers is actually criticism, especially if it's public; even a throwaway comment that hits a raw nerve.

One of the things we'll see on page 200 is that people running Imposter Syndrome are already really good at judging themselves and finding themselves lacking, despite external evidence that they are good. This means that their outward confidence and success can be precariously balanced on a combination of supportive comments from colleagues and willpower to see the positive in their abilities. This reliance on external validation (because their own internal referencing system has got out of kilter) means they are more susceptible to taking feedback badly.

In addition, they tend to take behavioural feedback as being about who they are, as a person (page 201). So criticism can trigger a complex PTSD response for them, as we'll cover later. This is why it's vital to have training in how to give feedback, if people in your team have Imposter Syndrome.

Is It Your Childhood's Fault?

Many experts believe that our childhood is where the root of Imposter Syndrome lies. They believe that children who were driven, high-achievers are more likely to develop perfectionism. This, combined with a need for parental or teacher approval is thought to create an externally-referenced measure of success.

However, I have found that working with clients to find a root cause in childhood risks keeping them stuck in those stories, treating Imposter Syndrome as a badge of honour. Unless there is a clear trigger event to be cleared, I much prefer to focus on the present moment and the future, rather than playing archaeologist with their past.

Triggers Aren't Guarantees

The existence of these triggers doesn't mean that Imposter Syndrome will definitely strike. When I look back at my own career, Imposter Syndrome was an issue for me in my engineering role; a job for which I was well-qualified and was getting great appraisals. But when I moved company to become Head of Market Research, a position for which I had no official qualifications and only guerrilla experience when I started it, I never felt like a fraud.

I had shifted industry, after six months of travelling in South America, so it was a completely fresh start. In that role I had a supportive boss, who believed in me (thank you so much, Lucy!) and who took the time to build my confidence, making sure I could see my natural skills reflected through her eyes. Not once in those years did I fear being 'found out', even though I 'should' have done.

Now you know how Imposter Syndrome happens and where it comes from, it's time to take a tour of what it costs us, as individuals and for businesses, so we are clear about why it's so important to lift the Imposter Syndrome taboo and do something about it.

What Does It Cost Us?

The Cost To People, Performance, Productivity & Profit

The fear of opening up the public discussion about Imposter Syndrome is the single biggest reason why so many people are left to struggle in silence.

When I was asking businesses to send the quantitative survey for the 2019 Imposter Syndrome Research Study around their teams, some were happy to oblige, whereas others reacted as though I had asked them to sell their Grandma. At first, I was confused by this response: couldn't they see how the research would help their teams; their employee wellbeing; their business' bottom line?

I asked some of the managers who refused whether it was something about the information I had given them about the survey. It wasn't. It was fear: fear that if they sent the survey round, it would either open Pandora's box and turn everyone into gibbering wrecks or it would get the 'lazy' (their words) and underperforming members of their teams using Imposter Syndrome as an 'excuse' for poor performance.

If I didn't know much about how Imposter Syndrome affects people, performance and productivity, I could see how raising the topic might feel like a bad idea. But it's the equivalent of suggesting someone avoid going to see their doctor for a check-up, in case they find something wrong.

The side effects of Imposter Syndrome aren't just a cost to the individual who is struggling with it. The results of the 2019 Imposter Syndrome Research Study indicate that it could be costing businesses billions a year. For example, 56% of respondents said they had not spoken up with great ideas at work as a result of Imposter Syndrome, which means their employer missed out on that potential to innovate or grow or to increase employee or customer satisfaction.

It can have a knock-on effect for productivity for that individual and in a wider team, as the team changes its behaviour to avoid criticism from the boss, who used to be brilliant, but has now turned into a micro-managing perfectionist. The team can become more risk-averse. Previously happy team members can even quit to avoid stress triggered by the manager's Imposter Syndrome.

It can stall a person's personal and professional development and even affect staff retention, as they blame the employer for their lack of advancement, despite it being Imposter Syndrome that led to them not taking the opportunities to shine.

It can lead to addictions and mental health issues, affecting performance and attendance. It can lead to subconscious self-sabotage at a personal level on projects that affect the company's bottom line.

And the research shows that Imposter Syndrome is a key factor in why we're not making the progress we had hoped for to close the gender pay gap and why women struggle with the glass ceiling: 45% of female respondents said they had not applied for a promotion they knew they were capable of, as a result of Imposter Syndrome, and 26% said they had not asked for or accepted a pay rise they knew they deserved. Even positive discrimination and quotas won't fix it. (There's a full article on this in the Reader Resource Vault[5] and we talk about it later).

Yet most businesses have a culture where talking about Imposter Syndrome is taboo – or even seen as a sign of weakness – and they have no strategy or employee training to deal with it.

And if you're an entrepreneur, setting up or running your own business, Imposter Syndrome is the single biggest reason why a business with a potentially successful business plan could still fail, as people subconsciously self-sabotage their success. 68% of solo-person business owner respondents in my research study said they have discounted their prices, without being asked, due to not feeling they could charge what they were worth. 64% said they had turned down opportunities for publicity or promoting their business, due to the fear of being 'found out'. A shocking 82% said they struggle with Imposter Syndrome 'daily' or 'regularly', compared with just 47% for the non-entrepreneur respondents.

There's a full white paper on how Imposter Syndrome affects entrepreneurs – and why they struggle with it more than people employed by companies – in the Readers' Vault.

---

[5] www.DitchingImposterSyndrome.com/vault/

How Imposter Syndrome Trashes Productivity & Performance

As we have just discussed, an attack of Imposter Syndrome triggers stress responses that make it harder to concentrate, to think strategically and to maximise your performance.

Imposter Syndrome's Four Ps also mean a person is more likely to procrastinate, getting distracted by less relevant tasks, to get stuck in paralysis, where they avoid an important task, to become a perfectionist, in an attempt to avoid mistakes and being criticised, or to over-commit, as a people-pleaser.

Classic time management techniques don't fix this, because the drivers to procrastinate, to avoid taking action with paralysis, or to feel like you have to over-prepare with perfectionism, feel like a matter of survival, at that 'identity' level of the Imposter Syndrome Iceberg. We know how to manage our time. But something inside us is driving us to ignore that, in order to protect ourselves.

You need to clear the triggers for the Imposter Syndrome and then the maladaptive behaviours it causes will no longer be needed. Change becomes easier.

Perfectionism means you're setting your standards impossibly high, on both performance and timing, in order to feel like you're finally *good enough* and will no longer be found out. People running this pattern may try to hide their mistakes or even to blame others, to avoid being seen as a fraud. Managers pass it on to their teams.

This is why we have to stop 'pushing on through' and pretending that Imposter Syndrome isn't there, if we're struggling with it. All of these factors make it even harder to succeed, feeding the very root fears that initially triggered Imposter Syndrome, making it much worse. We need to give ourselves permission – and the gift of time – to handle this, setting ourselves free from the productivity trap.

Yet in the professional world, it is seen as important to hide Imposter Syndrome and to pretend that everything is fine, despite your struggles with it.

Ditching Imposter Syndrome makes the difference between surviving and thriving.

We're going to cover the 'professional life' and 'personal life' costs of Imposter Syndrome next. But perhaps its biggest cost to us is energy. We use so much energy in worrying, feeling stressed, and in telling ourselves stories that hold us back from our dreams. Then years pass and we wonder why the same things are on our New Year Resolution lists, why others are over-taking us on the corporate ladder, and why we feel so tired all the time.

I don't want that for you.

Dealing with Imposter Syndrome is totally within your reach, using the five-step process you'll learn in this book, despite the myths that we'll cover later in this section. Making it easy for you to handle it at the 'emergency fix' level and at the longer-term root cause level is the entire purpose of Steps Two, Three and Four.

Why It Can Make You A Terrible Boss

There's nothing quite like a comfort zone stretching promotion to turn a formerly brilliant team member into a micro-managing, bully-boss. Add in the Four Ps with elements of workaholic perfectionism, procrastination, paralysis and people-pleasing, and you've got a recipe for teamwork disaster.

I have lost count of how many times I have seen this happen over the past fifteen years. A business promotes someone who was performing well and, within weeks, it feels like they have had a personality transplant.

A promotion requires us to make an identity-level shift: we need to change how we see ourselves as we step into a larger leadership role. For a few rounds of promotion, this will work fine. But there often comes a point where the rubber band of our comfort zone has been stretched slightly too far and it threatens to snap.

That's when previously dormant Imposter Syndrome kicks off.

The *who am I to...?* self-talk kicks in. *What if they find me out?* becomes our breakfast mantra. *What if they find out I don't belong here – that I'm a fake?* is our constant companion on our daily commute.

The Native Americans say that all criticism is borne of someone else's pain, as we'll discuss in more detail, later. This is one of the big challenges when a manager is struggling with Imposter Syndrome. The fear, worry and anxiety they are trying to suppress gets subconsciously projected outwards, onto team members. The struggling manager can become volatile, irritable and impatient.

Add in a dose of maladaptive perfectionism and their deep-seated need to prevent mistakes can turn them into an overly critical control freak who micro-manages every aspect of their team members' performance. They know that they are responsible for the results their team gets, so they're secretly terrified that someone else's mistake could lead to them being *found out*. This can create an environment with zero tolerance of mistakes, making the team risk-averse and stifling creative thinking. People become less likely to speak up with new ideas and the manager becomes less likely to suggest the changes that might be desperately needed to keep the business in front of its competitors in an ever-changing world. This can cause the business to miss out on opportunities its competitors seize. The team becomes defensive, in order to protect itself. 'Growth mindset' feels like facing a firing squad.

If the manager is running the workaholic version of perfectionism that so often comes with Imposter Syndrome, then the team quickly learns that you need to be *seen* to be working hard, because success equates with hard work. They sense that expectation from their manager, even if it's not explicitly voiced. If a team member's achievements look easy or flow or are fun, they risk public criticism or a bad appraisal. And the long hours and hard work have a serious effect on productivity and mental health.

All of this risks having a negative impact on team performance – and even on staff retention, as previously happy, high-potential team members decide to jump ship, rather than put up with a bullying boss.

How Imposter Syndrome Stalls Personal & Professional Development

For a business to grow, it needs its staff to grow, but Imposter Syndrome can stall a staff member's personal and professional development.

If you're secretly scared of being found out as a fake or as not being good enough and you're covering your imagined trail of mistakes with workaholic perfectionism, there's no way you're going to sit in your annual performance review and admit you have development needs. You are much more likely to get defensive, to try to cover up your perceived faults – the ones that make you feel like a fraud – and reject offers of training or coaching that could improve your performance.

You're less likely to speak up if you're stuck. You're more likely to go into paralysis and avoid tasks completely, leading to even more stress and anxiety. And if you don't understand something, you're unlikely to ask for help; instead, you'll try to second-guess the answer or what is needed. This can lead to costly misunderstandings and mistakes – even wasting time taking a project in the wrong direction.

Those who are struggling with Imposter Syndrome are more likely to quit a project before they succeed, to avoid the risk of being 'found out', even if that means justifying the decision to their boss. And they're much less likely than others to volunteer for opportunities that would give them a chance to shine – and stretch those comfort zones.

We have taught ourselves that we have to work super-hard to succeed, which keeps us stuck in that chronic stress pattern. It's then hard to get in flow – that performance space where brilliant ideas come from nowhere and we feel inspired to give our best. Instead, we're in survival mode. The manager of someone who is secretly struggling with Imposter Syndrome is unlikely to get the chance to see that team member's true potential.

When you look at the learning ladder[6] – how we go from not realising we can't do something through to subconscious mastery of it - Imposter Syndrome makes things harder at each level:

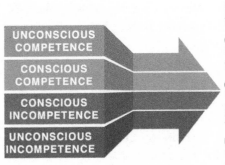

UNCONSCIOUS COMPETENCE
Results feel easy, so we write them off as 'fluke' or 'luck'.

CONSCIOUS COMPETENCE
We're trying hard to learn & this can trigger the 4 Ps.

CONCIOUS INCOMPETENCE
We know we can't do something others can and judge ourselves.

UNCONSCIOUS INCOMPETENCE
We don't know what we don't know - sometimes Dunning-Kruger effect.

---

[6] If you're new to the Learning Ladder model, you can find out more in the Readers' Resource Vault: www.DitchingImposterSyndrome.com/vault/

One of the key traits of Imposter Syndrome is that it particularly affects those who are already outwardly successful; it hits hard, *despite* there being external evidence that you're doing well. Why is that? Because we get a distorted perception of our abilities and our performance. We're so busy wiring those neural pathways with our self-critical inner dialogue that we've programmed the brain's filters to dismiss any positive feedback that contradicts how we see ourselves.

This is why positive feedback – either from a manager or in the form of affirmations – so rarely helps with Imposter Syndrome. If we see our entire success as being founded on fluke or luck or timing, we are not *owning* our own role in our success, seeing it as part of who we really are.

Our inner dialogue gets plagued with 'buts'. So someone telling us we did a great job at a presentation will trigger an internal 'but' response.

"You did a great job presenting that client pitch!"
"Oh, but I was lucky – they showed up pre-sold."

Positive feedback is, of course, still vital, but it won't produce much effect on self-belief or performance, because it is instantly dismissed by the self-talk habits that Imposter Syndrome has taught us. That external referencing system has become distorted. You need different techniques to successfully manage someone who is struggling with feeling like a fraud.

And, if things get too bad, the staff member will often leave. They have convinced themselves either that they're too much of a fraud to do the job, or that they only feel like a fraud because of some external circumstance, such as the company environment or a particular boss or team member. What they don't realise is that you take yourself with you. Changing role or company might allow Imposter Syndrome to go dormant for a while, but unless you have dealt with the deeper triggers, it will resurface, leaving you dancing the same dance to different music, at some point in the future.

Your Rising Stars Will Leave

When I talk to HR managers, they are often surprised that Imposter Syndrome might cause their 'rising stars' to leave, but it's remarkably common. One reason is that someone has been promoted beyond a level at which they felt 'safe' and is scared of being 'found out'. This can get them job-hunting for a role that feels like a better fit, especially if they believe that support to help them through the transition to a more senior role is not available from their current employer. This is particularly common in companies where there is no tradition of senior level coaching and no 'on-boarding' for employees when they are promoted into a new role.

Another reason is that some people, especially women, according to the 2019 Research, avoided asking for a pay rise in their current role, even though they knew they deserved it (26%). They were also not applying for promotion-level roles, despite knowing they were qualified to take them on (45%). They put this down to Imposter Syndrome. In the depth interviews, there was strong evidence that women in this position were more likely to apply for a job elsewhere, in order to get that pay rise and promotion, than to raise it with their manager in the company where they were otherwise happy.

The third factor in this was with high-achieving women, who had had a very 'visible' career within a company. The research showed that they were often reluctant to apply for a promotion in a public competition, for fear of judgement if they 'failed' and didn't get the job. Many felt that if everyone knew they hadn't got the role, they would feel they had to leave. This makes sense, given that 75% of senior women who said they had had Imposter Syndrome in the past year said they worry about being found out as not being as good as others in their field. They would rather keep that contest private by applying externally, so that no one at work would find out, if they don't get the promotion. In contrast, their male colleagues tended to just go for the promotion – and even rope fellow colleagues in to put in a good word on their behalf.

Addictions & Mental Health Issues

Much of the common advice for dealing with Imposter Syndrome, which we'll discuss in more detail soon, when we debunk the myths, centres around positive thinking, affirmations and reminding yourself that you're doing great. It tries – with the best of intentions – to deal with an identity-level root cause at the symptom-level of the thinking mind: mindset and attitude.

I'm not suggesting that we should stick with negative thinking, but this forced positivity sets up an inner conflict, where part of you is saying how you're not up to the job and you're scared of being found out, and part of you is trying to tell you you're wrong. It tends to lead to Imposter Syndrome shouting more loudly and you end up feeling like even more of a failure. As we'll cover soon, it's easy to end up feeling like a fraud for feeling like a fraud and not being able to turn it around.

But whatever advice you follow, the effects of long-term negative self-talk are not to be underestimated.

As we have already discussed, destructive thought habits create neural pathways in our brains for beating ourselves up, especially in that darkest hour of the night. And these thought habits also programme your brain to filter the information you perceive from the outside world, making us more likely to spot more of these negative triggers.

In times of stress and stretching comfort zones, this worry-based self-talk reigns supreme. I call it worry-based because it is often about things that have not yet happened. We are worrying about a future that we feel powerless to influence – and this is one of the keys with Imposter Syndrome. We give our power to 'they' and 'them'.

*What if **they** find me out?*
*What if **they** see I'm a fraud?*
*What if **they** figure out I don't belong here?*

We might be thinking about how last week's presentation went or how next week's client meeting might go, but where we're putting our energy and attention is on our concerns about how others will react. We're not lying in bed wondering how we can make the event go well or what we could learn from last week. We have given power over our self-worth, our sense of belonging and – ultimately – our happiness to forces outside of ourselves, over which we have little, if any, control.

These worry-thoughts have been shown to lead to anxiety and even depression, especially if our self-worth is taking a nightly knock.

And because we have trained those filters in our brains, no amount of positive reinforcement from our bosses is going to fix it.

Long-term, unsupported Imposter Syndrome can lead to clinical mental health issues.

Another common side-effect is escapism. We try to drown out the pain of Imposter Syndrome through distractions and addictions. These might include the gym or social media or binge-watching box sets.

Escaping into social media, for example, where it's easy to lose hours without noticing, gives us space from our inner talk, giving us the excuse to avoid taking the actions that are secretly scaring us. It sets us free from the silence that would otherwise force us to listen to our thoughts.

That escapism can turn into addictions, whether it's to sugar or Instagram, alcohol or online shopping, being a gym bunny or taking out shares in your local doughnut shop. We start to crave the dopamine hit that makes us feel that tiny bit better about ourselves.

If you suspect that Imposter Syndrome is getting to this level for you, then please do get professional advice and support. The techniques in this book will still help, but it's important that you don't take this journey alone.

How Imposter Syndrome Triggers Burnout

It's common not to consciously notice that we are running Imposter Syndrome until we hit burnout, because we're too busy to notice it.

Burnout happens at a mental, emotional and physical level. The physical side comes from the over-stressing of our adrenals, as we push on through yet another project, living in the chronic stress-state we talked about earlier. This is fuelled by the maladaptive perfectionism that often accompanies Imposter Syndrome, where we over-compensate for our perceived lack of ability, despite our achievements.

The emotional burnout stems from the anxiety that can form part of daily life when Imposter Syndrome strikes. It can lead to insomnia, which adds to the adrenal fatigue the next day, as you fuel yourself with caffeine, sugar and pure determination to counteract the knock-on effect of physical, mental and emotional exhaustion.

The mental burnout is exacerbated by the long-term over-triggering of the fight-flight-freeze response, which diverts the blood flow from the part of your brain that you need for strategic thinking, rather than short-term survival, as we covered on page 21. This inhibits concentration and makes it harder to retain information.

Burnout is a stress-related illness. The Imposter Syndrome cocktail of becoming a workaholic perfectionist, wasting time with procrastination, worrying half the night and the inability to concentrate and perform to your usual standard is a perfect storm for burnout. Tasks that used to come easily suddenly require superhuman effort and drain your energy reserves.

If you're an entrepreneur, growing your own business, then Imposter Syndrome can add to the perceived need to over-give, making it harder to have clear boundaries, draining your energy and making burnout more likely.

And there's the effect of social isolation: the fear of being found out as not belonging can lead to loneliness, anxiety and depression.

All of this is driven by fears that may have little basis in reality, but which still feel very real to your body and mind. Pushing on through, despite

Imposter Syndrome, triggers an inner conflict that adds to the emotional and mental fatigue. This is why I never recommend ignoring Imposter Syndrome or pretending it's not there. No one should need to go through this!

Making Simple Decisions Feel Impossible

We all have different ways of making decisions. Some of us make snap decisions. Some of us prefer to consider all options. Some of us ask for advice.

But when Imposter Syndrome strikes, making even simple decisions can suddenly become paralysing.

Our usual systems for decision-making can break down. We can find ourselves stuck, using the absence of the decision as a subconscious excuse to procrastinate.

"Oh, I can't do [scary thing], because I haven't made a decision about it yet."

And if we're clever about it, we can delay that decision *just* long enough that the opportunity passes and we can 'blame' the non-decision, rather than our secret fears.

If we don't make the decision, then we don't have to take the risk. But the new Imposter-Syndrome-driven delaying process causes stress, worry and anxiety. It gets your Inner Critic dancing on your dreams and telling you you're not good enough. It cranks up the effects of Imposter Syndrome until they flow over into areas of your life where you previously felt happy and confident.

We take our assessment of our actions – our behaviours – and turn them into identity-level statements about who we *are*. And then the identity-level self-talk kicks in:

"I'm no good at making decisions."

"I'm the kind of person who finds big decisions hard."

When that happens, this Imposter-Syndrome-specific behaviour becomes a new autopilot in your brain, causing more and more decisions to be difficult. The key warning signs for this are:

- A change in the emotions you feel about decisions
- A change in your decision-making process, leading to you being more cautious where caution isn't really needed

- A sudden drive to seek others' opinions, before you make a decision – often justifying this as being collaborative
- A shift in physical tension around making decisions (often in your gut or jaw)

'Pushing on through' and 'forcing' yourself to make decisions won't necessarily fix this; it could end up with you putting more subconscious effort in later down the line to sabotage the outcome of that big, hairy, scary decision.

Instead, it's better to look at the triggers for this indecision and to clear those, so that you are fully aligned with your yes or no and so that 'maybe' doesn't become a sleep-haunting monster.

The Real Cause Of The Glass Ceiling & Gender Pay Gap?

The 'glass ceiling' is where minorities, be they gender or race related, are seen as able to get to a certain level in a company, but not beyond. The gender pay gap is still prevalent, with men earning more than women, despite years of initiatives and legislation in the UK. But both of these are about more than discrimination, especially when we look at the gender divide. And positive discrimination won't fix it (more on that in a moment), because the research shows that Imposter Syndrome will still be a major cause.

Promotions are given to people who are seen as being confident, competent and credible. They are visible. They 'own' their role in successes. And they put themselves forwards for opportunities to shine.

Female respondents on the 2019 Imposter Syndrome survey who struggle with it daily or regularly reported that they:

- Choose not to volunteer for opportunities that would allow their skills to shine (30%)
- Put their success down to fluke, luck, timing or team effort (51%), rather than 'owning' their abilities and their role
- Do not apply for promotions for which they know they are qualified, for fear of being 'found out as a fraud' (45%) or public failure
- Are less likely to speak up with great ideas or controversial opinions, for fear of being 'found out' or criticised (61%)

Women who struggle with Imposter Syndrome are much more likely than men to deflect praise and to speak up more about their faults and mistakes, rather than their achievements.

These are all reasons why someone with talent might be overlooked when a promotion comes up. They are also all reasons why the gender pay gap is such an issue. High-achieving women who struggle with Imposter Syndrome will tend to avoid opportunities that would lead to promotions and are much less likely to ask for pay increases, to which they may be entitled.

Female respondents in the research also showed a strong tendency to becoming 'addicted' to getting more qualifications or waiting until they had more experience, in order to feel they were 'finally' ready to take the next step up; though that day often never came. Women talked about feeling the need to prove themselves, much more than men did. Women felt they had to be more qualified than a man, to be taken seriously and to feel good enough.

"When I'm qualified in X, *then* I'll feel good enough."

This is a very expensive form of procrastination, both for the individual and the business.

Positive Discrimination Can Make Things Worse:

If you promote someone who you can see is capable, but who is struggling with Imposter Syndrome, then you risk making their symptoms and stress worse. The Four Ps (page 30) may become more pronounced. The effects we have seen Imposter Syndrome as having on personal and team performance will increase.

So positively discriminating and promoting someone who feels like a fraud will amplify those feelings and their effects, especially if their colleagues gossip about it being positive discrimination.

This doesn't mean those people shouldn't be promoted. It does mean, however, that HR and line managers need to have clear strategies for identifying Imposter Syndrome and helping people to handle it, before the promotion starts.

I had never experienced Imposter Syndrome until I was in my mid-twenties, working in engineering. On paper, I had a first-class degree, a Masters, I had won an award on graduation, I had been promoted more quickly than my peers and my work appraisals had only ever been outstanding or excellent. Then, as you saw at the start of this book, Imposter Syndrome struck, though it was only years later that I discovered the feelings I had been having of not being good enough and risking being 'found out' had a name.

I became a workaholic perfectionist. I didn't have the option of pushing back deadlines, so procrastination and paralysis weren't available escapes for me. I had to push on through and pretend I felt fine. I felt ashamed of the fact I didn't think I was good enough and lived in constant low-level fear of someone finding out I was pretending to be ok.

Even when I was chosen to be one of the first people in Europe to be trained in Six Sigma design and manufacturing methods, that background worry about being a fraud, or not knowing as much as I should and pushing my luck beyond safe limits, like Icarus flying too close to the sun, was still niggling behind every action I took.

Each successfully completed project was accompanied by an inner fanfare of, "Phew! I got away with it again! I fooled them!" But the worry was always there that next time I wouldn't be so lucky.

There are those who hypothesise that this was because my fellow female engineer and I were trailblazers in an environment where we were outside of the norms – that we felt we had to prove ourselves. But it wasn't that at all.

Imposter Syndrome didn't strike because I was a woman in an all-male environment. It was because I had listened to the gossip that I had only got there *because* I was a woman; that somehow positive discrimination had been at play. Therefore I believed I was a fake; I wasn't good enough; I didn't belong, despite my qualifications, experience, results and manager feedback confirming the opposite.

When I was promoted to Senior Engineer, these symptoms sky-rocketed. I still did a great job, but the personal cost was huge. My coping strategies cost me emotionally, hurt my personal relationships and negatively affected my health. In the end, I felt I had to 'escape'. So I jumped ship and went travelling in South America for six months on a sabbatical, before leaving the company entirely. I left a career I loved and the factory lost a potentially great engineer. But never once was Imposter Syndrome mentioned or any support offered.

When You're Running Your Own Business

After fifteen years of running my business, I have seen thousands of entrepreneurs and freelancers who struggle with Imposter Syndrome, even if it was never a problem for them in their former corporate roles.

There's something quite unique about stepping out of a business environment where you have clear objectives and accountability structures, with a team around you to support (or sometimes hinder!) progress, then going solo and having so much choice over the actions you take – and trying to do it all yourself.

One of the key differences between entrepreneurs who struggle with Imposter Syndrome and those who don't is the emotional side of running a business. Those who struggle with Imposter Syndrome are likely to:

- Struggle with procrastination (70%), paralysis (53%), people-pleasing (58%) and perfectionism (16%) which means that achieving results takes much more time and effort.

  Perfectionism increases once they have a team, making it harder for them to delegate, meaning they end up doing everything themselves; a recipe for burnout. And Shiny Object Syndrome (see page 35) means they're less likely to complete projects and an incomplete project means you don't get paid.

- They are more likely to experience the stress-related symptoms of 'pushing on through, despite their fears', which can lead to anxiety and performance issues.

- They tend to struggle with pricing, often charging less than they are worth or discounting, without even being asked.

- They resist putting themselves forward for opportunities to shine, such as awards, speaking opportunities, interviews or PR – or even client pitches, even if they know, deep down, that they are doing a great job and are more than qualified.

- And they can struggle with boundaries (people-pleasing), meaning they over-give, often give too much away for free and can end up resenting their audience and the business.

The results of the research study were confirmed by research done by the UK's Nat West Bank, who concluded that 60% of women who want to start a business don't, because of Imposter Syndrome.

My full White Paper on how Imposter Syndrome is affecting entrepreneurs is available in the Readers' Resource Vault[7]. It shows that clearing Imposter Syndrome is a major factor in the success of a solopreneur or micro-business.

---

[7] www.DitchingImposterSyndrome.com/vault/

Myths: The Good, The Dodgy & The Downright Ugly

Why Imposter Syndrome Can Be Hard To Ditch

Imposter Syndrome's myths & bad advice keep us stuck staring into the rear view mirror, wondering why we can't see the road ahead of us.

Imposter Syndrome can feel hard to ditch, partly because of the beliefs we have picked up about it, over the decades. So, before we dive in with how to handle Imposter Syndrome, we need to tackle some of the most common myths around it. We're also going to talk about some of the mainstream advice that can unintentionally make it worse.

Good old cognitive bias and the backfire effect, which we'll talk about in a moment, mean that the final thing we need to do, before you dive in and start clearing out Imposter Syndrome, at both the emergency quick fix and the ditch-it-forever levels, is to ditch the myths that might otherwise keep you stuck.

If there's a mantra-like stream of limiting beliefs *about* Imposter Syndrome running in your brain, then they risk getting in the way of you setting yourself free from it. Your brain will trigger its heel-digging-in defence of its perception of status quo (remember – it thinks that keeps you safe) and the Reticular Activating System's filters risk stopping you from noticing the insights and ideas that hold the power to help you let go of feeling like a fraud.

This is part of what psychologists call *cognitive bias* and it is termed *confirmation bias*, meaning we subconsciously select to retain only the information that confirms what we already believe. We discount evidence that contradicts this.

The beliefs we pick up from the world around us – the received wisdom and well-intentioned advice – act as filters in the brain (good old RAS) through which we decide what gets our attention, as we discussed on page 23. So if you've picked up the belief, say, that Imposter Syndrome is impossible to heal and it's just something you have to 'push on through', part of you will work hard to prove that belief is correct and you'll risk sabotaging the success you could have with these techniques.

Why does that happen? There's a phenomenon called the 'backfire effect', a term coined by Professor Brendan Nyhan of the University of Michigan in his 2010 research on how misperceptions affect what people believe in politics. His team's work describes our innate ability to dig our heels in to defend something we believe, even in light of clear, factual contradictory evidence. In fact, being given contradictory information can actually make our position even stronger. His original research was at the time of the 'Weapons of Mass Destruction' reports with the Iraq war, but it proved equally valid in the UK's 2016 Brexit referendum, where people on both sides of the debate started to dismiss experts, whenever the evidence contradicted their own firmly held beliefs.

Clearing out the common myths up-front will give you as clear a mental workplace as possible to get maximum benefit from what you're about to learn. It will help to reduce your unconscious mind's resistance to the changes you want to make (or you wouldn't be reading this book).

Imposter Syndrome can also feel hard to ditch, because it runs at an identity level, with patterns that are deeply subconscious, whereas most of us have been using thinking-level techniques to try to clear it. But there are also barriers in the form of these myths and the unintentionally bad advice we are so often given.

So, in this section we're going to cover the myths and advice that prevail about Imposter Syndrome: the good, the dodgy and the downright ugly. Some of them are 'received wisdom'. Some come from well-intentioned experts who didn't have access to current data. Some are based on out-of-date understanding from the fields of neuroscience and performance psychology. Much of the research on Imposter Syndrome was done in the 1970s and 1980s. Our knowledge has moved on since then, but the 'old facts' still abound. It's time to set yourself free from other people's mental blocks!

The Good – Things You Need To Know

Wisdom is 'knowledge' with the benefit of hindsight and it's best served up with hope.

There are some key changes that have happened in recent years that it's important for you to know, because they will give you hope, even if Imposter Syndrome is something that you have been convinced can't be shifted.

It's Not In Your Imagination And Neuroplasticity Is Your BFF

Imposter Syndrome isn't in your imagination – it's hard-wired in your brain, as we have been discussing.

Neuroscientists tell us that when you have a thought, synapses in your brain fire off. And they have a saying, courtesy of Donald Hebb, a Canadian psychologist who specialised in researching how neurons in the brain affected behaviour and our ability to learn. Back in 1949 he drew the conclusion that neurons that fire together, wire together.

In other words, the more we practise a thought or behaviour, the more it becomes wired into the brain, so that it becomes automatic at a subconscious level. This is really useful for things like understanding how traffic lights work or learning to walk or learning how to use software at work. But it's not so useful for the destructive habits we run, like negative self-talk and Imposter Syndrome.

What neuroscientists and neuropsychologists have since discovered is that neurons firing together can overwrite old neurological pathways: neuroplasticity means you're not stuck with those brain-habits forever.

Neuroplasticity is your brain's incredible ability to change. There are those who say you can't teach an old dog new tricks, who use this as a justification not to change. But there's no reason why this should be the case, especially for humans, unless we believe it to be so.

There are ways to reroute your neural pathways, to change the filters in your Reticular Activating System, and to create new autopilot behaviours that are more empowering (that's the whole of Step Two). And there's a brilliant thing that happens when you make these changes: the brain 'deletes' the neural pathways it no longer needs, so those out-of-date habits literally disappear. It's called 'synaptic pruning' and it is the process whereby the brain strengthens the connections that are helpful and gets rid of those that aren't.

The step-by-step how-to is waiting for you in Steps Two, Three and Four. So if you've tried to ditch Imposter Syndrome in the past and it hasn't worked for you, it's most likely because you didn't know how to make the most of neuroplasticity. It will work for you this time, because you'll have the techniques and strategies you need to create this unconscious level of change.

The Dodgy – Stuff That Keeps You Stuck

So, we've done the good... And now it's time to move on to the 'dodgy'. In this section we'll tour the myths, beliefs and advice that *can* help, sometimes, but which can also make things worse.

The dodgy advice is well-intentioned, but it often doesn't work, which can make things worse as you beat yourself up, feeling like a failure when the advice doesn't stop you from feeling like a fraud... which makes you feel like more of a fraud.

It often comes from someone sharing their experience of what worked for *them*, without them understanding how or why it worked; what else they had shifted to *allow* that technique to bring them results. And usually the unintentionally dodgy advice we're about to tour is working at the cognitive, thought-based level, treating Imposter Syndrome as a 'mind-trap' or 'mindset' issue, rather than tackling the limiting beliefs, fears and identity-level blocks that are driving Imposter Syndrome. So it's like painting over the cracks on a damp wall and hoping you'll get a long-lasting, smooth finish.

Myth: It's A Predictor Of High Performance

The internet is brimming with articles claiming that Imposter Syndrome could be a sign of high potential. I even saw responses in my 2019 research from people celebrating having Imposter Syndrome, despite how it was hurting them, because it meant they 'would go far'.

My work and research indicates that there *is* a correlation between being a high-performer, seen as a rising star in your organisation, and Imposter Syndrome, but it is not a causal link. You can be a high-achiever without Imposter Syndrome. But if you're on the rise, and you haven't dealt with the blocks that create Imposter Syndrome, promotion can be a trigger event.

This myth is a problem because people then see Imposter Syndrome as a rite of passage, something that comes with the territory of being successful, and they believe they have to put up with it and all the damage it causes for them and their business.

Myth: You Have To Find Your Causal Event

In a moment, in Step One, we'll talk about why I don't care how you got Imposter Syndrome, but that doesn't mean I don't *care*. The belief that you need to find your causal event, in order to set yourself free from Imposter Syndrome deserves a special award in the 'dodgy myth' category, especially for those of us who are deeply into self-help and spiritual modalities.

Now, I can party with rainbow-farting unicorns at my 29th chakra like the best of them, but I'm not going to let you fall for the New Age myth of 'you have to find the original trigger event before you can heal yourself'.

Here's the advice I commonly hear from therapists and well-meaning advice-givers:

You have to find out *why and how* you have got Imposter Syndrome, *then* clear those mindset blocks / beliefs / fears / karmic debt / disturbances in your auric field, and *then* you can start to set yourself free from it.

Baloney.

> *You don't need to know why you first 'got'*
> *Imposter Syndrome to be able to ditch it.*

Yes, if there was an obvious causal event, then by all means let's clear the stuck-stuff from it, getting you to a place of acceptance and forgiveness, then setting you free to move on with a beautifully blank slate. But please, oh please, don't fall into the trap of believing that finding your causal event has to be part of the process, leaving you stuck letting Imposter Syndrome sabotage your dreams as you spend three decades hunting through your memory banks for your original trigger.

The beauty of the strategies you'll learn in this book is that you get to start from where you *are*, right *now*. You don't have to retrace your steps, desperately searching for something or someone to hold accountable – to blame (never a useful emotion, but that's a topic for another book, one day). You get to *choose* whether or not you want Imposter Syndrome to be part of your present and your future, *despite* what may or may not have happened in your past.

Myth: Just Visualise Your Past Successes!

One of the things that someone running Imposter Syndrome is brilliant at is the exquisite use of the word 'but'. It peppers their inner dialogue like chillies in a vindaloo.

Good cop self-talk:	*You did really well at that presentation!*
Bad cop self-talk:	*But you forgot to mention the point about shareholder value! (Will they ever drum that into me?)*
Good cop self-talk:	*Remember you increased sales value by 10% last quarter.*
Bad cop self-talk:	*But that was just luck. The Browns contract came up for renewal.*
Good cop self-talk:	*And what about the brilliant idea you had in the team meeting last week?*
Bad cop self-talk:	*But what if they find out I don't have a plan to back it up with?*

The word 'but' has the mysterious power to negate everything that came before it. Tell a loved-one, "No, darling, your bum *doesn't* look big in that, *but...*" and she'll be shrieking at you and slamming doors before you finish the sentence.

In the case of visualising past successes, the 'but' is your Reticular Activating System at play, triggering the backfire effect.

> *Your brain uses the 'but' to try to maintain its status quo.*

Your brain's ingrained neural pathways and filters will make it hard for you to remember positives, when you're feeling negative (another element of cognitive bias). The advice of your past successes can help you if it's a low-key dose of Imposter Syndrome, but only if you keep your 'buts' out of it. Plus it risks triggering the 'Icarus Effect', where we fear our luck won't hold, *because* we have had past successes.

When we have a well-developed Inner Critic, we are hyper-sensitive to the word 'but', because it pours ice-cold water on our burgeoning confidence. So if you're going to use remembering all of the things you're good at to counter feeling like a fraud, make sure you lock your 'but' away first, or it risks making you feel worse.

Myth: Have A Chat With Someone Who Likes You

Another piece of common advice is to go and have a chat with someone who *does* believe in you. This *can* work well if your Imposter Syndrome is just a minor wobble – if it is on a scale of three out of ten or lower. Having someone remind you of what you're doing well and why you *are* good enough can be enough to giving you back your perspective, calming your Inner Critic's ranting and getting you back on track.

But if you're in a full-blown feeling-like-a-fraud pit, it can risk making things worse.

When someone is struggling with Imposter Syndrome, they are usually well-qualified to fill the role they're in and are confident. But their 'internal reference system' – their ability to assess their own performance – has broken down. That's why they write off success as a fluke, set themselves near-impossible standards, and beat themselves up as a failure if they don't meet them.

They have trained their Reticular Activating System's filters to spot evidence to support them not being good enough, not belonging, and risking being found out. This makes it hard for them to trust the opinion of others who *do* think they're doing well.

So having a cuppa with someone who wants to boost your confidence presents the challenge that the positive feedback has to make it through your RAS' filters, your cognitive bias and the backfire effect (from page 68). Some will, but most won't, instead triggering the well-rehearsed inner dialogue of dismissing success as luck and silently justifying why the positive feedback-giver is wrong – the backfire effect we just discussed.

This gets the recipient running those well-trodden neural pathways of self-criticism again, reinforcing them and making their autopilots run even faster. It's one of the reasons why counselling or life coaching is unlikely to clear Imposter Syndrome.

It doesn't mean you shouldn't go and chat with someone who can point out your brilliance – it can be vital, especially in an emergency wobble. I keep a folder in my email system of unsolicited thank you emails from readers and clients for just such moments. But you *do* need to approach the session with an open mind, being highly aware of how your cognitive bias needs to be locked up for the duration.

If a colleague comes to you needing this kind of support with Imposter Syndrome, there are things you can do with your feedback to help it get past their subconscious filters and biases. You can find out more in the Reader Resources Vault.

Myth: It's A Girl Thing

I'll never forget the first time I realised that men 'do' Imposter Syndrome just as well as women. I was working with a non-executive director who told me how rarely he saw women in Board meetings. Later in the conversation, he explained how it had been a breakthrough for him to realise that pretty much every man in the room was sitting there with a secret mantra running in the background: "Don't let them *find me out*." He said the realisation that he wasn't the only one who had been judging himself as 'not good enough' freed him from his fears and also helped him to understand how to win over others, *despite* their fears. We discussed how his old mantra would have influenced the room's discussions, decisions and politics.

That was early on in my work with Imposter Syndrome, back in 2003, and I have since found that to be true at every level of business management and entrepreneurship.

Men get Imposter Syndrome, too, but they handle it differently to women.

The original 1978 research by Clance and Imes is partly responsible for the belief that it's a woman-only experience. They only interviewed women. Clance's subsequent research also included men and she found that Imposter Syndrome affects both genders, but this change in understanding hasn't yet shifted the initial assumption in the public's mind that Imposter Syndrome is a woman-only phenomenon.

Research by Mary Topping and Ellen Kimmel of the University of South Florida in 1985 looked at Imposter Syndrome amongst their faculty members and found the incidence was, in fact, higher for men than for women. The 2019 Imposter Syndrome Research Study has shown that incidence rates are similar for men and women, but that they don't respond in the same way. Of those who said they had had Imposter Syndrome in the past year, 46% of men and 49% of women had had it regularly or daily.

My work has shown that men are more likely to push down the emotions that come up when you're feeling like a fraud and will use 'taking action' as a strategy to push on through. It is widely believed that men do not openly acknowledge Imposter Syndrome and will suppress their negative thoughts, in order to uphold stereotypical masculine traits of being unemotional and strong.

As we have already discussed, 'pushing on through' and trying to suppress emotions triggers the Sympathetic Nervous System's stress response and can lead to long-term anxiety, performance issues and even physical illness, if that stress becomes chronic.

Women are more likely to get stuck in the mind-story fears and to overthink the problem and to get stuck in the Four Ps – procrastination, perfectionism, paralysis and people-pleasing. Men tend to keep doing what is necessary to move towards the goal. Women, under the same triggers, are more likely to worry about what others might think, to delay decisions, and to look for collaborative solutions.

Of course, these are generalisations. But they are a rule of thumb.

We discussed on page 62 how Imposter Syndrome can affect gender diversity in senior roles and how it contributes to the Gender Pay Gap. The data about how men and women behave differently shows how large a role the fear of being found out as not good enough will play for both of these.

This shouldn't be a surprise, if we consider the historical differences in how we have raised children. If a boy was upset, he tended to be taught to 'get over it' and go back to the game or task in hand. He learned to process emotions by switching them off and taking action. A girl was more likely to get sympathy and to be encouraged to talk about what she experienced: which can lead to the adult behaviour of over-thinking and over-feeling. This discussion could be a book, in itself, and I'm generalising here. But what we are seeing in adulthood with regards to the gender differences in Imposter Syndrome is, in part, the multi-decade effect of these types of unconscious messages.

The Downright Ugly – Advice That Can Make Things Worse

Now we're reaching the advice, myths and beliefs about Imposter Syndrome that I wish we could delete from our collective consciousness. This is the realm of ideas that, on the surface, might sound great, but hold massive potential to do harm, keeping someone stuck or even shifting them towards anxiety and depression.

Yet the advice in this section is also the most common response to Imposter Syndrome, shared by well-meaning colleagues and even some coaches. And when advice is given by someone we perceive as more expert than us, it can bypass the brain's usual filters, going in at a subconscious level, creating new limiting beliefs.

So are you ready to ditch the 'downright ugly'? I'm curious to hear how many of these have hit your inner radar!

It's Just Something You Have To Put Up With

This received wisdom nugget drives me crazy. It is the single biggest way to guarantee you'll be stuck with Imposter Syndrome forever. I have lost count of how many business leaders and entrepreneurs have told me, when admitting their Imposter Syndrome struggles, that it's simply something they have to put up with, because they'll always have it and there's nothing they can do about it. It breaks my heart.

Running this belief – given how effective the fear of being found out can be at subconsciously sabotaging our dreams and ambitions – keeps people stuck, potentially forever, in their comfort zones. It makes the risks of growing that box unthinkable.

The other disastrous side effect of running this belief is that it the strategies that *do* work to ease and clear Imposter Syndrome are less likely to produce results. The backfire effect and cognitive bias from page 68 mean we're less likely to notice the positive results.

Your brain won't let you make a change that it believes is impossible.

If you believe you can't ditch Imposter Syndrome, then your

unconscious mind will do its best to obey, taking that limiting belief as an instruction.

How can you turn this around? Without triggering your Inner Critic's backfire response?

"What if I *could* ditch Imposter Syndrome? What might that feel like?"

This simple shift opens up your brain's filters to imagine and notice ideas that could help you, to allow them to work, and to notice the results. Can you feel the difference it makes?

Fake It Till You Make It

One of the common Imposter Syndrome myths that leaves me confused is the idea that you get Imposter Syndrome *because* you are an imposter – a fraud – faking it.

That couldn't be further from the truth.

My work and research shows that:

> *Imposter Syndrome usually affects us when we are competent, qualified and capable of doing a task, but we have convinced ourselves we aren't, despite external evidence. There's nothing to 'fake it' about.*

Your internal reference system gets out of kilter and you're no longer able to assess whether you're doing a great job or not. We convince ourselves we aren't. Ironically, someone who knows they are pulling the wool over people's eyes, who is 'faking it until they make it', doesn't usually struggle with Imposter Syndrome.

With Imposter Syndrome, if we find something easy, then we convince ourselves that everyone could find it that easy, so we're nothing special. If we find something hard, then we convince ourselves it's because we're not good enough and we risk being 'found out'.

The key here is that there *is* external evidence that we are good enough (more than), but knowing our boss or clients believe in us doesn't make the feelings go away. You have high ability but low self-perception.

This is the opposite of the Dunning-Kruger effect, which has come to fame in recent years with some political leaders. With this, a person has low ability, but high self-perception. They over-rate their performance.

They bluster their way through projects they're not skilled enough to deliver. They are more confident in comfort zone stretching situations than their ability should permit. They have no idea that they *are* a fraud or that they're faking it.

You don't get Imposter Syndrome *because* you are *being* a fraud. You're just ('just'!) lying awake in the middle of the night worrying that you might be.

> *"Fake it till you make it" (super-common advice for countering Imposter Syndrome) will make everything worse.*

Doing this at a physical level by adopting the posture of someone who is confident *can* help you to feel more confident. Remember the 'powerful and strong' exercise from page 26? How you hold your body affects your biochemistry and your thoughts and can help you to feel more confident. In fact, the currently popular 'power pose' is a useful emergency quick fix, and if you base it on the yoga mountain pose (a method you'll learn on page 103) it can take you out of your mind-story fears and into your inner courage in under sixty seconds.

But the power pose only works if you already have a 'body memory' of feeling confident and calm in similar situations. Otherwise your body won't automatically fire off the biochemical reactions you need to generate the confident emotions that need to go with that posture. You'll risk standing in front of the client's team, knowing you're quivering inside your power pose.

And humans have congruence radars – the inner BS sensor. They can sniff out a fake at twenty paces. So if your tone of voice and words and actions don't match up with your power pose, people will know you're pretending. *You* have to *believe* you are confident and competent, for the shift to work. If you know it's an act, it won't work.

There are breathing techniques from the worlds of meditation and yoga that can help you to feel more confident and less stressed and we'll cover some in Steps Four and Five. With these exercises, you'll learn how to use them for 'confidence', but you can use them to choose any internal emotional state or inner resource that you need and they will use your body to fire off the biochemical reactions to create that internal state.

But the 'bluff you way through it' and 'fake it till you make it' version of faux-confidence doesn't work. When you consciously pretend to be something you're not, you trigger an inner conflict that affects every thought you think and each action you take. If you decide to 'fake it till you make it', you'll be forcing yourself to take actions that aren't supported by your thoughts, which are your Inner Critic's commentary. These actions are out-of-sync with your beliefs and they directly contradict who you see yourself as being, at that identity level of the iceberg. So your Inner Critic will ring its alarm bells louder than Big Ben and do all it can to get in your way.

"I have to fake it, therefore I'm not good enough to do it for real, so I must be a total failure!"

'Fake it till you make it' risks triggering you acting from a place of fear and the chronic stress response that creates (as discussed on page 26), making it harder for you to 'think straight', leaving you exhausted and irritable and making peak performance nearly impossible.

Telling someone who is struggling with Imposter Syndrome to 'pretend' they are feeling confident and competent and that it doesn't matter whether or not they themselves believe it, sets them up to feel even more like a fraud.

Do It Scared!

This one makes me want to drag my soap box out into the middle of the nearest crowded space and pummel my chest like Tarzan! "Do it scared!" is some of the worst advice you can give to someone who is already feeling scared and who is stressed about under-performing.

Now, I don't believe you should wait until you feel zero fear before you ever take action. That would lead to a very slow and boring life. But I also don't advise pretending your fears aren't there. We'll cover how to clear them – in minutes, not months – in Steps Two And Three. Before we do that, here's what your brain and body want to tell you about 'doing it scared'.

When we experience fear, we trigger the body's Sympathetic Nervous System and its fight-flight-freeze response. This, if you remember, gets your body ready to run from the sabre-toothed tiger or client pitch or newspaper interview or publishing your edgy blog post. It diverts blood flow from the pre-frontal cortex in your brain that does your brilliant thinking, insightful analysis and concentrating, prioritising the primal part that has kept you and your ancestors alive for millennia. And that bit is rubbish at presenting or giving intelligent interview answers or constructing a compelling argument for your latest brilliant idea.

So when you are feeling scared, but force yourself to take action, you're operating with the least effective part of your brain for strategic thinking. You'll find it hard to concentrate and think clearly about anything other than survival, you'll be hypervigilant to threats and there's no way you'll give your best performance.

And, afterwards, that will give us plenty to beat ourselves up about, in true Imposter Syndrome fashion, providing more evidence to back up the fact that we're a fraud on the verge of being found out.

But I hear people defending the need to 'do it scared' – apparently a bit of adrenalin helps them to feel they're giving their all to their performance. And I get that. 'Do it bored' is going to produce a very different pitch, interview or blog post. But you don't have to feel scared to get that buzz. We'll go into this in more detail on page 138, when we'll talk about the difference between 'good' and 'bad' stress.

The solution? Learn how to let go of the fears. Fast. That's Step Two. Get grounded and calm, to start turning things around. Forget 'do it scared'. How about choosing to 'do it excited', instead? It doesn't have to be crazy-toddler-in-a-sweet-shop excited – it's a sliding scale. Excitement triggers the low-level adrenalin kick that can help us to perform at our best, without the fight-flight-freeze penalties. And the difference between fear and excitement is about two inches, as you'll experience on page 139.

Smash On Through It!

The entrepreneurial world is flooded with the message that when you're feeling scared or feeling like a fraud, you should push on through those fears and take 'massive action'. Language like 'smash on through it!' is rife. And this attitude often spills into the mainstream business world, too.

Nearly twenty years of working with Imposter Syndrome have shown me that this advice nearly always comes from people who have never struggled with Imposter Syndrome – or who are in denial about it.

Again, I'm not saying you should wait until you feel zero fear before taking inspired action towards your dreams, but the 'smash on through it' advice is fundamentally flawed, for a number of reasons.

Firstly, if someone comes to you and has the courage to tell you they're struggling with Imposter Syndrome, telling them to ignore it gives them the strong message that their fears and worries don't matter, in your eyes. It makes them less likely to ask for help in the future and more likely to bottle problems up, until those problems become unignorable.

To be able to help someone, they need to feel we have *heard* them, without judgement. It doesn't mean we have to agree with them about their problem. But simply dismissing it out of hand and telling them to do the same risks them thinking we don't care and they don't matter.

For someone struggling with an identity-level issue such as Imposter Syndrome, where they fundamentally believe they are not 'good enough', despite external evidence to the contrary, this response risks making things worse, because they can take this response as also not being 'good enough' to be 'worth' you showing you care or wanting to help them.

Then there's the fact that 'smashing on through' is an adrenalin-fuelled, stress-inducing response, which will mean the body invokes its fight-flight-freeze mechanism, diverting blood flow to the primal part of the brain. This part of your brain is responsible for your 'animal instinct', rather than rational or creative problem solving. Its primary purpose is to keep you alive, not to help you to run a successful business or to get you an outstanding appraisal or lead your team. When we 'smash on through' using that part of our brains, the kinds of actions we choose are very different to those we would select if we were feeling, relaxed, creative, excited and inspired.

This is one of the reasons why I found that my engineering days were so crammed with metaphorical fire-fighting: everyone was running on low (or high!) levels of adrenalin, the whole time, because anything that could risk stopping the production line or affecting quality was a huge issue. And that stress (and related angry outbursts) were culturally contagious. The adrenalin rush was addictive. It was rare for people to be calm enough to sit back and consider what needed to be done (hence introducing Six Sigma to remedy that) and the actions people took when in their stress mode were quite different to those chosen when there was 'space' to be more reflective.

In the entrepreneurial world, 'smashing on through' tends to produce 'emergency' tactical responses that look – from the outside – like random actions, because the person doesn't have as much access to the frontal part of their brain that is brilliant at strategic thinking and inspired decision-making.

Then there's the fact that pushing on through – forcing ourselves to keep going, despite our fears can lead to burnout. And denying our emotions, forcing ourselves to do something that part of us has decided is a potential existential threat, can trigger mental health issues such as anxiety and depression.

There's always the option to deal with the triggers for our fears, to clear them out, and *then* to take action that inspires us. And sometimes we *do* need to take that time to step back, to rebuild our energy levels or to learn and grow. Sometimes we need professional support for this (please do get help if that is the case for you).

It would be much better for the person telling us to 'smash on through' to spend a few moments trying to understand what the block is, to help us to clear it, and then to agree an action plan that allows for growth, action and feeling inspired about our dreams in a way that feels empowering and safe.

Positive Affirmations Can Be Your Ticket To The Imposter Syndrome Pantomime

I asked my research respondents what they had tried to tackle Imposter Syndrome: what had worked and what hadn't. The most common response was 'positive affirmations' and only two respondents said these had made a noticeable difference.

If you already know my work, you'll know I'm seriously into positive thinking and I do recommend affirmations, if done the right way. I've even had a book published on how gratitude can turn your Inner Critic into your biggest cheerleader[8]. But I'm not a big fan of the craze for generalised positive affirmations. In fact, they can make things worse, especially if you apply them to something like Imposter Syndrome. There are three main reasons for this.

The first problem with positive affirmations is that they're often too vague and fluffy. To your brain and body, they can feel out of reach. Beautifully created card decks of affirmations often contain phrases like:

I am a creative being.

Love and abundance flow to me.

I am confident and strong.

They're such high-level concepts that it's hard to connect with them in a physical, practical way. If you say to yourself the affirmation '*I am happy*', what specifically are you asking your unconscious mind to do, to create that? What does the phrase even mean? What steps are you asking your below-the-surface self to take? It's like showing someone a photograph of a delicious meal and telling them to replicate it, but without giving them the recipe. It's likely to lead to confusion and non-action. And remember

---

[8] Book: A Year Full Of Gratitude

what we talked about on page 24 about how you need to add in a positive emotion to a thought to be able to change your neurology, like stamping through that muddy field? Highly conceptual affirmations rarely do that for us.

The second problem is that they can trigger the backfire effect we discussed on page 68. When someone has trained their brain to spot all of the reasons why they are, say, rubbish at presenting, their RAS filters will be super-sensitive to all evidence to support that limiting belief. Telling yourself you are a great presenter a couple of times a day won't touch the sides on washing away the belief that 'I'm a rubbish presenter', if you've spent a decade of rehearsing it, cranking up the fear-based emotions each time the word 'presentation' is mentioned.

The backfire effect will make your brain and self-talk defend that old belief even more vocally each time you run the affirmation, to prove it wrong.

Well-meaning advice often suggests we simply tell ourselves we're not a fraud, and not about to be found out, when Imposter Syndrome hits. Or we should talk to someone who believes in us, to convince us we're not faking it. It suggests using affirmations like, "I am not a fraud." Here's how the internal conversation tends to run, when we follow that advice:

> *I feel like a total fraud. Oh hang on, remember that affirmation? I am not a fraud. Hmmm... No, I'm definitely a fraud. Oh no you're not! Oh yes I am! Oh no you're not! Oh yes I am! It's behiiiind you!*

Cue pantomime villain lurking stage left.

If you've spent decades rehearsing the self-talk that trained your brain to spot all the reasons why you might be 'found out', then simply contradicting those fears and beliefs is not going to fix them. It's going to trigger the backfire effect we just talked about.

There's a final problem with this version of positive affirmation advice: right now, don't think of a blue donkey in a pink tree playing jazz on a saxophone. What happened? Which song was it playing? You thought of it, didn't you? And this is why:

> *Your unconscious mind can't process a negative.*

If a playground supervising teacher yells, "Don't run!" at a child, in order to process the instruction, the child first has to imagine the concept of 'run' and then 'don't'. They will rarely get as far as the second half. In fact, the teacher's instruction risks reinforcing the 'run', because imagining something creates similar neural pathways to actually doing it; it's the concept of mental rehearsal. It would work better if the teacher were to tell the child to 'walk'.

But this is exactly what we're trying to do as we dance the Imposter Syndrome pantomime, complete with corny songs, but minus the throwing sweets into the audience. To process 'I am not a fraud', your unconscious mind first has to imagine what 'I am a fraud' would look and feel like, and then the 'not' gets lost in the emotional response to the first part of this.

That's why in Step Two I'm going to give you my 'Magic Question' to turn this around, so you can laugh at the pantomime, instead of living it.

So many positive affirmations are formulated this way, trying to swap 'can' for 'can't' or 'am' for 'am not' and expecting Dumbledore-level magic to happen.

The problem is that 'can' is not the opposite of 'can't'.

> *"There's no such thing as can't, but that doesn't mean you can."*

My Great Auntie Yo was famous for being a teeny bit dotty, but she had a secret she shared generously, with all who would listen. I vividly remember the 'there's no such thing as can't' message being thrown back at me each time she spotted one of my excuses, as a kid. It took me years of objecting to realise she was teaching me that "I can't" was my excuse for anything I didn't want to do – or didn't believe I could do.

But taking the 'not' out of an excuse (code for a limiting belief or secret fear) does not suddenly make it lose its power to control our thoughts and our actions. It triggers the backfire effect, as above. But there's another problem with this strategy.

Say we're back on the presentations example: your inner mantra might normally be *'I'm no good at presentations'*. Your chosen affirmation might be *'I'm great at presentations'*. This is the classic 'affirmation flip'.

But if you try to do a U-turn from a negative to a positive, your Inner Critic will go all-out to resist it, digging its heels in to defend the decades of evidence it has collected. It can see you're trying to kick out the belief it thinks has kept you safe for decades and it won't give up without a fight.

We get stuck on a seesaw where our thinking mind tries to say yes, but our unconscious mind (which is running the show) says no.

If you try this flip with one of your "I can't" beliefs, you'll most likely notice this process creates physical tension in your body. For example, if you're used to telling yourself stories about "I can't write proposals," then telling yourself "I can write proposals" feels like a lie. It creates an internal conflict, contradicting the neural pathway thought habits and the Reticular Activating System's well-practised filters. The incongruous thought (AKA the affirmation) triggers your fear response, because the limiting belief was trying to keep you safe, and it fires off the stress-related biochemical reactions in your body that we discussed on page 21.

The answer isn't to do a seesaw. It is to clear the limiting belief in a healthy and empowering way, rather than trying to paper over the cracks. Then the affirmation won't even be needed.

And finally, unless a positive affirmation is specifically tailored to you and your needs, it risks being dismissed by your brain. For an affirmation to work, it needs to be specific and something you can have an emotional connection with. Remember what we said on page 21 about the neural pathways in your brain being like walking through a field of long grass, and that you create new autopilots more quickly with muddy boots, stomping on a rainy day than with light footsteps in dry weather? Your emotional connection with an affirmation is the neurological equivalent to the muddy boots. So unless an affirmation gives you goosebumps or tingling in your stomach or some other sense of relief and excitement, it's not going to make much difference.

All of that said, I'm a superfan of positive affirmations done correctly. Specific affirmations, tailored to your individual needs, with which you have an emotional connection, can fast-track the deep-acting change you are dreaming of and be a long-term solution to Imposter Syndrome. That's what I'll be showing you in Steps Three and Four.

What's The Worst That Could Happen?

I hear this question daily, in response to people's fears and worries about stepping outside of a comfort zone and taking risks towards their dreams. Given what you now know about how the brain's neural pathways are formed by repeated thoughts and the fact it can't process a negative, I'm sure you can guess what I'm about to say on this one!

"What's the worst that can happen?" requires someone who is already feeling potentially anxious to start imagining their private worst-case scenarios. And when you're dealing with an identity-level issue like Imposter Syndrome, those deepest fears are often existential: *if I do this scary thing I could die.* I know that sounds extreme, but if you work with someone through the layers of their Imposter Syndrome fears, the deepest fears – the ones their unconscious mind is trying to protect them from – are often at the 'will I cease to exist?' level.

When people tell us to imagine what's the worst thing that can happen, what they're actually looking for is for us to see how ridiculous our worries are and for that to give us back our perspective. That *can* work for someone who is basically ok and just having a teeny wobble that they need to laugh off. But if you have a well-trained Inner Critic who has excelled at 3 a.m. mind-stories, there's likely to be genuine fear behind the answers. We can't always tell from the outside of their head which of these camps someone is living in.

> *So, if I do the presentation, what's the worst that could happen? I could totally mess it up, lose the client, get fired on the spot, not be able to pay the bills, lose my home, have my spouse and children leave me and end up living in a gutter.*

And we want to risk someone imagining all of this, to make them feel better? When you look at it that way, the question itself is the ridiculous part.

The other side to this is the phenomenon of mental rehearsal. Clearly imagining a physical performance has been known for years to help people from the fields of sport, music and beyond to improve their performance, especially if you use multiple senses and add in emotions. The act of imagining can create new neural pathways and autopilot responses in your brain.

"What's the worst that could happen?" forces you to imagine – drum roll – various scenarios for the worst that could happen, which means we:

- mentally rehearse them
- fire off the same biochemical reactions in your body as though they were actually happening, triggering the Sympathetic Nervous System's stress response
- create new thought habits and associations in our neurology to keep us awake, worrying, in the middle of the night

- trigger the fight-flight-freeze mechanism
- which potentially reduces our performance, making the worst-case-scenario more likely

When you add all of that together, why on earth do we – as a culture – think that is a useful question? I rest my case.

But I NEED Imposter Syndrome!

Fact: no one *needs* Imposter Syndrome.

As we've already discussed, you don't need it to keep you humble (one of the most common justifications I hear). You don't need it to make you relatable and human. You don't need it to keep your ego in check. You don't need it to make sure you avoid others feeling bad about their lives. You don't need Imposter Syndrome to stop you from making bad mistakes.

The opposite of Imposter Syndrome is not arrogance. It is grounded confidence. The only thing Imposter Syndrome does for you is to keep you stuck, dreaming big but playing small. And feeling bad. Especially at 3 a.m.

It is totally possible to live and breathe the light and genius of who you really are in a way that shows compassion to others and which gets you out there making the difference you are really here to make, loving the journey. In fact, it's essential. And that's what you'll learn how to do in Step Five.

If you're finding yourself defending your *need* to *keep* Imposter Syndrome running, then you'll love the techniques in Step Four when we'll be talking about 'secondary gain' – the hidden reason why we stay stuck with beliefs and behaviours that secretly drive us crazy.

That wraps up the everything-you-ever-wanted-to-know-about-Imposter-Syndrome section of this book. Hopefully dealing with some of the myths and understanding how Imposter Syndrome happens – where it came from – has helped you already. There's an exercise in the companion workbook to help you spot what you have learned so far[9].

---

[9] www.DitchingImposterSyndrome.com/vault/

Why It's Going To Work For You This Time

Most change work takes place at the surface-level of the thoughts and perhaps some limiting beliefs. As we have seen with the Imposter Syndrome Iceberg on page 40, this means you're working with the symptoms – the 'effects' of Imposter Syndrome, rather than the root causes that drive it.

It means you'll get those triggers popping up and will have to then remember which different thoughts to think, to stop them from getting in the way. But by the point you become consciously aware of those thoughts, they are likely to have caused you to self-sabotage – or will at least have triggered the Sympathetic Nervous System's stress response and the anxiety and performance issues that leads to.

In this book, you're going to follow my five-step process for ditching Imposter Syndrome. You'll start with looking at the little-known key to success. It's the secret ingredient for keeping going, even if you're not in the mood, and it helps you to tip the 'change seesaw':

Nothing changes until the fear of staying the same is greater than the fear of changing.

Step One helps you to tip that balance. Then you'll move on to taming your Inner Critic in Step Two. It's much easier to do the deeper work, once you are having fewer thoughts (yes, you'll learn how to do that!) and know how to press 'pause' on those that make you feel bad. You'll find out how to tune your inner radio station, both at the emergency quick fix level and at the longer-term level, teaching your internal dialogue to support and encourage you, helping you to feel *truly* confident, rather than pretending.

But change that happens at the conscious, thinking mind, cognitive level has limits. It requires you to have high levels of awareness of your thoughts and actions, which most of us run on autopilot. It demands willpower and determination. True change happens when you go below the surface and work with the subconscious drivers of the surface-level thoughts and behaviours.

You'll start that journey in Step Three, where you'll move on to the subconscious elements of your mind – the part that hides the car keys in the fridge (or is that just me?) You'll discover how to spot exactly which limiting beliefs, out-of-date fears and unconscious excuses are keeping you stuck with Imposter Syndrome – and I'll teach you two of my favourite techniques for letting them go, without beating yourself up.

In Step Four you'll wave goodbye to Imposter Syndrome, having laid firm foundations in Steps One, Two and Three. This is where you'll discover how to easily take off the masks and armour that get in the way of authentic confidence, how to do the deep-acting work that creates lifelong change. You'll handle the single biggest reason why change doesn't stick – so that will no longer be an issue for you. In this section you're going to be working with the identity-level blocks that most people don't even realise are there to be worked with – and I hope you'll be surprised at how easy it can be.

Then, in Step Five, you'll wrap all of this together by exploring the Resilience Myth, the power of intention, influencing authentically, how to connect with your superpowers (fluff-free zone) and the power of Courageous Alignment to allow you to become the leader you were born to be.

To get the most possible from this book, it's important to play with each exercise and strategy; to try them on for size and to allow them to create shifts in your life. All I ask is that you bring an open mind and give this book permission to do what you have asked of it: to help you to Ditch Imposter Syndrome.

Shall we get started by finding out the secret to keeping yourself motivated on your Imposter Syndrome ditching journey?

Step 1: The Little-Known Key To Success

The entire premise of this book is that you will understand more about Imposter Syndrome *and* be able to do something positive about it. We're going to work at a deep-dive level, but I'll also be sharing some 'emergency quick fix' techniques, because there are times when you need something to press 'pause' right away, not in half an hour. The first one of those is in this Step.

Then you'll move on to the transformational, longer-term techniques from Step Two onwards.

Here in Step One you're going to figure out whether or not you are actually running Imposter Syndrome, how to avoid one of the most common reasons why people stay stuck in it, and how to connect with your inner motivation to keep you going through the exercises in this book – and beyond – on your Imposter Syndrome ditching journey,

Do You Have It?

"I can't do that, because I've got Imposter Syndrome."

With a recent paper in a psychological journal suggesting that Imposter Syndrome could be a sign of high potential (we've just talked about why that's nonsense), plus more high-profile women admitting they have struggled with it, suddenly it's as though everyone wants a slice of the Imposter Syndrome pie.

The thing is that Imposter Syndrome is a really specific type of problem. Just because we're doubting ourselves, it doesn't mean it's Imposter Syndrome. Just because we go through a phase of lacking confidence, it doesn't mean it's Imposter Syndrome. Just because we have to stretch a comfort zone, it doesn't suddenly mean we're going to get Imposter Syndrome. Just because we secretly believe we don't deserve to be successful, it doesn't mean we've got Imposter Syndrome.

And this is brilliant news – because it sets you free to clear out what was causing your doubts and wobbles and then to move on.

What I see so often with people who genuinely struggle with Imposter Syndrome is that it's a constant worry-soundtrack in the back of their thoughts, as it lurks – silent as Vesuvius until Pompeii had its final days. We know that the threat of Imposter Syndrome is there. We avoid taking risks that might trigger it. We stress about it coming back and overwhelming us. It affects the thoughts and actions we have every single day, even if it's not currently active in our lives.

When I'm working with someone and we find out it's *not* Imposter Syndrome they're struggling with, the look of relief on their face is always wonderful to see.

Society and experts have tried – with the best of intentions – to tell us that Imposter Syndrome is forever; that we can never 'get rid' of it and we'll be stuck with it for as long as we live. By the end of this book you'll know that's not true. But it's also why I want to make sure you don't give yourself the Imposter Syndrome badge unless you are actually running it.

And there's a fact that people aren't talking about:

Whether or not you run Imposter Syndrome depends on what you're doing. Imposter Syndrome is context dependent.

It might be crucifying you in the context of writing a book, but it may have no effect whatsoever on your ability to iron a shirt.

It might make sure you don't speak up with your brilliant idea in a meeting at work, but it may have no impact on you sharing ideas with your friends.

It might get you discounting your fees without even being asked, or not asking for the pay rise you know you deserve, but it may be of no consequence when you're networking.

This is brilliant news.

This means there is an aspect of you that isn't affected by it at all – and part of you that is. If part of you isn't, that means that Imposter Syndrome is not who you *are*. It's something you sometimes *do* or *experience*. It doesn't need to get mixed up with your sense of identity. You can do something about it.

When you weave something into your sense of self – how you see yourself as *being* – then it becomes part of your identity. The idea of letting go of that 'something' triggers self-preservation instincts. "But that's who I *am*!"

On my garden boundary, there's a very old fence to keep the forest deer out. It is probably older than I am. And there's an old beech tree that grew next to one of the metal fence posts. Over the years, the tree grew and the gap between its trunk and the fence wire narrowed. Now the tree has swallowed up the fence post and the adjacent wire. The two are so entwined that you could no longer remove the fence post without damaging the beautiful old tree.

This is what happens when we mistake Imposter Syndrome as being part of who we *are*, as a person. We grow and wrap ourselves around it until it becomes such a part of us that we believe it would be impossible to let it go.

But it's not. When you see Imposter Syndrome as being something you *do* and *experience*, rather than part of who you *are*, it's much easier to step away from the 3 a.m. thoughts and self-sabotaging behaviours, as you'll learn in Steps Two and Three.

But first, let's find out whether you've actually got Imposter Syndrome.

How To Spot Imposter Syndrome

There's no brain scan that's going to tell you whether or not you have Imposter Syndrome, so the most useful indicators you have are your self-talk and your actions. Here's an overview of how respondents in the 2019 Imposter Syndrome Research Study described their experiences with it, so you can see how you compare.

As we covered on page 17, there's a difference between Imposter Syndrome and self-doubt. The chart below shows how this can be seen in your self-talk:

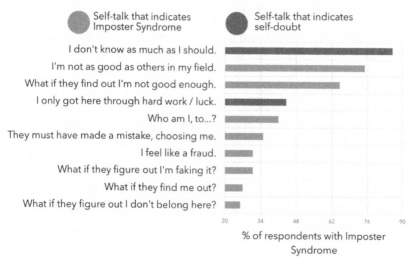

% of respondents with Imposter Syndrome

And here are some common behaviours that people report, as a result of Imposter Syndrome:

Note: in addition to this data, think back over what you've covered so far in this book, especially with the 4Ps of Imposter Syndrome on page 30, and make some notes about which behaviours have resonated with you.

Do You Have It? Hint: It Doesn't Actually Matter

If you're drawing the conclusion that you're low on the Imposter Syndrome scale, please celebrate! This book can still help you with:

- taming your Inner Critic & negative self-talk
- cranking up your confidence to stretch comfort zones
- clearing out the hidden blocks and limiting beliefs that keep us stuck, so you can be more of who you *really* are and make a bigger difference in the world

And if you think you've got a major dose of Imposter Syndrome, you're about to go through the five steps to ditching it, which will make a huge difference for you.

Why I Don't Care How You Got It
– And Nor Should You

There are times when looking for root causes is useful, and times when it keeps you stuck.

Back in my engineering days, I specialised in lean manufacturing (including 'just in time') and Six Sigma, designing products and processes so they could be made as efficiently as possible, with quality standards 'guaranteed'. Root cause analysis was the bread and butter of my team's work. When something went wrong on a production line that cost $2,000 a *minute* to stop, we needed an emergency quick fix to keep things run at the right quality level, but then we took the time to dive in and find out why it happened and fixed it, so it couldn't happen again.

And the 'why' wasn't something like 'Joe put the wrong widget on the wrong fitting' – that's just a surface-level symptom. There's a 'why' and 'how' beneath that. How was it possible for Joe to make that mistake? How could we alter the design of the component or the process, to make it something Joe didn't ever need to think about again, even if someone had just distracted him or he was tired from a long shift? Digging through the layers took us to the genuine root cause of the mistake that had stopped the production line. When we fixed *that*, the problem would never happen again. In manufacturing, this investigative structure is called the 'Five Whys' technique.

When I'm working with business leaders on Imposter Syndrome, I make sure they have those 'sticky plasters' – the emergency quick fixes they need for when they're about to walk into a client pitch or make a suggestion for a radical improvement in a meeting. Their performance in those moments is as important as keeping that production line moving, with the right quality coming out at the end.

But I also work with them at the deeper level, understanding the core triggers for Imposter Syndrome – they're unique to each of us – and clearing those out, so that they no longer have to handle Imposter Syndrome. Because, unlike Joe's production line, we don't have machines checking for quality and mistakes as Imposter Syndrome triggers our subconscious self-sabotage behaviours. We often don't spot it is running until it's too late; until we've turned down that golden opportunity or justified not negotiating a pay rise or convinced ourselves that the brilliant idea we held back from suggesting was rubbish, anyway.

And, just like Joe's work situation, the bits of Imposter Syndrome we are consciously aware of, such as our behaviours and self-talk, are surface-level symptoms. Trying to solve the problem at that level isn't really a solution. The triggers will still come up and we'll be facing a constant battle of willpower and gritted-teeth determination, alongside our 3 a.m. self-talk nightmares.

That's why you can't 'fix' Imposter Syndrome at the thinking level, with positive thinking or contradicting your own self-talk or even trying to change limiting beliefs. Pretending and pushing on through doesn't work with Imposter Syndrome, because it tends to cause the damage before we even realise it's come out to play. It's running at the deeply subconscious identity level – 'who am *I*, to...?'. Dealing with it at that level clears out the root cause triggers.

I have a confession to make. I don't care
how my clients got Imposter Syndrome.

I'm not interested in diving into 'causal events', looking for someone to blame or hold accountable. I won't spend clients' time on finding the trigger that allows them to say, I've got Imposter Syndrome, because..."

I'm not negating the trauma, PTSD or core belief-triggering experiences that may have happened. But I *am* saying that we move towards our destination by looking out front, not by getting lost, gazing into the rear-view mirror.

Imagine going to your chosen health professional for help with, say, lower back pain. You will most likely be given something to ease the current pain and inflammation and then, hopefully, be referred to someone to find out what is causing it, so it can be healed. But imagine if that showed up it was the way you're sitting at your desk at work, but before they would help you to fix this, the professional insisted on knowing *why* your boss had set the desk up this way and what happened in your childhood to mean that you accepted having an uncomfortable desk and didn't complain about it or didn't even notice it? We'd feel pretty narked at being forced to navel-gaze, when what we want is a solution. Yet that's what so many of us unwittingly do with Imposter Syndrome. Because sometimes it feels safer to look for an event to blame than to set ourselves free.

With people, the '5 Whys' style of questioning is like asking a child why they threw the marble through the plate glass window of the display cabinet and then fibbed about it being their older sister (I clearly still have baggage to clear on that one). With a child under five, the answer is likely to be a genuine 'I don't know why'. With an older child, you're likely to get a lower-lip-pouting 'because'.

When we spend our time and energy
asking why we run Imposter Syndrome,
looking for the original trigger event (hint:
there often wasn't one), it risks setting us up
to feel like a victim, handing our power over
our present performance to some person or
problem in the past that caused us to pick
up that limiting belief.

It risks Imposter Syndrome becoming a 'badge of honour', as we tell ourselves stories that justify and validate why we can't achieve our dreams. We talk about 'my' Imposter Syndrome and I 'have' it. It is like a treasured possession. Those mind-story dramas become our excuses for playing safe and being hemmed in by our fears, as we remind ourselves that we can't do 'X', because... And, as you'll see in Step Three, this keeps you neurologically stuck, hard-wiring those stories into your brain.

Looking for someone or something external
to blame does not help you to heal
Imposter Syndrome. It digs you in more
deeply.

In fact, blame doesn't help in any way, ever. It disempowers us, because something was done *to* us, *by* that external force.

If you have an obvious trigger event for your Imposter Syndrome, then clearing the emotional pain and effects of that is certainly worthwhile. Taking time to resolve the emotions that may have come with it, to reach a place of acceptance and forgiveness can be vital. But there's no point in putting time, effort and energy into playing detective if the answer isn't obvious, when you could put those resources into setting yourself free from Imposter Syndrome, instead.

Why Do You Want To Ditch It?

If you're a bookworm, like me, Simon Sinek published a great book called *It Starts With Why*. It's his take on how successful brands and organisations need their teams and their customers to have bought into their 'why' – the 'because'.

It's the key to you ditching Imposter Syndrome, too.

When we connect deeply with our Big Why – that 'because' – we are connecting with something that is important to us at the 'values' level of the Imposter Syndrome Iceberg. The more passion and energy we put into a value, the more power it gives us to create change. And that's why I want you to connect with your Big Why for ditching Imposter Syndrome, before we move on to dispelling the myths about it.

When I'm working with clients and they're stuck, going back to their 'because' helps them to find that extra bit of courage to keep going – and the breakthrough they were dreaming of is often much closer than they had thought.

Knowing your Big Why helps you to choose where to 'spend' your attention and energy: "Do I really want to feed that mind-story fear more than I want to feed my dreams?"

Your Big Why is about more than getting a flashy car or a bigger house. It's at that deeper value-identity level, connected to your 'why am I here?' question.

Your Big Why doesn't have to be your perfect, definitive, forever Big Why. It just needs to be something that creates a positive emotional pull for you, creating a sense of relief and excitement in your body, which will connect you with that passion to keep you going, even if you're not in the mood.

We'll be coming back to your Big Why regularly throughout this book, so it's really worth taking a few minutes now to explore it.

The following guided visualisation is designed to help you with this. And there's an MP3 of it in the Readers' Resource Vault for this book. So make sure you've signed up to download it and your companion workbook now: www.DitchingImposterSyndrome.com/vault/

Guided Visualisation: What's Your Big Why For Ditching Imposter Syndrome?

Start by taking three deep, sighing breaths, in through your nose and out through your mouth with an 'ahhh'.

Thinking about Imposter Syndrome, how does it currently affect you? Think of two or three examples.

Now imagine you can move forward in time to a year from now, when you have cleared out Imposter Syndrome and it no longer gets in your way.

How does life feel? What kinds of things are you doing differently?

Which version of 'you' have you allowed yourself to become?

Now imagine you can move forward in time to five years from now, once Imposter Syndrome is such a distant memory you can barely sense how it used to get in your way.

How differently are you living now, without Imposter Syndrome?

And allow the answer to the following question to bubble up, without editing:

I want to ditch Imposter Syndrome, because (write it here):

The 'because' is your Big Why for this book. That which you can imagine, you can create. And the how-to for getting you to that Imposter Syndrome-free experience of life you have just been imagining is what currently lies in your hands with this book.

Emergency Quick Fix

As promised, it's time for one of my emergency quick fixes for Imposter Syndrome. This is the technique you need if there's no time for navel-gazing or even thinking. You need something that works fast, even if it's a bit of a sticky plaster. It helps to reset the Sympathetic Nervous System's stress response, which means you can think more clearly.

Maybe you're about to walk into a client pitch. Perhaps you're about to click 'send' on an email that could change your life. Maybe you've just had a brilliant idea and you're desperate to speak up in the middle of the meeting you're in.

Then this one's for you.

The rest of this book teaches you what to do to tame your Inner Critic, to let go of out-of-date limiting beliefs (there's no such thing as an 'in-date' one!) and to clear out Imposter Syndrome properly. For now, here's your one-minute, near-magic-wand fix.

There are three keys to this technique. The first is getting grounded. That helps to rebalance your Autonomic Nervous System, so that your fight-flight-freeze response is no longer screaming for attention. The second element is pressing 'pause' on the negative self-talk that triggered the Imposter Syndrome outbreak, because there's no point in calming down your stress response if you're going to keep thinking the thoughts that created it. Then you can use a visualisation technique to instantly boost your confidence and shift your Inner Critic from the beat-up zone to cheerleader mode.

This technique allows you to crank up your confidence, to connect with your Inner Genius, and to perform at the standard you know you can achieve. Once you're familiar with this, it takes less than sixty seconds.

Resource: Emergency Quick Fix Video & MP3

There's a video, and MP3 and a downloadable cheat sheet for this technique, waiting for you in the Readers' Resources Vault. That's where you will also find a downloadable workbook for all of the exercises in this book, with space for you to write down your answers. www.DitchingImposterSyndrome.com/vault/

Exercise: Your Emergency Quick Fix

Step 1: Getting grounded

Stand up tall with your feet about shoulder width apart. Become aware of the points of contact between your feet and the floor.

Imagine you are growing roots from the soles of your feet into the earth beneath you, connecting you, bringing you back into your body and out of your stress head.

When you're ready, take three deep sighing breaths, to bring you back here, right now. Breathe in through your nose and out through your mouth with an 'ahhh'. It's ok to smile while you do this!

With your next in-breath, imagine you are breathing in through the soles of your feet, from deep in the earth, the confidence, the groundedness, the wisdom and the strength of a mountain. Allow this to travel all the way up through your legs to your belly.

On each out-breath, imagine any tension, stress or worry is being released through your belly, down through your feet and into the earth, letting it go.

Continue in your own time for a few breaths.

Step 2: Pressing Pause

Now imagine you're looking at a movie screen and an actor is playing the 'you' who has been experiencing the Imposter Syndrome gremlins. Watch the acting out of ONE of those thoughts and ask yourself: "Is this really true?"

Let your body give you the answer. If it's not true, that will often feel like a release of tension. If you believe it is true, somewhere in your body will tense up.

If it's a yes, make a commitment to go and do something about it, later, when you have time!

If it's not true, breathe it out through your legs and feet into the earth and let it go.

... continues

Step 3: Visualisation

When you're ready, think about something you feel grateful for about how you are living your life right now – something that brings you that sense of happiness and joy and gladness. Imagine it starts as a soft, warm, golden light in the area of your heart and your chest. As you think about that thing you feel grateful for about, allow that sensation of soft, warm, golden light to expand through your chest.

Think of another thing you feel grateful for about how you're living your life and with each breath allow that soft, warm, golden light to effortlessly expand through your abdomen, your pelvis, your thighs, your calves, your shins, your ankles, the tops of your feet, the soles of your feet and the tips of your toes.

And as you think of one more thing you feel grateful for about how you're living your life, allow that soft, warm, golden light to expand from your heart and your chest to expand, filling your shoulders, your upper arms, your elbows, your forearms, your wrists, your palms and your fingertips, up through your neck, your throat, your jaw; relaxing your face, the muscles around your eyes, your scalp and out through the crown of your head.

Breathe in the confidence, the calm and the stillness of the earth, feeling every cell of your body being washed through with that soft, warm, golden light of gratitude, for who you really are.

And as you prepare to release this process, open your eyes, if they've been closed, give yourself a stretch and a really good yawn. Then stamp your feet on the floor a few times to really come back here, now. And know that this process is here for you, whenever you want to feel more confident, get grounded, get out of your stress-head and back into your body, and connect with your Inner Genius.

Imagine if you started your day with this technique, each day for a week. How might it start to become second nature? How might it shift your experience of your day? The choices you make? Your ability to be even more 'you'?

The key is to play with this regularly, so that if a time comes where you actually *need* it, it's already second nature; you're anchored into the process and it takes under sixty seconds to turn things around.

What did you notice as you did this exercise? Which shifts could you feel in your body; your thoughts; your emotions?

Some people like to read through this book without doing the exercises. And it will still produce results for you as the insights and lightbulbs help you to understand how to set yourself free from the games your mind has been playing with you.

But those who get the best results – the transformations that last a lifetime – actually pause to do each exercise, as they go through. They are specially designed to help you create breakthroughs in just a few minutes, and they're the kinds of things we would be doing together, if I were able to support you one-to-one on this.

So if you find yourself wanting to skim through and not do the work, pause for a moment and ask yourself what you're getting to *avoid* or *keep* by not putting in this tiny bit of extra effort to ditching Imposter Syndrome. Then check out the 'secondary gain' section on page 195 to find out why it's important to deal with that unmet need, for change to work.

Remember: there's a downloadable PDF workbook in the Readers' Resource Vault for you to make notes and write your question answers down. It's worth spending a moment now to get your copy – and other resources that go with this book:

www.DitchingImposterSyndrome.com/vault/

Now you've got clarity on how Imposter Syndrome has been affecting you, you've connected with your Big Why and how life will feel afterwards, and you've got an emergency quick fix, it's time to dive in with Step Two – taming your Inner Critic.

Let's crack on with making sure those emergencies don't need to crop up!

Step 2: Taming Your Inner Critic

What Is Your Inner Critic?

*"The words we speak will become the
house we live in." Hafiz
And that goes for your self-talk, too.*

Most people don't notice the conversations they have in their heads. It's like that radio station in the background – you're vaguely aware of it and would notice if it switched off, but hours can pass without consciously noticing a single word. It's only when that inner conversation yells to get your attention or if you do something to silence your outer world, such as go on a meditation retreat, that you finally notice how talkative your mind really is.

That would be great, if that internal conversation involved a team of virtual cheerleaders. But that's rarely the case. Normally it's your Inner Critic setting the agenda and chairing the meeting. As we'll cover in this section, that can do untold damage to your confidence, your actions and even how you handle Imposter Syndrome.

Yet most people have fallen for the myth that there's nothing you can do about 'negative thinking' (we'll cover why that's not a helpful term). So they put up with how their self-talk makes them feel bad, play small and have to push on through their fears. The cumulative effect of this over the decades is immense.

So, in Step Two you're going to learn how to tame your Inner Critic – in under sixty seconds – how to make friends with it (yes, it can be helpful), how to understand the role it has been playing for you with Imposter Syndrome, and how to turn it into your biggest cheerleader, without white-washing, pretending or having a daily hissy fit at it.

Your Inner Critic comes from the semi-subconscious conversation you have in your head. It can be in words or images or physical sensations – or a combination of these. It can be a running commentary on the world around you, describing what you see. It can evaluate what you're seeing – "Ooh! Interesting lipstick choice with that dress!" It can analyse what is happening. It can replay past events. It can play 'what if' scenarios and try to predict the future.

This dialogue is a collection of habitual thoughts. Thoughts are electrochemical reactions that fire off in the brain's trillions of synapses (tiny gaps), which connect its billions of neurons (nerve cells). Even neuroscientists aren't sure where thoughts 'come from'. But we know they are often triggered by sensory stimuli – from the breeze in your hair to the photons produced by the words on this page reaching your retina and being encoded by your brain into words that (hopefully) make sense.

As we discussed on page 24, these thoughts have autopilot shortcuts, like motorways in your brain, so that, for instance, you don't have to figure out what a red traffic light is and what it requires you to do, every time you see one. That's a good thing. But when it comes to your internal dialogue, those thought habits can cause problems. When these thoughts become self-critical, your Inner Critic comes out to play, with its well-rehearsed scripts.

We've also talked about how the filters in your brain's Reticular Activating System influence what we notice – and hence what we think. And we've covered in the Imposter Syndrome Iceberg how our beliefs, what's important to us, and who we see ourselves as being affect our thoughts. Step Three will take you through how to handle the limiting beliefs that could be getting in your way and Step Four tackles the identity-level issues. To make the shifts you'll get to create in those steps much more effective, it really helps to start by taming your Inner Critic – being able to choose which thoughts to feed. That's what we're doing here in Step Two.

If you're running a self-critical series of thoughts, you can't force them to shut up. By trying to 'get rid' of negative thoughts, you're giving them all of your attention, effectively handing them the power to choose which actions you'll take. Your Inner Critic loves a good fight – its food is drama. So trying to push it down or telling it that it's wrong will trigger the 'backfire effect' we talked about on page 68, making it increase the volume and ferocity of its message to prove its point.

Similarly, you can't white-wash it into positive thinking. That creates internal conflict, as we covered with the Imposter Syndrome pantomime on page 84. This risks making the Inner Critic worse. That's why the techniques you'll cover in this section are specially designed to avoid that.

The world of meditation often describes this inner dialogue as the 'Monkey Mind' or your 'grasshopper mind', as it jumps from topic to topic, throwing in random ideas, and generally causing havoc. One of the key benefits of regular meditation is being able to calm those thoughts, as we'll cover later in this section.

When I was nine, I was in the junior Girl Guides, called the Brownies. I was a 'sixer' (team leader) and my team was called the 'imps'. I remember back then wondering if that gave us permission to misbehave. Apparently it didn't. But I used to spend a lot of time day-dreaming about the way imps might behave. Now, decades later, I sometimes feel my inner dialogue is like having a bunch of imps running around in my head, getting in the way and turning my goals upside down. When I describe those thoughts as being like imps instead of a critic, it makes them feel softer and more playful – mischievous instead of intentionally damaging.

I don't personally believe that 'negative thinking' is a helpful way to describe this inner dialogue, especially if your self-talk is far from supportive. For most people, their thoughts feel random and out of their control. Describing these as 'negative' is a form of self-judgement, which is a major causal factor in Imposter Syndrome (we cover this in depth in Step Four).

You risk ending up judging yourself for having a thought that was judging yourself.

Also, many people believe that they *are* their thoughts. So if those thoughts are 'negative', then that becomes an identity-level judgement, which is a recipe for stress, anxiety and Imposter Syndrome.

The other issue with judging your self-talk as negative is that you risk missing the gifts it holds for you. Yes, I know it doesn't feel like much of a gift when your Inner Critic has you wanting to hide from the world or give up on your dreams. But, as you'll discover in this Step and Steps Three and Four, there are ways to unravel your Inner Critic's dialogue to discover which simple shifts can create breakthroughs for you.

So instead of hating your Inner Critic and feeling like it's an enemy, it can really help to make friends with it, to listen to it (without diving into the drama) and to work with it to clear the blocks that have been keeping you stuck.

The Secret Power Of Self-Talk

... and the risks of letting it run wild!

Your self-talk is the expression of your subconscious – the part of you that wants to keep you safe from danger, as we discussed on page 21. It uses the dialogues we have rehearsed over the years to communicate with us. The tone of the thoughts and even their content are something we can change, which is what you'll discover later in this step.

But it's important to know that your unconscious mind takes your self-talk as unfiltered instructions. Remember the saxophone-playing donkey? If your inner dialogue is all about how tired you feel, your unconscious mind will obey by triggering the biochemical reactions that keep you feeling tired. If you're telling yourself stories about how you don't deserve success or you're not as good as your peers, it will find ways to help you to self-sabotage and support that self-talk.

All of this is automatic. As babies, we're curious, but naturally programmed to keep ourselves safe. We have reflexes that alert us if our brains detect that we might fall. We flinch at loud sounds. Things that scare us make us contract – to try to become smaller. As we grow, these self-preservation reflexes expand to cover not just our physical world, but our mental and emotional worlds, too. We are wired to protect ourselves from emotional and psychological pain, not just physical danger. We don't just stick with flinching at loud noises, we flinch – contract – at other things that scare us, too, causing us to play small or hold on tight to a familiar comfort zone. And all the time your self-talk is training your RAS filters what to be scared of.

The link between your thoughts, your emotions and your body's physiology are governed by the Autonomic Nervous System, which means they're involuntary and not normally within our conscious control. So you won't be able to think a criticising thought and feel a happy emotion at the same time. As we discussed with the Imposter Syndrome Iceberg, these thoughts affect your actions and the results you achieve.

*If your thoughts flinch at the idea of a goal,
your body does, too, setting off a fear-
based response.*

When you think critical thoughts, this triggers the body's stress response to protect you from a perceived threat. That sets off the biochemical reactions that get you ready to fight, fly or freeze.

Your body doesn't care whether that response was triggered by a hypothetical 'what if' discussion in your head. It doesn't care if it was your mind replaying a past event. It gets you ready to run, right here, right now. That's why fear-based thoughts create tension in your body, as though winding up a spring. You might notice it in your belly or your jaw – or even your fists.

Your body feels every thought you think, without filtering. It can get addicted to those biochemical reactions, especially those triggered by cortisol, which is why so many high-achievers love the thrill of leaving things to the last minute and 'forcing' themselves to then achieve Herculean feats to get their 'to do' list done.

Over time, though, the adrenalin and cortisol hit that we get from our mind story drama has less effect. So your body helps your mind to ramp up the stories in your self-talk to trigger higher levels of the hormones it craves. Those imps in your head turn into gremlins, without your consent, wreaking their unique blend of self-talk damage. It can feel impossible to press 'stop' on that train.

One of the ways your brain cranks up the drama – and hence the biochemical reactions – is to take things personally. When criticism becomes about who you *are*, as a person, rather than your behaviours – what you *do* – it hurts more. It triggers higher levels of the involuntary stress response. It turns a little bit of self-doubt into a massive dollop of Imposter Syndrome.

Remember we talked about how adding in hefty emotions to a thought habit turns it into a motorway in your brain – a brand new autopilot that stops you from speaking up with your great ideas or seizing the opportunity to shine. That's the power of your self-talk.

And there's another layer to this:

*The level of drama in your self-talk about
your emotions directly affects the level of
stress your body feels.*

The language we use to describe our emotions – to ourselves or others – keeps us stuck in the cortisol cycle. When something goes wrong, it's easy to use phrases like, "I was *devastated!*" instead of thinking about being 'a bit miffed'. We might say, "I felt *distraught!*" when what we actually mean is we felt quite upset. Just as 'tired and weak' had an effect on your body, emotions and self-talk stories, so will adjectives like *hysterical* or *shattered*, where *agitated* or *tired* would suffice.

The more extreme the words you use to describe your emotions, the bigger those muddy boots are, stomping their way through the field in your brain, creating autopilot motorways. If this is something you struggle with, make sure you pay special attention to the techniques on page 142 where we'll be talking about how to retune your inner radio station. And if you often use the worlds 'I am' in front of your emotional adjectives, make sure you read page 241 where you'll find out how this can accidentally keep you stuck forever in those emotions...

If chronic, long-term stress and self-critical self-talk are features of your life, then these can make Imposter Syndrome nigh-on inevitable – with the hypervigilance trap.

Falling Into The Hypervigilance Trap

The human body is designed to handle stress. If it weren't, the human race wouldn't have survived for very long. But it's designed to handle stress only in *short* bursts – the whole system is intended to come back to equilibrium – homeostasis – once the danger has passed.

Our modern lives mean we rarely switch off and it's common to be glued to a screen (or multiple screens) from the moment you wake until long after lights-out. The effect of this is that the body's 'stress reset' system doesn't get to do its job. The stress response is governed by your HPA Axis. HPA stands for Hypothalamic- Pituitary-Adrenal. The hypothalamus and pituitary glands are in your brain; your adrenal glands sit just above your kidneys. Between them they help your body to regulate the stress hormones, including cortisol and adrenalin.

The clever bit about how they work is a feedback loop that makes sure you don't overload your system on cortisol and its buddies – bringing you out of the Sympathetic Nervous System's stress response and back into that balanced homeostasis of feeling relaxed, but alert. That's really important, because when the Sympathetic Nervous System kicks in, it switches off the body's non-essential mechanisms (like healing, digestion and cellular-level regeneration), to give more energy to the muscles, heart and lungs to get ready to run. Getting back into homeostasis brings the Parasympathetic Nervous System (your body's relaxation response) back into the game and your body gets to look after itself again.

But if you spend years running with stress and low-level mind-story fears your 24-7 companions, this feedback loop struggles to cope with the near-constant cortisol and your body struggles to regulate the stress hormones, taking you *out* of balance, into allostasis, with the Sympathetic Nervous System triggered most of the time. This leads to what is called 'toxic stress'.

Medical research is showing that this HPA Axis imbalance can trigger anxiety, recurrent infections and even weight gain, as the body's natural healing mechanism is disrupted by the low-level stress we experience.

When the body is running on adrenalin, it is looking for perceived threats – its focus is avoiding danger. It doesn't give two hoots about next week's presentation or the review meeting with your boss. It cares about your survival. This constant 'high alert' state (even at low levels) trains the RAS filters in your brain to spot more threats. Unless you know how to press the reset, this can lead to hypervigilance.

Hypervigilance is a state of constant sensory awareness, looking out for danger. It is often connected with PTSD (Post-Traumatic Stress Disorder). Back in 1941, Abram Kardiner – a psychiatrist who researched the effects of war and trauma – noticed that after trauma people could develop a chronic vigilance for and sensitivity to threat. This causes someone to become jumpy, irritable and anxious. It can also cause them to become more sensitive to perceived threats, easily becoming emotional and over-reacting.

But more recent research is showing that hypervigilance doesn't only occur after single trauma incidents: it can be the result of chronic, long-term stress, hard-wiring your body and brain to be in its fight-flight-freeze mode, looking for threats. When we live under those conditions, the stories we tell ourselves about our fears of what might happen (AKA worrying) can trigger mini-traumas, multiple times a day. Hypervigilance makes us more likely to pay attention to these self-talk stories and these self-talk stories make hypervigilance more likely to kick off.

Here's the bad news: having a well-trained Inner Critic that has convinced you that you might be found out as a fraud or which sings you to sleep with stories about how everyone else knows more than you increases the likelihood of this hypervigilant response. Your brain is desperate to protect you from harm – which includes being judged or rejected.

So a throwaway comment from a colleague might trigger an emotional outburst or the prickling of tears, because you've hard-wired the hypervigilant response into your nervous system and you're already on high alert.

There is evidence that Imposter Syndrome's repeated fears can create a series of mini-traumas that lead to what is termed 'Complex PTSD'. This Complex PTSD can trigger hypervigilance and the HPA Axis imbalance, above, as well as anxiety and even clinical depression.

In reverse, chronic stress can trigger hypervigilance – the heightened awareness of threats – which can make you more likely to take 'feedback' personally, making it more likely that Imposter Syndrome will strike. In such cases, Imposter Syndrome is effectively trying to protect you from harm. That's why it's so much more than a 'mind-trap' or something you can 'think' your way out of – it's much more complex than that. The five steps in this book are there to help you, even if you're running Imposter Syndrome at that level.

Many of my business leader clients have been stuck in this cycle, without realising, and they risk ending up using addictions such as alcohol, gym workouts or sugar to self-medicate and try to combat that stress response.

Hypervigilance is a hormone-driven response to threats, triggered by the Autonomic Nervous System, which means it is outside of our conscious control. To clear it, you need to be able to desensitise yourself from the stress, getting your nervous system back into balance – including the HPA Axis cortisol response. It is utterly exhausting, which – ironically – means we rely more heavily on adrenalin and caffeine to keep going, which makes the hypervigilance and HPA Axis imbalance worse.

To clear this, you need to be able to reduce the sensitisation caused by the stress or Complex PTSD and to reset the HPA Axis, so you can get your hormone-driven stress response back into balance. Long-term, techniques from the worlds of yoga and meditation are really helpful, especially belly breathing techniques. There's more on this in the Readers' Resource Vault.

And one way you can start this for yourself is in being able to press 'pause' on the mind-story fears and drama in your self-talk, to reduce how often your stress response is triggered, which you will know how to do by the end of this section.

So, instead of ignoring your self-talk and hoping it will go away (which is what most people do), I invite you to dive into the strategies you're going to cover in the following steps to set yourself free from your Inner Critic, to retrain your brain to become your biggest cheerleader, and to experience how to ditch your mind-imps, before they turn into gremlins. And we're going to start by playing detective: uncovering how you *do* Imposter Syndrome.

How Do You Do Imposter Syndrome?

Have you ever noticed how when you feel confused about how to do something, it can feel like an impossible task? But as soon as you 'get' the how-to, the steps can fall into place?

It's the same with creating change in your life: to change a habit often requires us to understand how and why we do what we're already doing – dragging ourselves back into the conscious competence or conscious incompetence zones from the learning ladder on page 56. Carl Jung said that awareness is the key to change. So the first step towards ditching Imposter Syndrome is dragging it out of your subconscious autopilot habits into your conscious awareness, so you can choose where to make changes.

This isn't about spending the next three months deep-diving on your navel-gazing or over-thinking the way you do Imposter Syndrome. It's about understanding the process, as though it were a manufacturing line, so you can spot the triggers and take 'corrective' action, earlier in the process.

That's an important distinction. You don't 'have' Imposter Syndrome. If you did, it would be something you could give away (that's not a gift you'd ever get a thank you note for). It's also not really who you *are* – you aren't actually a fraud or a fake. We just *see* ourselves that way when it's running. Imposter Syndrome is 'just' a series of thought and behavioural habits that you *do*. That's much easier to imagine changing than something you *have* or *are*.

It's really important to do the exercise in this section with a sense of fun, rather than over-thinking. Remember: I'm not interested in *how* you 'got' Imposter Syndrome or even *why* you do it. Over-thinking and over-analysing can lead to Imposter Syndrome paralysis.

It's time to have a chat with an alien. This idea behind this exercise is to help you get 'out of your own head' and to decode the steps you take on your own version of the Imposter Syndrome autopilot, so that you can more easily make changes. Remember: Imposter Syndrome is something you *do*, rather than something you *have*, so it's time to map out your how-to, by teaching your version of Imposter Syndrome to an alien.

This exercise, like all of them, is part of the companion workbook that you'll find in the Readers' Resource Vault. The workbook includes the exercise questions, with space for you to write your answers: www.DitchingImposterSyndrome.com/vault/

Exercise: How Do You Do Imposter Syndrome?

I want to imagine that you've met an alien, who is visiting earth, and you've been chatting about how we get in the way of what we want. Let's call him / her / it Glurg. Glurg simply doesn't get it. It's not a problem they have on their planet.

And Glurg wants to understand more about this concept. So you paint them a verbal recipe for 'doing' Imposter Syndrome. Do this with self-compassion: it's about awareness, not beating yourself up.

Use the questions below to map out the Imposter Syndrome journey. And this is about how *you* do it, not humans in general.

Start by explaining to Glurg how you know that Imposter Syndrome has come out to play. What are your early warning signs? What kinds of things are you thinking when you realise it? What are you seeing? Saying?

Now Glurg wants to know the details of the steps you take to *do* Imposter Syndrome. Imagine you're going back in time to the start of an episode of Imposter Syndrome. What triggers that autopilot? Stick with a single example for now.

Once that trigger has been nudged, what's next for you? How does it affect your thoughts and feelings and physical sensations, in the early stages?

Is there a point at which you can press 'pause'?

If there isn't / you don't, what happens next, as Imposter Syndrome goes from 'early warning signs' to 'ready to deploy'?

.. continues

What happens next, as it gets to 'full launch'? What kinds of thoughts are you thinking? What kinds of things are you doing? What kinds of things are you *not* doing? What makes you make those choices?

Then at the end of an episode of Imposter Syndrome, how do you know that the rocket boosters have powered down? How do you feel afterwards? What kinds of things are you thinking? And saying? And doing?

Because Glurg is a kinda positive chap / chapess / chapit, describe to Glurg how your life will be once Imposter Syndrome is no longer an issue for you – if you could live like Glurg?

And finally: look back through your answers. Is there anything that surprises you? Anything you could let go of right away? Any lightbulbs? If you could change the journey that Imposter Syndrome takes with your mind-story fears and your dreams, where could you make changes to have maximum impact?

We'll be coming back to your answers from this exercise over the next few steps. For now, just 'park' them; there's no need to change them yet, aside from letting go of what is obviously no longer serving you.

Whenever I'm designing a training programme, be it online or in the corporate world, I start with a process flow chart (you can take the girl out of engineering...) It usually begins as a series of coloured paper notes on the floor, mapping out the journey the delegates need to take to achieve the desired outcome. In fact, this is also how I mapped out this book.

Once the flow chart or process is there in front of me, it's easy to shift things around, seeing what's going to take them towards the goal or move them away from it and distract them – or derail them. If you do the same for how you *do* Imposter Syndrome, there will be elements you know you can simply screw up and chuck in the recycling. There will be triggers you can remove. There will be places where you can press 'pause'. I'll be showing you how to do this, later in this step.

Bringing how you do Imposter Syndrome into your conscious awareness gives you back your choice over how to respond to life's curve balls. That's why we're going to dive in with your Early Warning Signs. They're a great place to start.

How To Spot Your Early Warning Signs

There's a thing in engineering called 'gain'. It's not about getting stuff. It's about what gets amplified in a system. I used to live in a very old house. With a straw hat for a roof (thatch). It was so old that it was already 100 when Henry VIII was crowned. It was listed in so many directories of 'interesting old houses' that it wasn't uncommon to look out of my bedroom window to find an elderly gentleman or three pointing geriatric Box Brownie cameras at us, from across the road.

It also had a dreadful TV picture. I was half-convinced that my favourite drama stars lived in a fuzzy parallel universe where everything crackled and hissed and everyone looked kind of the same. My inner engineer knew the cause was obvious – the cable from the aerial on the chimney was close to being perished, so the signal had to get past those electronic hurdles to reach my TV set. Engineers call that 'noise' – it's stuff you want that gets in the way of the outcome you want.

I figured an amplifier would fix the problem – something to add 'gain' to the signal, so that we finally had a watchable TV picture.

But, as every control systems or electronic engineer knows: where you add gain in the system is critical to the output you get. In other words, put the amplifier in the wrong place and you'll make things worse.

Normally an amplifier would go near the TV, because it's inside the house and they like to be warm and dry. It amplifies the signal from the local TV transmitter. But this would have trashed our TV picture. Why? Because as well as amplifying the signal from the TV mast however many miles away I'd also have been amplifying the 'noise' from the damaged cable. It wouldn't have fixed anything and could even have made it worse.

What was the answer? To place an amplifier as close as possible to the aerial, to boost the TV programme signal, despite the noise, so that the noise from the damaged cable had less of an effect.

The earlier in a process you can fix a glitch, the smaller its effect will be on the end result. Otherwise its 'noise' (negative impact) gets amplified by everything else down the line – including our autopilot habits and self-talk scripts and our mind-story fears. So in the case of your Imposter Syndrome work from the previous section (courtesy of Glurg), if you can press 'pause' at the Early Warning Signs stages, Imposter Syndrome will have a much smaller effect. You're no longer amplifying the 'noise' it creates with your mind-story dramas.

The sooner you spot those EWS (think 'eeuww', as in 'yuck', to get how I'd love you to be saying this!), the easier they are to handle. But don't worry – it's never too late to press 'pause'.

Exercise: How To Spot Your EWS

Go back to your Glurg exercise and start with your answers to the first section. Start by explaining to Glurg how you know that Imposter Syndrome has come out to play. What are your early warning signs? What kinds of things are you thinking when you realise it? What are you seeing? Saying? Write these down.

Now think of a specific example of Imposter Syndrome that was a three or four out of ten for you in terms of seriousness.

As you walk through the EWS of how you realised that Imposter Syndrome had come out to play, tune in to your self-talk and your body-tension link. What do you notice? Where in your body is that tension? What happens with your breathing? What kinds of thoughts are you thinking? Which emotions are you feeling? These are your Imposter Syndrome 'tells'.

Go through the grounding exercise from your Emergency Quick Fix on page 103, imagining you're growing roots like a tree into the earth, then doing your three deep, sighing breaths. Imagine you can breathe in and out of the place in your body where that tension is. Imagine you can breathe in the calm of a mountain (like you did in your Emergency Quick Fix) and then as you breathe out you can release that physical tension, letting it flow into the earth. Do this until you feel that the area of tension has relaxed.

Notice the shift in your thoughts. What has changed?

Now ask yourself: how do I want to *feel,* instead?

Allow that feeling to grow in your body, putting the smile back onto your face.

Can you imagine being able to do this whenever those EWS come out to play? Can you sense how it means you'll no longer be amplifying the effects of Imposter Syndrome thoughts and feelings, by knowing how to turn it around, fast?

This still counts as an 'emergency quick fix', rather than a permanent solution. But if you do this little and often, you'll be training your brain and your body to instinctively know how to press 'pause' on those autopilots, and it becomes a preventative measure for Imposter Syndrome as you rewire your neural pathways, changing your autopilots.

The process you have just followed will help to press 'reset' on the stress response from your mind-stories, rebalancing your nervous system and setting you free from the fight-flight-freeze of the Sympathetic Nervous System. I'm curious: how might you remind yourself to play with this?

Once you know how to spot and handle your Early Warning Signs for Imposter Syndrome, it's useful to have some emergency stop buttons up your sleeve. Here are four of my favourites.

Four Emergency Stop Buttons

If you spot an Early Warning Sign of Imposter Syndrome, it's incredibly helpful to have the mind-equivalent of 'reset buttons', to press 'pause' on the autopilot cycle between your thoughts, emotions and physiology, getting you off the Imposter Syndrome hamster wheel.

You've already got my Imposter Syndrome emergency quick fix (page 103) and in this section I want to give you ideas for other 'reset buttons' you can use. They work for those times when Imposter Syndrome is nagging, rather than yelling, and they can reset your self-talk to let go of the drama and the emotions, stopping a bout of Imposter Syndrome before it does damage.

This resets that Sympathetic Nervous System fight-flight-freeze response, helping you to relax, feel calmer and stop the stress response. Here are four ways you can press 'reset', without having to pretend or fake how you're feeling. Please note that these strategies are 'quick fixes', rather than something to genuinely clear Imposter Syndrome from your life, but they're really helpful steps.

1. Keep A 'Wins' File

Whether this is something you drag out of your drawer or save on your phone, keep a folder of 'wins' – times when you did really well.

The key to making this work is to be specific about the role you played in that success. So this isn't about your team's wins; it's about what *you* did to help create that outcome. Make adding to it a priority, so your Inner Critic can't dismiss it as out-of-date.

One of the symptoms of Imposter Syndrome is that our internal reference system, responsible for assessing our performance, gets out of balance and becomes overly critical. So both the creation and the updating of this folder of achievements is an important way to help redress the balance.

And, no, keeping this folder won't suddenly make you arrogant or big-headed. But it can boost your confidence, right when you need it most, countering the self-talk of 'who am *I*, to...?' and 'what if they find I'm not good enough'.

2. Thank You Letters And Praise

The companion to your internal reference system is the external reference system. When you're listening to this, it means you're placing your decision-making trust in the opinions of others, rather than deciding for yourself. It's a context-dependent thing: if you always read reviews before buying a book, you're running an externally referenced decision process. If you instead prefer to make up your own mind and ignore star ratings, then you're running an internally referenced pattern – in *that* context. But in another context, your preference might be reversed.

Generally, it's a sliding scale and we do a bit of each in most situations. But with Imposter Syndrome that internal referencing system gets out of balance, so it's important to be able to reference objective, external validation to help rebalance your inner view of your performance and who you are.

Keeping a folder of thank you letters and praise, no matter how small, can remind you that others think you're doing well. Looking back through it whenever your Early Warning Signs pop up can help to stop a bout of your self-talk imps turning into post-midnight-feasting gremlins.

And if you're stuck in an Imposter Syndrome slump, find a way to ask someone you trust to boost your morale. It might be your boss or a trusted colleague or mentor or a friend. The key is that, at some level, you trust them to be accurately evaluating your performance, otherwise their feedback won't get past your Reticular Activating System's filters! (See page 23).

3. The Woolly Jumper Test

Sometimes it's a piece of feedback that throws us into an Imposter Syndrome spin. A single 'but' can invalidate half an hour of praise.

Why is that? Because if we're already running RAS filters that we're somehow not good enough or are about to be found out as a fraud, we've programmed our brains to spot evidence to support this. So that piece of well-intentioned 'constructive criticism' (anyone else hate that phrase? How can criticism *ever* be constructive?) rips the rug from beneath our precariously balanced feet.

Also, the brain is wired to respond to threats and danger; to pay extra attention to them. So the niceties of how wonderful you are float on past with a glowy feeling, but the moment *criticism* hits our inner radar, the mind, body and emotions go onto high alert. Someone who is struggling with Imposter Syndrome alongside chronic stress or anxiety can become hypervigilant and hypersensitive to criticism.

And sometimes that criticism comes from within, courtesy of our very own Inner Critic.

In either of these situations, you can do the 'woolly jumper test'.

When I was at university, my Grannie was convinced that me being vegetarian would mean I was always cold. I studied engineering in Sheffield in the northern part of England, so it was quite a bit colder than the near-south-coast area where she lived. But I rarely felt the cold, despite my dietary preferences. Even so, she would lovingly send me a jumper as a gift each autumn. And it was always far too small, as though she had forgotten I was now in my twenties, no longer a ten year-old.

My Grannie was very special to me. So I would try to wear the jumpers, even if they threatened to cut off blood supply. But in the end, I had to give up (and deal with the guilt I felt). The jumpers didn't fit. I had to let them go. And, no, I never told my Grannie.

It's the same with 'feedback'.

In business, people often think they're giving you a gift with their 'but' – it's a chance for you to improve.

Do the woolly jumper test: try the feedback on for size – without your defensive prickles barbing the wool as you drag it over your head. If it fits, find a way to do something about it. If it *genuinely* doesn't, let it go and move on. Don't give it even more energy through your mind-story drama. (The grounding technique from the Step One Emergency Quick Fix can help with this).

And there's another aspect to this. There's a Native American saying:

> "All criticism is borne of someone else's
> pain."

Happy people don't rip others to shreds. Internet trolls are not hanging out in bliss. Critical people rarely remember how it feels to smile.

This doesn't justify criticising behaviour, but it helps us to see that it's often not really about us; it's about the other person needing somewhere to project their pain, as a release.

You don't have to take their woolly jumpers, just because they're lobbing them at you. But you also don't have to chuck them back at them. You can allow them to drop at your feet and to walk away, with your dignity and confidence intact.

You certainly don't have to let *their* pain trigger Imposter Syndrome for *you*.

4. Just A Minute

There's a radio show in the UK that has run for decades called 'Just A Minute'. In it, panellists have to speak for sixty seconds on a nominated topic without repetition, hesitation or deviation. It's quite a skill, as more seasoned panellists prove when compared to new members, and it can be hilarious.

You can use a similar technique to press your 'reset' button with Imposter Syndrome:

Exercise: Genuine Self-Compassion

What if, just for the next sixty seconds, you could allow yourself to be completely free from Imposter Syndrome; allowing your self-talk to run without judgement, criticism or comparison; bathing yourself in the unconditional love you would show to a newborn baby.

What kinds of things would you say to yourself?

How does that feel?

These, then, are four reset buttons you could start to use today, for whenever Imposter Syndrome is lurking with intent. But there are more! Spend a moment noticing the reset buttons you have already designed and practised:

Exercise: Your Favourite Reset Buttons

Thinking about a time in the recent past when you have experienced Imposter Syndrome, what did you do to turn it around?

And what else has worked for you?

What have you seen friends or colleagues doing, which might work for you?

And how might you remind yourself to play with these reset buttons, when your Early Warning Signs come up?

So, now you've got a good supply of emergency quick fix 'reset' buttons for when Imposter Syndrome threatens to come out to play, it's time to start taming your Inner Critic. This is much easier to do when you're not in the middle of a fight-flight-freeze adrenalin rush, which is why we've covered the 'reset' buttons first.

I want to teach you a magic trick that will help you to choose which thoughts to feed. This is the key to Rockstar confidence. When you're telling yourself stories about being good enough, clever enough, experienced enough, and having the connections you need to turn your dreams into reality – and *believing* those thoughts (Steps Three and Four), you're much more likely to take the inspired actions that create the breakthroughs you need.

To get started, you just need to know how to choose which thoughts to feed.

The Key To Rockstar Confidence

It was 2007 and *The Secret* by Rhonda Byrne was all the rage, teaching people about the 'Law of Attraction' and how the thoughts you think can change your life. I had already been an NLP Trainer for a few years by then, so its message wasn't new to me. But it was making the stuff I taught more mainstream.

I remember sitting on the sofa in my lounge with a dear school friend, talking about how our thoughts create our experience of reality. My friend had been reading *The Secret* and she got it – she needed to change her thinking to change her life (actually her actions, too, but that wasn't part of the book).

I'll never forget the way she looked at me, with fear in her eyes, as she demanded: "But how can I change my thoughts? They just happen! I'll never be able to do the stuff in here!" she said, waving the book as though she wanted to throw it against a wall.

The message was that you had to change the thoughts you were thinking, but no one was talking about *how*. The world was consumed by a wave of understanding that positive thinking was the way forward, but how could you do that with your Inner Critic blaring in the background?

Her question set me on a mission and the answer is what I'm about to share with you.

Of course, you already know that the neural pathways we

subconsciously create multiple times a day in our brains become our thought habits. And we have the RAS filtering system that governs what we pay attention to. And we've talked about how neuroplasticity means we can change all of this, just as we learned to ride a bike or read and write.

And now we're going to go into *how*.

You're going to start by discovering how to press 'pause' on loud-hailer thoughts. Then we'll look at practical ways to start turning your Inner Critic into your biggest cheerleader (hint: it's one word and it's not 'pretending'). I'll share with you my mentoring questions to turn your mind-story fears from mountains back into molehills. Then we'll explore how to retune your inner radio station, so that you can shift frequencies at will to get out of an Imposter Syndrome self-talk rut.

And we're kicking off by going back to the ABC.

Tame Your Inner Critic In Under 60 Seconds

One of the biggest myths I come across as a meditation teacher is the belief that to be able to meditate, you have to make your mind go silent. I regularly meet people for whom that's their second biggest excuse after not having enough time (by far the #1 favourite).

But it's not true. You can't *make* your mind go blank. Try to force those thoughts out and they'll grab their swords and fight right back with tongues of sharpened steel. Dive into the drama of why they won't go away and those inner whispers will turn into wails faster than a kid who just got a 'no' to their request for yet more chocolate.

After years of meditation practice and applying the simple techniques you're about to learn, I *can* get my thoughts to pause. But I don't *make* them stop. I *let* them. And when it happens, I instantly notice my breathing calms, my body relaxes and tension melts away. Suddenly I have a sense of clarity that had been hiding when my mind was full. The stillness in those gaps between thoughts is where my power to choose my future lies.

It doesn't particularly matter to me whether that inner silence lasts a nanosecond or an hour. It's the act of getting to press 'pause' on a thought that sets me free from its subconscious autopilot. And that's what this exercise will teach you to do.

I have taught this strategy to thousands of people from all backgrounds and even to children. The thing they all have in common when they play with it is that they get to start choosing which thoughts to feed. And when you know how to consciously pick which thoughts to feed, you can press 'pause' on the internal dialogue that accompanies a bout of Imposter Syndrome and turn things around, without pretending.

So we're going to do the ABC. This process presses instant 'pause' on destructive self-talk, shifting it to be something more positive, without white-washing or faking it.

The best time to apply this technique is as soon as possible after your Imposter Syndrome EWS kick off – or any time your Inner Critic comes out to play. It helps both as an interim fix, pressing 'pause' on negative self-talk, and also as a preventative, because practising it regularly starts rewire your brain and RAS.

A is for Accept.
As soon as you notice yourself thinking a thought that is making you feel bad, accept it.

Our natural tendency is to join in the discussion, to try to argue that thought away, to resist it and fight it. When we do that, we're giving it all of our energy and attention, diving into the drama-stories and mind-story fears that are that thought's best friends. We're cranking up the thermostat on the body's corresponding biochemical reactions and we're amplifying the emotions that made us feel bad. And we're stamping through that neurological pathway field with muddy size 15 boots in the rain, reinforcing our autopilot motorways.

You can't fight away a negative thought.

Similarly, you can't 'Pollyanna' over it – pretending it wasn't there – putting your fingers in your ears and singing "la la la I'm a positive thinker!" hoping it will stop baying for attention.

When you accept that thought, unconditionally and without judgement, it ceases to trigger hormones and emotions. It loses its prima donna central stage role. Its power over how you're feeling dissipates.

It becomes 'just another thought'.

"Oh yeah, that's an Imposter Syndrome thought."

This is a really useful strategy: allowing you to name the thought or emotion, thereby acknowledging rather than resisting it, but without diving into its drama-story.

When you stop resisting it and just let it 'be', accepting it without judgement, the thought loses its power, instantly.

B is for Breathe.

By this point, your Autonomic Nervous System may be well into its stress-related fight-flight-freeze routine. Your body may be teeming with cortisol and adrenalin and your senses may be on high alert for signs of danger.

One of the simplest ways to press reset on this is with your breathing. Remember those three deep, sighing breaths you took in technique in the Emergency Quick Fix on page 103? Scientists have now proven what meditators and yogis have known for thousands of years: that mindful belly breathing (letting your focus gently rest on breathing in and out at your diaphragm, becoming aware of the physical sensations of breathing) can reset your Parasympathetic Nervous System (relaxation response) and get it back in balance in just sixty seconds.

It's really important to do this, because, as you know, mind, body and emotions are linked. If your body is still flooded with stress hormones triggering stress- and fear-based emotions, that cycle will keep feeding stress-related thoughts. By spending a few moments to reset your biochemistry with mindful breathing, you set yourself free for the third stage, which is:

C is for Choose.

Consciously choose to think a thought that makes you feel better and brings you a sense of relief. It might be something you're feeling grateful for in your life – the more specific the better. (There's an article to explain why this is in the Readers' Resources). It might be a happy memory. It might be something you're looking forward to.

If you get stuck, my magic question can unlock one for you, in the context of what you were previously thinking about:

"What do I want, instead?"

Make it something within your control and positively phrased. Remember the saxophone-playing donkey? Your unconscious mind can't process a 'not'. A phrase like "I want him to stop using that tone of voice" means you first have to imagine that tone of voice, taking you back into the stress response and your inner critic's mind-story dramas. The 'not' or 'stop' or 'don't' get lost.

And here's the secret sauce: take this thought from *thinking* to *feeling* it in your body. Allow that sense of relief, ok-ness, and even happiness to wash through your body from the crown of your head to the tips of your toes. This fires off your body's version of happy hormones, creates strong new neural pathways in your brain, and rocket-powers the likelihood that your next thought will be a happier one, too.

A ninja tip on this is to make sure that the thought you choose doesn't start with 'but' or your Inner Critic will sense you're up for a fight and charge back into the arena. If you need a conjunction to start that sentence choose 'and'.

So that is how you choose which thoughts to feed – pressing 'pause' on your Inner Critic in under sixty seconds. You use ABC to press 'pause' on a subconscious stream of thoughts and then consciously choose a new thought that brings a sense of relief and happiness.

And if you want *even* more, the next layer of this technique (once you've played with it a few times) starts to train your Inner Critic to become your biggest cheerleader. Fast.

Plus 1-To-3

If you want some icing and a cherry on top of your gluten-free, dairy-free, vegan choosing-which-thoughts-to-feed cupcake, you'll love my 1-to-3 technique. It's ideal to use at the 'c' of choose, once you're familiar with the ABC technique. This is what helps you to retrain your brain (physically, mentally and emotionally) to tell you stories that help you to feel more confident, rather than beating yourself up.

This is perfect for when your 'negative' thought was judging yourself, as it often is with Imposter Syndrome.

The 'one' is the self-judging thought. Maybe you were comparing yourself to someone else. Perhaps one of your Imposter Syndrome mantras had kicked off. Maybe you were beating yourself up for not speaking up with a great idea. It doesn't actually matter what 'one' was. Run through Accept and Breathe for it.

Then for Choose, it's your three:

One at a time, consciously choose to think about three things you're proud of about yourself, that you've been doing well, that you are grateful for, no matter how small. The key is to make them specific and to really connect with the physical and emotional feelings of *being* that version of you. The more specific you can be with this example, the more your brain will fire off the mental-rehearsal biochemical reactions that create that feeling of past confidence right here, right now.

For the first one, let that thought and the feelings grow. Then as you're cranking up that dial, shift to the next one. Rinse & repeat.

Do this for sixty seconds and you're super-charging new neural pathways in your brain with all of those positive emotions, you're reprogramming your Reticular Activating System to spot stuff you're doing well, and you're gently but firmly training your Inner Critic to dig out the pom-poms and become a more-than-occasional cheer leader.

I'm curious: how might you remind yourself to practise this, little and often, each day?

This technique starts to use gratitude to retrain your Inner Critic to become your biggest cheerleader. Daily gratitude practice – going beyond just keeping a journal – can be transformational. If you'd like to learn how the power of gratitude can turn your Inner Critic into your biggest cheerleader, one thought at a time, creating breakthroughs in the next few weeks, you can find out more in the Readers' Resource Vault[10].

And once you've played with the 1-to-3 strategy, it's time to learn my favourite self-mentoring questions for turning your Imposter Syndrome mind-story fears from mountains back into molehills. Are you ready?

---

[10] www.DitchingImposterSyndrome.com/vault/

Honey, I Shrunk The Mountains!

In this section, you'll find out how to turn mind-story fears around. As we discussed on page 15, there's a difference between legitimate fears – *is jumping out of this plane with a fancy tablecloth on my back **really** a good idea* – and mind-story fears – *what if I mess up this presentation*. But your body reacts the same way to both.

In one of the very first meditation courses I went on, a former Buddhist monk taught me that a thought – left to its own devices – will pass on through in sixty seconds. It was the same for emotions. All I was supposed to do was to observe the thought, without engaging with it. At the time, I was skilled at keeping a grumpy or victim-based story running in my head for hours, if not days and months (you'll find out why when we cover 'secondary gain' in Step Three). So I didn't treat this pronouncement with the gratitude it deserved. I kicked back and defended my position – effectively my 'right' to feel stressed, miserable and a bit angry. (Good old backfire effect).

... because, if he were right, then I had been putting myself through all of those emotions for no reason.

What he forgot to say is that such a level of non-attachment to your mind's drama stories takes quite a lot of practice to cultivate. But I now know he was right.

The more I studied meditation to become a certified meditation teacher, the more I realised that the only reason why a thought or emotion persists for so long is because of the stories we use to feed it. And those mind-story dramas trigger biochemical and emotional reactions that are physically addictive – such as running on adrenalin when we push ourselves to the wire to get our 'best work' done to a long-standing, long-ignored deadline.

The simple act of an "I'm not good enough" thought triggering an Imposter Syndrome drama-story (it's like a soap opera in the brain) can turn a worry-molehill into anxiety-mountain. And that's how mind-story fears are born.

We often don't notice it happening until we half-crash into the base of that mountain, that looming obstacle in the path towards our dreams and goals. We can choose to go around it, which can be a massive and demotivating detour. We can climb over it, which costs time and effort that could otherwise be spent on taking action towards those dreams, or we can smash on through it, which is what has to happen when we fight that fear and do the things that scare us, anyway.

But there's a fourth way – and it amazes me that this one isn't standard: We can shrink that mountain back down to the size of a molehill and step over it with near-zero effort. And it's easier than we might think.

Now you know the ABC process to press 'pause' on negative thinking, you can use that as soon as you spot yourself feeding a mind-story fear. It's important not to judge or beat yourself up or to dive into the drama-stories of 'oh I'm doing *that* again', or it's the equivalent of grabbing a pickaxe and expecting to tunnel your way through Mont Blanc by tomorrow lunchtime. You will be making your metaphorical mountain scarily real. Instead, there are some simple self-mentoring questions you can ask yourself.

Exercise: Turning Mountains Back Into Molehills

Start by imagining this mind-story fear you're feeling is a mountain. You might want to pick one from your Glurg exercise on page 116 or one of your Early Warning Signs from page 118.

What size is it as you start this process?

Thinking about the specific mind-story fear you're focussing on, ask yourself: **is it *really* true?**

Watch out for the backfire effect on this. There's a part of you that has a vested interest in proving it's real.

So you don't want the answer to come from your thinking mind. Let it come from your body. Often a 'no' to this question will produce a sense of relief in your abdominal area or jaw, or wherever else you were holding tension.

If what comes back is a 'yes' (somewhere in the body tenses), the next question allows you to play detective:

What evidence am I basing that on?

It can help to jot down notes at this point, to stop the discussions in your head triggering a stress response.

... continues

Then, looking at the 'evidence', you'll be able to simply cross out much of it. The act of writing it down has shown you it's nonsense.

For whatever is left:

Is this evidence biased? For example, is it simply a thought-habit or down to the filters in your RAS or cognitive bias due to the backfire effect?

If there is anything left on the list, *gently* ask yourself (remember, you're not going to war over this):

What do I want instead?

Make this something positively phrased and within your control (you can't change others, only yourself).

Now focus on how that will *feel*. And give your attention to the next action you could take towards creating the context for that feeling.

Notice how the former mountain has become more of a molehill.

You might need to do this every ten minutes if you're in a high-stress situation. But the more you play with it, the earlier in the mountain-growing process you'll spot what's going on and the sooner you'll be able to take action, so those mountains don't grow beyond hillocks any more.

This exercise helps to reset your Sympathetic Nervous System's stress response, getting your cortisol and adrenalin back into balance. This helps you to think more clearly, to take the emotions out of a situation, and to feel calmer and happier.

Now I know how simple it can be to shrink a mind-story fear or worry-mountain back to the size of a molehill, I often wonder why would anyone would force themselves to 'push on through' those fears. We'll explore the secret reason why we do this is on page 195, when we talk about Secondary Gain.

So, now you know how to turn mountains back into molehills, you no longer have to *embrace* your fears or fight them or push them down or pretend they're not there. You simply shrink them back down to a sensible size so they no longer need to get in your way.

Three Ways We Accidentally Feed Our Mind-Story Fears

These three categories of words are red flags that a thought is about to grow a mountain, yet we rarely notice we're using them, until that biochemical and emotional chain reaction has fired off.

Generalisations

This is where your mind takes a single thought or experience and turns it into a universal law.

> He **never** says anything positive about my presentations.
> She **always** gives me **that** look when she thinks I'm wrong.
> I mess up **every** time I'm asked to put a client pitch together.

These generalisations become filters in the Reticular Activating System: it looks for evidence to support them. They become autopilot pathways in your brain, creating habitual thought shortcuts. And they create the perfect environment for the backfire effect to have something to defend. The generalisations are assumptions we use to build the box within which we choose to experience life – at a deeply unconscious level. They are a fast-track for turning those worry molehills into anxiety mountains.

But if we're honest with ourselves and set aside the drama and the emotions, they're not true. It's highly unlikely that he *never* says anything positive about your presentations. It's more likely that he *sometimes* says things you experience as negative, but that there's also at least neutral, if not positive, stuff in there, too.

It's really unlikely that you mess up *every* client pitch, or you wouldn't be asked to do them. It's more likely that perhaps one went wrong or was less than perfect and you are subconsciously generalising that experience.

When we challenge these assumptions and call them out, it's easy to apply the self-mentoring we've just used to shrink the mountains back down to a step-over-them level. The key is to be specific:

'What *specifically* is the problem with this?'

'Really? *Always? Never?*'

This helps to bring a generalisation mountain back down to manageable molehill size.

Distortions

Have you ever been out on a walk and thought you saw a snake, only to find it was a stick? Or seen a shadow in the dark and been convinced it was someone about to attack? Or heard the heating creak and been convinced you weren't 'home alone'? That's distortion.

Another example is hearing what we *want* to hear, even if it's not what we'd consciously want to hear. It's down to confirmation bias, where we look for evidence to justify what we already believe; filling in the gaps based on what we expect to hear. This can cause two people to hear the same message but interpret it differently.

The typical human response to ambiguous information is to try to make meaning from it – to try to read something into it. We (often subconsciously) choose that meaning based on the brain's RAS filters and our autopilots.

The context in which we hear a message is another factor in how we distort it, as is someone's body language and tone of voice. Say a manager has just come from a meeting where there was anger and tension, then they see a member of their team and ask them to come to their office in ten minutes' time; the team member will process that message differently to if the manager had been in a happy, relaxed mood. It risks triggering their defence mechanisms and giving them ten minutes of mind-story hell. They have distorted the request to go to the office, based on their perception of the manager being tense and angry. They assume it's because they have done something wrong. This will be further magnified if the team member is running Reticular Activating System filters for this kind of behaviour, based on past experience.

Email and text messaging are further opportunities for distortion. In a world where picking up the phone almost seems weird, most of us rely on texting and emails for our business conversations. I have lost track of how many times I've seen people in social media groups asking friends what they think someone *meant* with xyz phrasing, as they overlay their assumptions and biases onto the tone and the typed words, potentially distorting the message. Offence is easily taken where none was intended. This is distortion.

A classic example of this was one of my students: Julia. She struggled with her co-worker, Lee. He was often late on deadlines for information she needed. He seemed grumpy, sometimes even sullen, and would never apologise. It got to the stage where, in her head, Lee couldn't do anything right. She would lie awake at night, recounting his office sins and misdemeanours. She kept mental count of every look, every sigh, every tense word. And Julia was quite convinced that Lee didn't like her. In fact, she strongly suspected he was being late with the work she needed as some way of making her miss deadlines, to get her fired.

She had been in this position before with a former boss at her old company who had taken a dislike to her and she wasn't going to let it happen again.

What Julia didn't know was that Lee was in the middle of a very difficult divorce and that his wife had had an affair. He was at risk of losing his children and his home. He was on antidepressants and his boss was fully aware of his request to keep working, albeit not at his usual standard, rather than be signed off sick.

His behaviour and reduced work performance were nothing to do with Julia, but she experienced these as personal attacks. Julia was projecting her inner assumptions onto Lee's behaviour, distorting it to become a personal attack and even risking her employment. By helping her to see what was *real* versus what was the projection of her inner mind-story fears, she was able to be less reactive to Lee and to improve their working relationship, without him needing to change.

It's really important to be mindful of distortion in your mind-story fears. It's why the self-mentoring questions include, 'is it *really* true?' and ask what evidence you have for it.

In the meditation world this is called the difference between *perception* and *projection*. What we perceive through our senses gets distorted by what we *expect* to see. It then suffers a further level of distortion with what we *project* from our previous experience. It's like we add filters to overlay the sensory information.

Deletions

Deletions are, unsurprisingly, the bits of our self-talk conversation that we miss out. We might be telling ourselves a story about how 'Fred doesn't like me!' and find ourselves lamenting that 'it's not fair!' The deletions are the pieces of information that are missing from that sentence. What is 'it'? What does 'not fair' actually mean?

When our self-talk includes deletions, it opens up the space for generalisations and distortions to fill in the gaps.

Generalisations, distortions and deletions feed your mind-story fears by cranking up the drama. Once you know how to spot them in your inner dialogue, you can use the ABC technique to pause the story and then ask yourself the self-mentoring questions from the mountain-to-molehill exercise on page 132.

And that leads us to looking at why we so often defend our right to feel scared.

But Fear Helps Me To Perform!

This is another one of the myths that lead people to hold onto Imposter Syndrome: that we need the fear and adrenalin it triggers to achieve peak performance.

Fear doesn't help you to perform. Not ever. Fear puts you into the fight-flight-freeze mode, and we've discussed a number of times now why this is such a threat to peak performance and learning. What we really mean when we believe we need fear and stress to bring out our best work is that a little adrenalin helps. We actually mean something called 'eustress' – and you can get a boost of this from excitement.

Hungarian-Canadian endocrinologist Hans Selye coined the term in the 1970s, referring to the difference between stress experienced in response to a threat – distress – and the stress triggered by a challenge which we perceive as positive and a chance to grow – eustress. In my work, I have seen that classic stress ('distress') is triggered by fear, whereas 'good stress' (the actual meaning of eustress) is driven by excitement. This can motivate us to stretch comfort zones in a way that feels empowering, rather than terrifying.

Which of these two options we experience comes down to how we perceive the challenge we are facing: whether it triggers fear or excitement. People can respond differently to the same activity, which is great news, because it means we have the power to choose.

I don't know about you, but I'd much rather take a step outside a comfort zone based on feeling happy and excited, rather than stressed and scared. The difference in our biochemistry, emotions, physiology, posture, confidence and performance is huge, depending on which of those options we choose.

Fear is the emotional symptom of an underlying limiting belief or block. Your fears dictate your limits.

Pushing on through your fears, rather than releasing them, seems a crazy idea, once you realise how easy it can be to let them go – and the difference between fear and excitement is about two inches.

The Difference Between Fear And Excitement

Exercise: The Difference Between Fear And Excitement

Just for a moment, I invite you to pick an Imposter-Syndrome-driven mind-story fear that's around a **three** out of ten – perhaps a task that you've been putting off because you secretly feel scared. Tell yourself that story. Allow yourself a few thoughts to embellish and what-if and dive into that drama and worry.

Notice where in your body you *feel* that fear. Put a finger on that place. Even if it seems a weird thing to do.

Now let go of that finger, shake off that story and smile.

Next I want you to think about something you're excited[11] about or have been excited about in the past. Allow yourself to dive into those positive thoughts and emotions. Turn up the dial a bit. We're talking 'happy anticipation', rather than 'kids who just saw the pile of Christmas presents' crazy excitement.

Now notice where in your body you *feel* that excitement and anticipation. Put your finger on that place.

What is the difference between the two spots?

For many of us, it's about two inches.

... continues

---

[11] If you have clinical anxiety, then don't anchor yourself into excitement, because the energy of that can be too close to that of anxiety. In such cases, really focus on the breathing out of the fear – getting grounded using the technique from the Emergency Quick Fix technique on page 103 – and then work with a sense of 'calm ok-ness' instead.

Now here's where the magic happens. Rather than having to do the cognitive strategies we covered in the last few sections, you can shift from fear to excitement by moving your finger. Here's how:

Take that mind-story fear you started with and place your finger where you were feeling it in your body, keeping your mind focused on the topic that triggered the story. Imagine you can take a deep breath in to that area of your body and then as you breathe out through your feet, allow all of the tension in that area to flow into the earth. Repeat two or three times until you feel calm.

Now, still thinking about the same topic, move your finger over your skin to the point where excitement was. Allow those emotions to wash through the scene of the mind-story fear and notice what shifts. What happens in your body?

When you play with this technique, the task remains the same, but the way you *allow* yourself to experience it can shift dramatically. It can take you from distress to eustress, bypassing the fight-flight-freeze response.

Since our emotions are chemical reactions in the body, they are inextricably linked with our physical experience. Our language even talks about this – we talk about *butterflies in the stomach* when we're nervous or having *a gut instinct* about something. When your mind is telling you stories about being 'scared' or 'anxious', you can shift that emotion to 'anticipation' or 'excitement' by intentionally working with your body.

When you remove the filter of fear (with its generalisations, distortions and deletions triggering mountain-building), and replace it with the filter of excitement, it resets the fight-flight-freeze response, calms your stress levels, helps you to think more clearly and opens up the option for peak performance. And moving from fear to excitement doesn't just make you feel better, it shifts your focus away from problems and towards possibilities.

Fear and excitement fire off similar reactions in the body and you can use this to your advantage. Sometimes the mind can't solve a problem it unintentionally created. In those situations, moving into physical-body solutions can hold the key to change. The more often you play with this, the easier it becomes, until it is an instinctive reaction – and life becomes much less difficult and serious. It becomes more fun and playful. And this helps to rewire those neural pathways in your brain.

Ninja Strategy:

There's another layer to this strategy, to help you shift from fear and worry into anticipation and confidence. It's a single-word self-talk swap.

When you're climbing mind-story-fear-mountain, your inner dialogue is often about all the things you *have* to do – the must, ought, should of self-talk. I call this suffering from 'shoulditis'. It triggers those sinking feelings of guilt, resistance and even resentment-filled obligation, as your subconscious choice of words reinforces the fact that you are about to do something you would rather not – and that you don't feel it's optional.

This fires off the fear-based stress hormones in the body that turn the molehill into a mountain. It's particularly common with Imposter Syndrome if you feel that you're having to *force* yourself to push on through the fear and the doubt.

Once you're comfortable with the ABC from page 127 and the fear-to-excitement technique we just covered, there's a single word in that self-talk you can swap, to set yourself free from 'shoulditis'.

Allow your "I have to'" to become "I choose to" … and notice the shift in your body and your thoughts.

In this single word shift you are reclaiming your inner power over the action you're about to take. You'll instantly press 'pause' on the fear-cycle. You'll shift to acting from a place of gratitude, rather than the negative emotions that had been running the show. And the mountain shrinks, effortlessly.

Retuning Your Inner Radio Station
AKA How To Stop Beating Yourself Up

Now you know how to press 'pause' on your self-talk, it's time to look at how to retune that inner radio station to a more supportive frequency. If you practise the techniques in this section a couple of times a day for a week, you'll start to notice a shift in your unconscious self-talk, with near-zero effort.

The simplest way to do this is to tune into the loving voice that is whispering in the background all of the reasons why you *can* do what it is you want to achieve. It gets drowned out by the yells of your Inner Critic, but it's still there. When you consciously listen out for its kind and encouraging words, you'll find they are uniquely aligned with what you most need to hear in that moment.

If your Inner Critic tries to get in the way, use the ABC technique from page 127 as far as the Accept and Breathe, then ask yourself:

If my inner voice of encouragement could speak to me right now, what would it say?

People often find it easier to think of this voice as starting quietly and being encouraging, rather than 'arriving' with the full fanfare and fun of a cheerleading squad, because that would be such a strong contrast that the backfire effect might kick in. The more you experiment with listening to your inner voice of encouragement, the more you'll be creating the neural pathways and RAS filters that means it can become your go-to self-talk.

Thoughts As Passing Clouds

When you have fewer thoughts, they are easier to manage. Sounds obvious, doesn't it? But how do you do it? Learning how to let your thoughts pass on through is one of the keys to taming your Inner Critic, reducing your stress levels, and ditching Imposter Syndrome. So I want to share with you one of the techniques I teach to my meditation students, both online and 'real-world'.[12]

---

[12] You can find out more about this in the Readers' Resources Vault: www.DitchingImposterSyndrome.com/vault/

It isn't our thoughts that create the pain; it's our attachment or resistance to them.

Basically, if we don't feed the stories that keep those thoughts coming, they will drift on through, like passing clouds, creating space for the next thought. And that gap, as we've discussed, is a great place to play with the ABC / 1-to-3 technique.

The key to letting thoughts float on through is to become the non-judgemental observer of them. Have you ever noticed on social media that if you try to engage with a 'troll', they fight back harder? Their need to prove they are right becomes their immediate purpose in life. And responses don't have to be rational. The more you try to engage with them and help them to see another world view, the more they get energised from the argument and the more loudly they shout.

It's the same with your brain.

Catch a thought that you don't want to be having and try to convince it to go away and you're turning it into a neural pathway troll. It will fight back. It sends emergency memos to your memory banks to find examples to support its point of view. And before you know it, a casual, throwaway thought has become a campaign for inner world domination.

When you fall into the trap of experiencing your thoughts as part of who you *are*, you get so emotionally invested in them that they take over your physical and emotional experience of life. Yet their triggers are subconscious, so it's easy to feel like a canoe in a storm on the ocean.

Instead, if you take a step back and imagine you're watching your thoughts on a movie screen, you can choose whether or not to emotionally engage with them, or to simply observe them and let the scene pass.

When we choose not to engage with a thought, it doesn't get the chance to trigger the biochemical reactions that create our emotions and lead to us feeding our inner drama stories. But it's not about fighting or rejecting them – or about forcing them to go away – or about making a fuss about ignoring them. It's about cutting the emotional and energetic tie you have to that thought, so it can melt away.

Resource: Thoughts As Passing Clouds MP3

It's hard to learn this from a book, so there's a meditation MP3 waiting for you in the Readers' Resources Vault to guide you through how to do it. It's one of the meditations from my online meditation course (there's more to meditation than the guided visualisations you get on apps) and you can download it to take it with you, whenever you need it. It's a great emergency fix for Imposter Syndrome.

Want A Magic Wand For Worrying?

We've talked about how our mind-stories can create fear and drama, but we haven't yet covered one of its favourite other jobs: worrying.

Esther Hicks, a motivational speaker and author, has a great definition of worrying:

Worrying is a way of creating a future you don't really want.

When you worry, you're running 'what if' scenarios in your brain, triggering the same neurological connections as if the event were really happening – triggering the same biochemical reactions and emotions in your body. It's a form of accidental mental rehearsal for something you really don't want to happen – which makes it more likely to happen, because you're creating the neural pathways to support it.

Many of my business leader mentoring clients are 'natural born worriers'. They believe that the self-talk stories which keep them tossing and turning at 3 a.m. are important – a way of avoiding mistakes and making sure they get things right. Yes, there can be gems in the middle of a worry-story that are things we need to remember or pay attention to. But you don't need to rehearse worst-case-scenarios to spot these.

You don't have to do the worrying, to know which actions to take. That's just a justification that makes us feel better about worrying. It's time for my magic wand for worrying.

Exercise: Magic Wand For Worrying

When you find yourself worrying, play with these self-mentoring questions:

Is it really true?

Which specific elements of this story I'm telling myself are actually true?

Writing it down gets it out of your head (remember your companion workbook in the Readers' Vault): state the facts, minus the drama and emotions.

Then: **is this what I really want?** (Chances are it's a no!)

Then: my favourite magic question: **What do I want instead?**

This shifts you from worrying about problems to focussing on solutions. Follow the guidelines from the exercise on page 133 for this.

Finally: commit to take action – today!

Meditation can really help with this because it helps you to connect with the gap between your thoughts. And in that gap (even if it's a nanosecond) lies your power to choose which thoughts to feed next. It helps you to stop watering the seeds of worry. If worrying is a big issue for you, there's information in the Readers' Resources Vault about a meditation MP3 that can guide you from problem to solution in under five minutes.

The more regularly you meditate, the easier it is to spot and deal with those worry-thoughts, before they turn into worry-mountains.

And if you combine your meditation practice with some of the gratitude techniques that you'll cover in Step Four, then you'll create lifelong, genuinely positive shifts in your inner radio station's frequency.

So now we've covered how to treat your thoughts like passing clouds and created a magic wand for worrying, let's get retuning that inner radio station!

Your inner dialogue has the power over what you achieve in life and who you allow yourself to become. Yet most of us have no idea how to retune that inner frequency.

If your brain is subconsciously tuned to 'shock-jock FM' then you're going to struggle to feel anything other than stressed, angry and argumentative. If it's tuned to 'über-Zen FM' then you'll find it hard to get motivated to take inspired action towards your dreams.

The body is in its neutral balance point (homeostasis) when we are relaxed but alert. In fact, one of the first things I do with my meditation students it to teach them how to move from hyper-alert to 'calm and safe'.

You can do that at a physical level with breathing techniques like the one on page 258. At a mind-level, we do it by changing the nature of your inner dialogue. We're not looking to change the actual thoughts you're thinking. We're going to shift the way you experience them.

Back in 2003 a friend taught me something that blew my mind.

We were sitting in a cafe, soon after I qualified as an NLP Trainer. Although I had plenty of tools to help, my Inner Critic still ran the show. I loved to tell myself stories about not being good enough, how I wasn't ready, I was too young or too old or too tired or too busy.

My friend, Steve, sat in the cafe and looked at me as though he could read my mind. In some ways, he could, because we give away micro-clues to our inner dialogue in our physiology, our choice of words, and the way we speak them.

And he taught me how to turn off the volume on my Inner Critic.

It was as simple as imagining I had a volume dial in my mind and consciously turning it down. And it worked.

Some people think in pictures. Some think in words. Some think in physical sensations. Some of us have a mixture. For example, I can't 'see' pictures in my mind. But I *can* imagine what that image might *feel* like. Most of my thoughts are words. I have great conversations with myself.

I have also worked with clients who have no verbal inner dialogue. For them, it's all about pictures.

For ease of reading, I'm going to call all variations on these options your 'inner dialogue'.

This self-talk has patterns that are easy to recognise, when you know how. For example, happy thoughts might have a smiling tone of voice, be at a gentle speed and have colourful images. Angry thoughts might have a shouting voice, faster and more 'punctuated' sentences, and jagged, fast-moving images.

To retune the inner radio station of your thoughts, all you need to do is to work out what the 'settings' are for your happier thoughts. As you go through this exercise, it doesn't matter whether you are consciously aware of hearing or seeing or feeling your thoughts. Ask yourself the questions and notice the shifts in your body to draw your conclusions:

Exercise: Retuning Your Inner Radio Station

Start by thinking about a happy memory; one that feels great. Allow yourself to fully experience it, imagining what you are seeing, hearing and feeling.

Now notice what you notice about your thoughts.

If they are words, become aware of the speed, the volume, the pitch, the tone of voice, any pauses, the length of sentences.

If they are images, notice the colours, if there is movement and what it's like, whether it's a panorama or a framed image, whether you're 'in' the image or looking at it from 'outside' of yourself.

If it's a physical sensation, where in your body is it? Is it constant or is there a rhythm? What kind of sensation is it? How strong?

Pause and make notes on the key things you noticed from this list.

Now, thinking of something that has been stressing you, based on Imposter Syndrome, make it maximum a four out of ten the first time you play with this: repeat the questions above and make notes.

One at a time, swap these factors over. So if your happy memory was a moving image with smooth movement and sunshine-filled colours, but your Imposter Syndrome thought was staccato screenshots with a grey filter, swap it for the happy image factors. Go through each of your swaps and note down which have the biggest impact.

Apply each of these, one at a time, to your Imposter Syndrome thoughts, consciously choosing to change your experience of that mind-story.

... continues

You will know it has worked when you feel a sense of relief in your body, emotions and mind, letting go of the stress and tension of those negative thoughts.

What has shifted?

Which change made the biggest difference?

This will be your shortcut swap, whenever negative thoughts start playing without permission. Run that swap to retune your inner radio station, fast, reclaiming the power from your Inner Critic, like flicking an inner switch.

The more often you play with this, the faster and more effective these switches will become. They can be a near-instant way of pressing 'pause' on the mind-story dramas, so you don't have to dive into your stress response and trigger a bout of Imposter Syndrome.

Four Imposter-Syndrome-Feeding Words Hiding In Your Self-Talk

These are four very short words that crop up in far too many self-talk sentences – and if you're running Imposter Syndrome, they can make it worse, trigger an episode, or even justify keeping yourself stuck! Here's how to turn them around, so that they lose their power over your thoughts, emotions and actions.

If

'If' is a great word for implying doubt. "*If* the presentation goes well…" opens up the option for it not to go well. Remember that pesky unconscious mind, which takes your self-talk as unfiltered instructions? Guess how it responds to an 'if'!

When you're running Imposter Syndrome, the 'if' in your self-talk *can* be useful for opening you up to the possibility of success, if that is something you have previously struggled with. But if you're in a 'good place', it can lift the trap door on that slippery slope back into self-doubt.

The alternative to 'if'? When. Try a statement about something that triggers Imposter Syndrome for you, using 'if' and 'when', and notice the difference in your body.

But

It's time to ditch your buts!

As we saw on page 74, the word 'but' has a magical power that most of us don't notice: it can negate everything that came before it – including positive, encouraging self-talk.

"*I agree with you, but…*" No, you don't!

"*I am good enough, but…*" No, I'm not!

"*I feel confident, but…*" No, I don't!

What can you use, instead? **'And'.**

It's not about white-washing. You don't have to be über-positive. It's about acknowledging and honouring the whole of your experience, rather than denying it.

Try

If at first you don't succeed, try, try, try again.

There are two major issues with this childhood proverb: firstly, there's no point in trying again unless you have figured out why it didn't work last time. As Einstein reportedly said, doing the same thing over and over, but expecting different results, is a sign of insanity.

And the second problem with this proverb is the word 'try'. Ask your body how it feels for a moment to say, "I'll *try* to get that done." What do you notice about your level of commitment to whatever 'that' is? How likely is it to happen?

'Try' is an Imposter Syndrome get-out-of-jail-free card. If you're stuck in the Four Ps (see page 30), 'try' gets you off the hook. 'Try' effectively means 'I'll give it a go, but it's fine if it doesn't happen'.

If your self-talk is about *trying* to do something, it's a flag that – at some level – you're either not fully committed or you're feeling scared. And it's a classic early warning sign for Imposter Syndrome.

What's the alternative? As Yoda said:

"Do. Or do not. There is no try."

Just

'Just' is a great way to stay stuck, playing small. It feels like an apology. 'Could I *just*…?' 'I *just* want to ask…'

Whilst it won't trigger Imposter Syndrome, it can be a sign that you're not standing in your full personal power and confidence. Adding 'just' in a sentence feels mouse-like and if it's in your self-talk, it can make you contract, seeing yourself as smaller than others.

What's the alternative? Nothing! Let it go! And if you find yourself hanging on to 'just', it's worth doing some work on why it's so important to you. The 'because' exercises in Step Three (page 169) will really help with this.

Avoiding Toxic Positivity

In a world where 'positive thinking' is supposed to fix almost as much as a 'nice, hot cup of tea', there's a genuine risk of your self-talk falling into the toxic positivity trap. Social media is overrun with its memes: think beautiful people in sunny locations with inspirational one-liner quotes, intended to inspire – and also to show us we're still not 'there'.

All too often new clients tell me in our first session together that they feel bad about negative thinking. They have been beating themselves up because their thoughts aren't positive enough. They see each self-critical thought as a personal failure. And that makes their negative self-talk even worse.

I mentioned earlier in this section that I'm not a fan of the term 'negative thinking', because it means we are judging ourselves, based on the 'positivity' of our thoughts. Thoughts are just thoughts and they don't hold any emotional charge until we attach emotions to them or feed ourselves stories about them. Like the clouds in that earlier exercise, they can pass on through.

As soon as we judge our thoughts as positive or negative, we become attached to them. We reject some and chase others. Those that we reject as negative suddenly have our full attention and we subconsciously engage in a fight, which gives them more power. Those 'positive' thoughts that we try to cling to won't hang around for long unless we have built up the neural pathways to support them – which you're on your way to doing – and if they disappear, we feel bad again.

But one of the most worrying trends I have seen in the past decade is that of toxic positivity. In my childhood we used to call this being a 'Pollyanna' after the frustratingly cheerful child from a book from 1913, later made into a film, where the heroine's world falls apart, but she remains unfailingly positive.

This saccharine-sweet version of positivity preaches the importance of feeling positive, all the time. However, it's effectively about denying your emotions, unless they're upbeat. It's about pretending you feel fine, when inside you might be feeling lonely or worried or confused or overwhelmed. And it leads to people judging themselves, if they fail to conform with this hyped-up version of fake happiness. We can end up feeling ashamed at our inability to always see the silver lining and pull ourselves together, knowing that 'happiness is a choice' and 'everything is perfect'.

'Stop worrying and focus on your happy thoughts!' means you're trying to use the power of your mind to do a biochemical U-turn in your emotional state – whilst still judging yourself for the worry-thoughts. You're asking the impossible from your body. 'Good vibes only!' means you're rejecting the part of you that is trying to get a message through to you, with those less positive emotions. Toxic positivity increases the stigma around mental health issues by implicitly judging and rejecting anyone whose inner thoughts and feelings don't match the ideal of the super-glossy Instagram feeds we are bombarded with.

This deep rejection of any form of negative thinking or emotions leads to what is sometimes called a 'spiritual bypass', where people use their inner journey to justify denying their shadow side – those aspects of us that are ready to come up for healing and release.

We use positivity to pretend that everything is great, when we're secretly hurting inside.

And this spiritual bypass denies us the chance to learn and grow from our less-than-fabulous experiences, making it more likely that we will subconsciously recreate them at some point in the future – 'same story, different actors'.

When we experience emotions like disappointment or jealousy, for example, these are inner warning signs that something is out of kilter and that we need to take action. Emotions are often a sign that we're wearing a mask that it's time to let go of (spoiler alert for Step Four).

Why is toxic positivity so popular? Because facing our genuine emotions can feel scary. If you don't know how to handle them, it's easier to pretend everything is fine. But this 'pushing down' of emotions can cause the communication between your cells to shut down (more on that in the Readers' Resource Vault) and it teaches us that we're somehow broken or not good enough to honour what we're really thinking and feeling. That self-honesty and vulnerability can feel frightening.

Toxic positivity is one of the reasons why I fundamentally oppose classic 'resilience' being taught in schools or in companies (you'll find out why in Step Five). Anything that requires us to deny the truth of who we are and what we are experiencing – or even to numb out our emotions – in order to be able to bounce back more quickly or be more thick-skinned is a potentially dangerous direction to take. That's like walking around wearing inch-thick emotional armour.

I'm not suggesting we should wallow in misery. But the techniques you have already covered in this section will set you well on track to know how to choose which thoughts to feed, be able to press 'pause' on the mind-story dramas, and retune your inner radio station to feel more positive. Optimism is a wonderful attitude to cultivate, especially in a team environment, but toxic positivity will hurt you and others.

There's more on toxic positivity, how and why it happens, how to cultivate optimism in a team, plus resources to help you if you're on the receiving end of it in the Readers' Resources.

Emotional First Aid

I vividly remember the power of the emotions I felt for months after my mum died. After the initial grief, I could still be emotionally knocked off my feet by triggers as simple as seeing something in a shop that I might have bought for her. And those emotions felt like a tsunami – arriving with near-zero warning and washing away the rest of my world while they swamped me.

You don't need a major event like bereavement, though, to feel powerful emotions. What my time as a meditation teacher has taught me is that an emotion really can pass through in minutes, no matter how strong it is, as long as you allow it to. I know that's the kind of statement that could get you lobbing rotten tomatoes at me. But as we've discussed earlier in this section, it's the stories we tell ourselves, attached to those emotions, which keep the pain going for days, months or years.

When those emotional tsunamis hit, I would breathe through them. Sometimes it was simple, at other times I had to dig deep, to trust that the emotion would flow through and I wouldn't be stuck with it forever. And it always worked.

The strategies you have covered in this section will help you to get off the emotional roller coaster, day to day. But if a strong emotion comes up for you, the first two parts of the ABC are your best friends: accept and breathe. Rather than fighting the emotion and telling yourself the story about it – or the story about how you're fed up with that emotion – accept that it's there and it's a chemical reaction in your body. Then breathe – the grounding breath from the Emergency Quick Fix technique on page 103 is ideal for this, breathing out the emotion with each exhalation.

Once the main wave of the emotion has passed, go for 'C' and choose a thought that brings relief.

Another tool I use for emotions if they feel 'stuck' is EFT – Emotional

Freedom Technique, also known as 'tapping'. This works incredibly well if you're an over-thinker. Because body, mind and emotions are inextricably linked, if you have a powerful emotion running and the mind-stories have kicked in, you can use EFT by tapping on key points of your body to clear the emotion's effects there. I have found this immensely powerful for myself, my family and my clients and students. It can also help you to clear the triggers that created that emotional response.

To find out more about EFT and how you can use it, both for emotional first aid and to create shifts in your life, you'll find resources in the Readers' Resource Vault[13].

Above all, if you're struggling emotionally, please reach out to someone you know and trust to help you. Suffering in silence, pushing on through, and pretending everything is ok is a painful way to live and the support you need is there, waiting for you, as soon as you let it in.

The Vital Ingredient For Success

Turning your Inner Critic into your biggest cheerleader is best done 'little and often', rather than as an occasional blitz. And it takes time, patience and perseverance. To help you stay motivated through this journey, there's a vital ingredient for success: celebrating your 'micro-wins'.

This is something my clients find hugely helpful and it also helps to rewire your brain and those Reticular Activating System filters, to help you spot others things you're doing well, too. So it's a win-win and can help to reduce the likelihood of Imposter Syndrome.

What do I mean by 'micro-wins'? I mean the tiny successes that are sprinkled through your day. Most of us wait to celebrate the really big goals – the kind that happen a few times a year. But if you want to train your brain, your body and your emotions to *truly* support you, then you need to tune your inner radar to actively look for smaller things to celebrate, on a daily basis.

When we shift from waiting until the 'ultimate' success of something we want to do, achieve or create, it's like going on holiday and refusing to eat anything but dry crackers and water until the final day. Our journey through life is surely as important as any destination.

---

13 www.DitchingImposterSyndrome.com/vault/

This 'waiting to celebrate' is exacerbated if you're also running perfectionism, because you'll have set yourself such a high standard that you're never likely to get to the partying part.

Celebrating micro-wins means consciously looking out for what you are doing well and the step-by-step successes, each and every day. For example, you might come out of a meeting and ask yourself what you contributed, what difference you made. You might choose to notice the positive response someone gave to an idea you shared. Or it might be as simple as celebrating the fact that you stayed awake when everyone else was dozing off!

It actually doesn't matter what your micro-wins are. What matters is that you consciously choose to seek them out and to spend a minute or so telling yourself a story that celebrates them.

As I have been writing this book, I have celebrated each day's word count, I've celebrated each lightbulb idea, I've celebrated each interview, each survey analysis, each section's completion, each confusion-into-clarity moment, and each section's completion. I could have chosen, instead, to focus on how challenging it can feel to write 90,000 words on a topic, to structure a book so that it flows, to overcome writer's block, to deal with my worries and fears about how the book might be received, to beat myself up when first-draft words wouldn't flow, to worry about trolls. Had I done that, this book would never have been published. Yet that's how most of us live our lives, focusing only on the struggles and challenges, forgetting how far we have come.

Celebrating your micro-wins is transformational. Same journey, very different experiences.

You can celebrate your micro-wins as you go through your day or at the end of your day. What really helps is to write your micro-wins down, so they feel more 'real' than just fuzzy thoughts in your head.

You might choose to celebrate your micro-wins with an end-of-week email to a mentor or accountability buddy, so that you're not celebrating on your own. Some of my students make this celebration the first thing they tell their loved-ones, when they get home from work, rather than complaining.

However you choose to celebrate your micro-wins, the absolute key is consistency. Your brain's neural pathways are formed by repetition, with strong emotions – like the pathway through a field that we discussed on page 21. So if you celebrate micro-wins at least once a day and allow the physical emotions of that celebration to flow through your body, you're fast-tracking yourself to becoming Imposter-Syndrome-proof. And it will help you to become truly resilient, rather than 'pretendedly' resilient (more on that in Step Five).

By celebrating micro-wins, not only are you retraining your RAS to spot what's going well and your Inner Critic to be more encouraging and supportive, you're also resetting the primary trigger for Imposter Syndrome – that out-of-balance internal metric for your performance that meant you used to beat yourself up, even when others said you had done well. If you play with this a few times a day for a week, having done the previous work in this book, I promise it will be transformational for you!

If you celebrate three micro-wins at the end of a day, before you fall asleep, you'll be acknowledging the progress you're making. You'll be resetting those RAS filters in your brain to spot more micro-wins. And, over time, you'll teach your Inner Critic to become your spotter-of-micro-wins – AKA your biggest cheer-leader.

Celebrating daily micro-wins also helps you to notice and track your progress, being consciously aware of the changes you have made, which will help you to stay motivated on your journey to ditch Imposter Syndrome and become the leader you were born to be. Some examples of micro-wins might include:

- Not reacting emotionally when a colleague presses a 'button'
- Speaking up in a meeting where you might previously have waited for others to share their ideas first
- Taking an action that would normally have been derailed by the Four Ps (perfectionism, procrastination, paralysis and people-pleasing), without drama or fear

Exercise: Celebrating Your Micro-Wins

Take a moment to think about three micro-wins you could celebrate from the past 24 hours. Write them down here, being specific about what they are and why you're celebrating them.

1.

2.

3.

Now go through each in turn and allow yourself to *feel* the thank you as you focus on celebrating that micro-win.

Notice what shifts in your body, your thoughts and your emotions, when you have done this.

Research by Joel Wong and Joshua Brown from the University of Berkeley in the USA showed that as little as four weeks of regular gratitude practice, especially for those who wrote it down, produced a measurable improvement in the mental health of a group of college students who were attending counselling, compared with control groups who did not practice gratitude. Keeping a daily gratitude journal – which can include celebrating your micro-wins, can change your life. There are more resources on the power of gratitude to change your life in the Readers' Resource Vault, including information on my book: *A Year Full Of Gratitude*, which is a gratitude journal, combined with a year-long course to make gratitude your new way of living.

And we'll come back to celebrating micro-wins and how they can turn your Inner Critic into your biggest cheerleader in Step Four.

To wrap up Step Two, here are some questions to ask yourself:

Exercise: Wrapping Up Step Two

What have you learned in this section?

Any surprises? Lightbulbs?

What are you going to be doing differently now?

And what's your next action?

That's all for Step Two. I hope it has inspired you to get taming your Inner Critic and that the strategies we have covered are already producing results for you.

Now it's time to go a level deeper: it's time to learn how to spot and clear your hidden limiting beliefs, fears and excuses – the ones that feed your Inner Critic's conversations – before they trash your dreams.

Step 3 – The Sticky Stuff: Clearing Out Your Hidden Blocks & Fears

A belief is basically a filter in your brain. A core belief is like an autopilot highway. Back in the Imposter Syndrome Iceberg (page 40) we talked about how our beliefs shape our thoughts and influence our actions. So why did we tackle taming your Inner Critic, first, if it's just the effect and not the cause? Because it's much easier to shift limiting beliefs once you know how to press 'pause' on your self-talk drama-stories.

In Step Three, you're going to cover why dealing with our hidden blocks is so important and how white-washing and 'pushing on through' can lead to future problems. You'll learn how to spot them – with a super-simple mentoring question, plus two different ways to release them. And you'll discover how to create more empowering beliefs – ones that your body buys in to.

Our beliefs can limit or empower us and we rarely consciously choose them. They influence the filters in the Reticular Activating System area of our brains, causing us to filter out sensory evidence that contradicts a particular belief, making it stronger. That's why Henry Ford's quote about 'whether you believe you can or you believe you can't, you're right' resonates so much. Beliefs create your expectations about how life will be, govern your major decisions, and influence the actions you take towards your dreams.

Knowing how to spot beliefs that are holding you back – and how to healthily clear them – is an essential step on your Ditching Imposter Syndrome journey. So, let's start with a story about an elephant and a tent peg.

The Elephant And The Tent Peg

A baby elephant arrives in a circus and has a chain fitted around its front left ankle. The chain rubs. It's uncomfortable. The baby elephant struggles, trying to get the chain off. But it can't. And that chain is tied to a wooden tent peg. The baby elephant soon realises that if it moves too far from the tent peg, the chain bites its ankle. That hurts.

The baby elephant keeps trying to get to the fresh, green leaves that are just beyond its reach. But the chain and the wooden tent peg stop it. The elephant soon associates reaching beyond its easy range with pain, so it gives up trying, living in a literal comfort zone.

Over time, the skin under the chain toughens with callouses, but it still hurts if the elephant tries to pull away from the tent peg. It longs for the freedom of the jungle – a distant memory that it now wonders if it imagined. Tentatively, it stretches to try to reach those fresh, green leaves. But it is scared of the pain. So it makes do with what is within its reach. Again.

As the baby elephant grows, the chain is still there. And the tent peg. The adult elephant remembers the pain from years gone by, when it used to try to stretch too far and the chain tightened around its ankle. Circus visitors marvel that an animal strong enough to uproot a fully-grown tree can be tethered to a tiny wooden peg.

Back on page 26 we talked about how your body *feels* every thought you think – and how the brain triggers the same autopilot reactions, whether something distressing is currently happening or just being replayed or imagined. That's what happened to the young elephant. It was the *fear* of remembered pain that kept it stuck. And that's how our limiting beliefs keep us stuck, too.

Our hidden blocks often come from experiences we had when we were young or after a major life change, such as a big promotion or becoming a parent, although, as I said earlier, it's not important to know the causal event, in order to be able to clear them. Psychologists believe that the majority of our 'core beliefs' are formed by the age of seven. These become our guiding principles for life and how the world works. The rest of the beliefs we pick up over the course of life become attached to those, like the seeds from 'sticky weed' (the plant also known as cleavers).

Our beliefs can come from our family and society – based on values concerning what's right and wrong. They can come from our sense of who we really are. They can be formed by repeated thoughts, creating those neural pathways and Reticular Activating System filters. And they can come from outside-world experiences, especially those attached to strong emotions.

Although Imposter Syndrome is an identity-level issue, there is plenty of belief work to be done. Those beliefs are like the baby elephant's tent peg: they teach us about what our unconscious mind believes is safe or dangerous and prompt us to moderate our actions, to avoid fear and pain.

A stressful or distressing experience can cause us to shut down, making a subconscious vow to avoid that situation again. This shutdown closes the door to other options, creating a comfort zone, which becomes the box within which we experience life.

Imposter Syndrome intensifies these beliefs and comfort zones by taking them out of the 'behavioural' level and turning them into identity-level blocks. That's why mindset work often doesn't do as much as you might expect with Imposter Syndrome – because the beliefs that feed it have become 'stuck'.

Limiting beliefs are directly connected to the fear-zone in your brain, triggering the unconscious mind to protect you from the danger it wants you to avoid, kicking off the stress response (and much more[14]) in your body. And this builds our excuses – the reasons why we can't do what we secretly want to do or become who we, deep down, want to become.

They feed the stories about who we will allow ourselves to be. They grow the coping strategies that might have worked when we were seven, but which keep us stuck for decades doing things that no longer make sense. Those coping strategies often lead to subconscious self-sabotage and Imposter Syndrome.

Given that, as I mentioned, most of your core beliefs were formed when you were really young and that these beliefs are still influencing the choices you make and the actions you take today:

The biggest decisions in your life are probably being made by your inner seven-year-old.

You're sitting in a meeting and the perfect solution to a problem is bubbling up inside you. You sense the excitement growing. Part of you desperately wants to speak up. But another part of you is yelling, "Move. Away. From. The. Spotlight." It's telling you stories about times in the past when you spoke up and were ridiculed; times when you shared your ideas and people didn't get them; times when you got 'the look' from your old boss that reminded you not to bat above your rank or people will reject you for showing off. So you sit, in silence, and the moment passes. The inspiration is wasted. But you're safe.

What you don't consciously realise is that the whole scenario was sparked off by a teacher who publicly ridiculed you when you were ten for using the word 'apologise' instead of 'sorry' and spelling it incorrectly (yup – that's one of my t-shirts). The ten-year-old you vowed never to let that happen to you again. So you hide your talents and your inner genius. You risk just enough to grow, but not enough to thrive. That shutdown gets so well-rehearsed that it becomes part of who you believe you *are* and it sets

---

[14] If you want to find out more about the scientific research behind how beliefs affect our physiology, there's more on this in the Readers' Resource Vault.

itself up as a future Imposter Syndrome trigger.

We all have stories like this one. The purpose of this section is to help you to understand how they're getting in your way and to give you the tools to set yourself free from them and the limiting belief boxes they accidentally created for you.

Five Ways Your Limiting Beliefs Are Triggering Imposter Syndrome

Fear is the emotional symptom of an underlying limiting belief or block. Your fears dictate your limits. Clear the block and the fear will disappear.

Limiting beliefs are a trigger for the fight-flight-freeze response, linked to our fears of perceived threats and danger.

The 2019 Imposter Syndrome Research Study made it clear that there are five core fears that drive most people's Imposter Syndrome behaviour. All of them are attached to limiting beliefs. Once you know how to spot them, you're on your way to setting yourself free from their subconscious self-sabotage effects.

If any of these fears have been a pattern you have struggled with, run them through the second of the two belief-clearing processes we will cover in this section to gain insights and to start to let them go.

1. Fear Of Failure

This one leads to the Four Ps of Imposter Syndrome. It can cause us to procrastinate, because if we don't finish something, we can't fail. It can turn us into perfectionists, setting unrealistically high standards. It can leave us paralysed into inaction, avoiding the project completely. It triggers the "I'm not good enough" self-talk that is one of the most common Imposter Syndrome responses.

The classic response to fear of failure is to ask someone: what's the worst thing that could happen? But now you know what you know about worrying (see page 87), the mental rehearsal of worst-case-scenarios is not going to be useful.

2. Fear Of Success

This particular fear sits squarely in the 'secondary gain' camp, which we'll explore on page 195. It is protecting us from losing something that is important to us – or from gaining something that part of us believes would be dangerous.

This one plays hard with our fears of visibility and with owning our successes or allowing our light to shine. It triggers Imposter Syndrome in the form of not taking credit for our achievements and not going for potential opportunities to shine.

3. Fear Of Criticism

This is the fear that gets you not speaking up with your brilliant ideas, or keeping quiet, even if you know you have the answers.

The challenge with criticism is it doesn't even have to have happened for you to feel scared of it. Seeing others being trolled on the internet, for example, can trigger a fear of criticism in someone who has only ever experienced praise, especially if they're naturally empathic and can sense the pain it causes others.

Remember that your biggest critic is the one inside you and you've just spent the whole of Step Two learning how to tame it.

4. Fear Of Rejection

We are hard-wired to want to be part of the tribe – that's how our ancestors stayed alive. If you're running a fear of rejection (which most of us do, at some level), then it can trigger Imposter Syndrome in the form of not speaking up or letting our light shine, because we don't want to be seen as different. Or maybe we share the credit for our success with the wider team, in order to feel accepted.

"What if they figure out I don't belong here?" was one of the most common self-talk responses for those struggling with Imposter Syndrome, in the research study.

5. Fear Of Lack Of Money

Maslow put money in the foundation levels of the pyramid for his famous Hierarchy Of Needs (see page 196), because feeling financially secure is a precursor to the higher needs. In the worlds of yoga and meditation, this is described as the 'base chakra' – our need for safety and security.

It's hard to take action towards your dreams when you're secretly worrying about how to put food in the fridge.

In terms of Imposter Syndrome, this fear triggers seemingly crazy behaviour like discounting prices before being asked or not asking for pay rises we know we deserve, because we are scared of losing the sale or the salary that we *do* have.

It can also trigger the common self-talk of "What if they find out they made a mistake in hiring me?" and "I only got here through hard work / luck."

Of course, there is overlap between these five fears – many of us are running more than one. And these five core fears play a further role in Imposter Syndrome: they set our expectations via the pesky Reticular Activating System in your brain. And, as we discussed on page 23, we usually see what we expect to see. So if you're running a fear of failure, your brain will automatically filter in external sensory information to show you examples to back that up, so your self-talk can make the fear a self-fulfilling prophesy.

When we take the cognitive approach to clearing Imposter Syndrome – treating it as an attitude issue, it's easy to forget that our limiting beliefs are accompanied by powerful emotions – the strongest of which is fear. If you try to clear the belief whilst ignoring the emotion, your body will continue to want the biochemical reaction it has become used to (which triggers the emotion – see page 21) and will find a new way to get that fix. Most advice ignores this, which is why so many people find they have previously tried to ditch Imposter Syndrome, but not succeeded. And, in fact, it can be dangerous advice to tackle something as emotionally-charged as Imposter Syndrome solely at the cognitive level, because those emotions will seek another outlet, leaving you forced to push them down, again, with the physiological, emotional and mental health risks that brings.

I don't want that for you. It doesn't have to be that way. That's why everything in this book is about the *whole* of you, not just your head. The techniques you're going to find in this step for clearing those limiting beliefs will help you to release the stuck emotions, too – the missing link in most personal growth work – in a way that is safe and brings a wonderful sense of relief.

And the great news is that releasing a hidden fear is a very similar process to clearing a limiting belief, which is exactly what you'll discover in this section. The two processes I'm sharing with you in this step work really well for fears, too.

As a caveat, though: if those fears are triggering anxiety for you, it's really important to get yourself professional support to clear them. You are not alone!

Now you've got a handle on how the five core fears can trigger Imposter Syndrome, it's time to explore my favourite way of uncovering hidden blocks and limiting beliefs.

The Secret Power Of Because

In 1977 Ellen Langer at Harvard University conducted research that has since been dubbed 'The Copy Machine Study'. Everyone who works in an office knows the feeling of waiting in the queue for the photocopier when someone tries to push in. Imagine the scenario:

The queue for the photocopier was long. The queue was dull. The queue was where mad-Kevin (every photocopier queue has one) liked to hang out and torment people, who felt forced to stare desperately at their shoes. Ok, so maybe Kevin wasn't there. But it was probably the only office worldwide where he wasn't[15].

And then Someone (name changed to protect the innocent) simply walked up and *dared* to ask to jump the queue.

What the...? You can imagine the looks. The shock. The incensed huffs and puffs that silently spread through the line. Had this been in the UK, there would have been a very polite and low-key riot at such a ridiculous

---

[15] Kevin is lovely, really. He's just a bit over-talkative in the copier queue.

request.

Someone got a 'no' around half of the time. Yes, the researchers risked Someone's safety by asking him to do this more than once. Sometimes Someone got a yes, but only if the person in front of them hated their job so much that standing in the queue for longer was better than going back to their desk. Probably. The researchers forgot to ask.

Then Someone changed their tack.

Same photocopier. Still a queue. Still the foot-staring and finger-tapping. But this time Someone used the word 'because' after their request.

What came after the 'because' wasn't particularly creative. They weren't running late for a Board meeting and risking being fired, unable to feed their sympathy-invoking children. They weren't hurrying to pitch an idea to the firm's favourite client that could keep everyone in a job for the next hundred years. They weren't behind with a project that could end world hunger by Friday.

"*Because I'm in a rush,*" was the best Someone could manage (scripted by the researchers).

And, like the red sea before Moses, 94% of the time, the queue parted and allowed Someone instant access to the Xerox machine, while everyone quietly returned to studying their shoes.

Then Someone experimented some more: "... because I have to make copies." This wasn't quite as effective as a semi-genuine reason, but it still got people agreeing to let Someone jump the queue 93% of the time.

The researchers were confused. Someone's 'because' was – frankly – pants. It was a non-reason. But it held a magical power to achieve the unthinkable, without objections or delay.

And, no, they hadn't deliberately picked the office's Nice People for the queue that day.

The researchers proved what we instinctively know: that when you give people a *reason* – a *because* – it gets attention; it reduces resistance; it makes them listen; it gets them supporting the 'because'. It's an un-blocker of stuckness and a cranker-upper of excitement for your big vision ideas.

'Because' can get people taking action, without questioning. And it can make them *fear* taking action, without questioning.

Interestingly, it works in the other direction, too. If your 'because' is more of a 'but' – "I can't do that, because..." – then it reinforces a limiting belief; a hidden block; a fear; an excuse. And remember that your 'Big Why' from Step One is the 'because' that keeps you motivated on your journey to ditch Imposter Syndrome.

For this section, we're going to look at the power of 'because' to unlock your hidden blocks, excuses and out-of-date fears.

*I can't do the interview, **because** I'm too busy.*

*I can't give the presentation, **because** no one would want to listen to me.*

*I can't apply for that promotion, **because** I'm too old / young.*

What comes after the 'because' is an excuse that defends the limiting belief and is trying to keep you safe. So the word 'because' has the power to both unlock what you most want and to keep you stuck, missing out on your goals and dreams. And that's why it's such an important word in your self-talk:

Your 'becauses' hold the key to the limiting beliefs that are keeping you stuck.

Our limiting beliefs are rarely in our conscious awareness, so being able to spot them and release them, before they cause us to self-sabotage, is really important. Let's find out what your becauses are!

Remember: all of the exercises in this book come with a downloadable workbook with space for you to write your answers. It's particularly useful for an exercise like this one. If you haven't downloaded your copy yet, you can get it here:

www.DitchingImposterSyndrome.com/vault/

Exercise: How To Spot Your Limiting Beliefs

Take a deep, sighing breath, to settle you back into this moment and your body. Then, thinking about a goal you want to achieve where Imposter Syndrome is getting in the way, ask yourself:

What do I believe about my ability to achieve this?

Am I the kind of person who can do that? Yes / no …. Because….

Complete the following statement about this goal, listing at least seven answers, letting them bubble up, without editing:

I haven't done that yet, because….

It's ok if some of those answers feel strange. If you feel you get stuck, take another deep sighing breath and imagine you're dropping down into the next level of answers, letting them come to the surface, without judgement.

If you want to prompt a few more, you could ask yourself: "And if there *were* more, what might they be?" The deeper, core beliefs often don't pop up until answer seven or later.

Now go through your list and look at each 'because' in turn. Some of them are so patently not true that you can draw a line right through them (ask your body, not your mind! Your gut knows the *real* answer). For the rest, just let them be for now and we'll come back to them with the two belief-clearing exercises you'll cover in this step.

Look back at your answers to your two Glurg exercises on pages 116 and 119. How do your answers to this exercise tie in? What insights are your answers giving you?

The 'because' endings from this exercise are the limiting beliefs, fears, excuses and secret comfort zones that are running behind the scenes, keeping you stuck. There's nothing wrong with them – you're not somehow 'broken' and in need of 'fixing'. They just *are*. Looking back at your first Glurg exercise on page 116, might any of these beliefs have been getting in your way on a wider Imposter Syndrome scale?

And if they are no longer serving you, then it's time to let them go. That's where my favourite Italian word comes in.

My Favourite Italian Word

If you've hung around with me for a while, you'll know what my favourite Italian word is. But if you're new to working with me, you're in for a treat. My Grannie's family was Italian and I have studied the language, on and off, for years. There's one word that stands out as my all-time favourite – and there's no real English equivalent. And, no, it's not *vino*.

This word can get you off the emotional rollercoaster in just seconds. It can reset your Autonomic Nervous System to get you back into homeostasis. It can get you unstuck, even if limiting beliefs are ruling your world. It has the power, in just five letters, to change your life, fast and forever.

It saves you having to wait to hit rock bottom, before you make the decision to bounce back, saving you potentially decades of pain, frustration and regrets.

My favourite Italian word is:

"Basta!"

It's pronounced like 'pasta'. But that's where the similarity ends. The word has the same meaning in both Italian and Spanish and my kids know it well. In English it means:

"Enough!" or *"Stop it!"*

When I use it with my boys at home, they know it's the final warning before things have gone too far. When you bring it into your self-talk, it's a brilliant way of halting your Inner Critic in its tracks and making the clear choice to change something. But it's important to say it playfully, rather than angrily, so it doesn't fire off your Sympathetic Nervous System's fight-flight-freeze response!

In my workshops I talk about how change doesn't happen until you have a 'basta-moment'. This can either happen *to* you, as a life melt-down or disaster or trauma. Or you can create it, right here, right now, by making the commitment to let go of a habit that's no longer serving you, or to firm up a boundary.

Once you've had your basta-moment, the change starts to feel more real, more possible. It triggers your Reticular Activating System's filters to start noticing ways you *could* create and support that change. It acts as an instruction to your unconscious mind to help you to let go of the past and focus on your future.

So how about – right now – picking one of the blocks that came up for you in the last exercise and having a basta-moment chat with it? Imagine the classic Italian grandmother giving that block a super-stern look, with a cheeky glint in her eye, as she waves a hand across her body, as though sweeping that block off the table and onto the floor – letting it know that its time is done.

And when you've done that (extra points for theatrical performances), it's time to find out how to clear that block from your thoughts, your emotions and your physiology.

Why I Don't Want You To Get Rid Of Your Limiting Beliefs

When you want to clear a limiting belief, there are two ways to approach it. You can look at it at the cognitive level – that conscious thought level – which we now know from the Imposter Syndrome Iceberg (page 40) is just a surface-level symptom. You can try to understand the belief at a cognitive level, analysing its impact, looking at how you got it and going into its stories.

But that leaves all of the belief's dangly bits still lurking below the surface, looking for a fresh batch of thoughts to feed. It also risks triggering the backfire effect that we met earlier in this book, where your unconscious mind and Inner Critic join ranks, digging their heels in to defend your status quo. So over-analysing your belief can risk it becoming more deeply entrenched. There's a high risk that we'll find someone to 'blame' for the limiting belief and may even treat it like a badge of honour, to which we become attached. It keeps us stuck in the mind-story drama and fears.

Any change made above the surface level of the Imposter Syndrome Iceberg – at the thoughts and actions level – requires effort and willpower to make change at the 'effects' level, overruling the below-the-surface 'causes' that were supporting and driving the old behaviour. This is why 'attitude' alone is not enough. Yet this cognitive approach is the one most of us pick, because we love to analyse and understand.

Or you can go below the surface and deal with the root cause and triggers as you clear out that belief quickly and easily. Then your Reticular Activating System gets 'updated'. You create new neural pathways in your brain. This shifts what you notice in your sensory environment, changing the thoughts you think and the actions you take – with near-zero effort. The change is fast and it's sustainable, without you having to remember to do things differently – you have *become* more of who you really are by clearing out that hidden block.

This way is so much more fun than trying to control each and every thought you think or trying to 'conquer' or 'slay' the bits of you that were getting in the way, with brute force and gritted-teeth determination.

And by going below the surface, you get to clear out the essence of that out-of-date belief, even if it was created and stored at a non-verbal level. This is the case for many of our core beliefs if we picked them up when we were too young to be chatting to ourselves in our heads.

I'm going to share both methods with you in this step – the cognitive version, which works for lots of limiting beliefs, especially if you're ready to let them go, then the deeper-acting version, which is one of the most potent change-tools I have ever found in nearly two decades of teaching this stuff.

But first, I have a confession: I don't want you to get rid of your limiting beliefs. Yes, you read that right. 'Getting rid' of them risks setting up a long-term inner conflict and can trigger anxiety and self-worth issues.

That old limiting belief has, most likely, been part of you for quite a while. The bit of you that picked up that belief did so, thinking it was making the best possible decision to keep you safe. That belief was there to protect you from the perceived threat. So if you think about 'getting rid' of that belief, you're rejecting a part of yourself – part of you that was trying to help you. It means you'd be doing this belief work from a place of anger and resentment and possibly even hatred. There's no way that's healthy.

That doesn't mean you should hang on to the belief just to keep it happy in some misguided attempt at gratitude. But it does mean we need to be mindful of the way we talk about changing our beliefs. And that process needs to honour the journey that part of us went through and the effort it has made to keep us out of danger for so long.

The more you can treat your inner self with love, compassion and acceptance, the happier you will be. This also has a bonus side-effect of reducing the effects of Imposter Syndrome. You can't turn back time, so there's no point in being angry with yourself for having believed something about yourself and your abilities that you now realise isn't true.

So, instead of 'getting rid' of your limiting beliefs, I invite you to *choose* to *let them go*. Thinking about *releasing* that old energy which is no longer serving you is a much healthier approach than going to war with part of yourself.

Clear A Limiting Belief In Under Five Minutes

I want to begin this section by congratulating you! The exercise we just did about how to spot your limiting beliefs is something very few people ever bother to do. And you've done it! (Squirrel back to that exercise right now, please, if you haven't). That puts you way ahead of most people and gives you a great head start on your Ditching Imposter Syndrome journey.

We're going to start with the cognitive version of the process. This works for most beliefs, unless they're 'sticky' (more on that soon). And because you're playing with this strategy for the first time, I invite you to try it out with a belief from your list in the exercise on page 169 that's a three or four out of ten, so you can learn the process.

Note: if any of your answers to the exercise are real 'biggies', go and get yourself some mentoring or other support to work through them. You don't have to do this on your own.

Exercise: Clearing A Limiting Belief

Looking through the list of the 'becauses' that came up for you in the exercise on page 168168, look at the ones that remain.

For each of them, ask yourself: is this *really* true?

... no story, no drama, no emotions!

Sometimes, just becoming aware of a 'because' is enough for it to melt away. If that happens with some of yours, celebrate!

For the 'becauses' that are left on your sheet, one at a time, ask yourself these questions:

Who says?

You've already told yourself it's true – but who says it's true? Do you really want to give that person or that experience power over your present and your future and who you can become in life?

If not, it's time to reclaim your power and ask:

What do I want to believe, instead?

What do I want to believe about myself and my ability to create that goal? Make it something that your **body** *believes in. It will tell you with tension, if it doesn't!*

How could I collect evidence to support that new belief?

Which thoughts might I think?

Which actions might I take?

How does it *feel* to be free from that old belief?

So, that's the cognitive process, where you use logic and your thinking mind to help you to clear an out-of-date belief. How did you get on with it? What did you notice?

Did you spot how we totally ignored how you *got* the belief? That's because you really don't need to know that, to be able to clear it, unless it's a deep-seated trauma, in which case you'll know what it was, anyway, and will probably need to do some forgiveness and acceptance work around that (more in Step Four).

Once you've played with this, there's another layer that can help you to choose your new, empowering belief.

A belief is like a box within which you experience life.

Outside of that belief box is stuckness. Even the most empowering belief in the world can keep you stuck at some point in the future, when you outgrow it. You'll cover techniques to do this when we tackle positive affirmations in Step Four.

The second option I promised you gets you out of your thinking mind and into your body. Given how closely they are linked, clearing something in one affects the other. It allows your unconscious mind to release the belief without your thinking mind getting in the way. This process can work more deeply than the cognitive process. There's an MP3 to guide you through it in the Readers' Resource Vault[16].

Getting back into your body can be easier than the cognitive approach, because the body doesn't over-think things. With the thoughts-emotions-physiology cycle we discussed on page 21, you can press 'pause' at any one of these and pause the other two. Stopping an emotion can feel difficult. Pausing the roaring juggernaut of your Inner Critic mid-track can be tricky. But your body is always there as a back-up option to let things go.

The following exercise is intended for beliefs that feel safe for you to work on, on your own. If your insights have shown you some 'biggies', please make sure you get professional support to clear those blocks. There are processes I use with my 1:1 clients for this and you can find out how to work with one of my certified Imposter Syndrome Coaches in the readers' resources vault.

---

[16] www.DitchingImposterSyndrome.com/vault/

Exercise: Melting Away An Out-Of-Date Belief

Choose a belief that no longer fits – an 'I can't do this, because' that has survived the last step.

Take a deep breath in through your nose and out through your mouth with a sigh. Do this three times.

Thinking about that belief, notice where in your body you *feel* that belief. I know that might be a strange question! Become aware of those physical sensations.

Now, wherever it is in your body, allow that area to soften and relax. You might like to imagine that you're breathing in and out of that part of your body.

And as you allow that belief to soften, maybe asking yourself: "Is it *really* true? Do I really want to keep believing this? Or is it time to let it go?"

And you might want to say to yourself, "I choose to let go of this belief. I don't need it anymore."

Continue in your own time until you feel that belief starting to soften and melt away, like butter in the hot summer's sun.

Then you might like to get curious: "What would my *future me* like me to believe, instead?" It's ok if that question sends your head into a spin. Gently play with new ideas – try them on for size – and notice the kind of thoughts they make you think.

How would it be if you were to start thinking those thoughts, right now?

Imagine that you could incorporate them into your daily life, with that new belief. If you imagine taking a step into the future, how does that feel? What kinds of actions are you taking? Which thoughts are you thinking?

Allow yourself to stretch this as you experiment with the curiosity of a young child, as you choose your new, more empowering belief.

And then all you need to do is to remember to keep playing with that new, empowering belief. It can be easy. It can be fun. It can be playful.

... continues

And as you take another step into your future, really experience what it feels like with those new thoughts and those new actions.

And when you're ready, opening your eyes and giving yourself a wriggle to come back to this moment, you might want to write that new belief down – along with anything that you noticed from this process. Writing it down is the first step of your commitment to that future 'you'.

Now you've got two clear tools to let go of old beliefs, it's worth covering some of the common traps that can derail people. Whatever the block, we can get attached to it.

Baggage isn't just something you take on a plane. It can stop your dreams dead in their tracks.

When we get attached to our baggage – the stories, the drama, the self-talk, the biochemical responses, the emotional rollercoaster – it can keep those out-of-date beliefs stuck. Psychologists call this 'secondary gain': what is it that the old belief is *doing* for you, that you need to achieve in a new, healthier way?

*Sometimes, if a belief doesn't shift easily, it's because it **thinks** it's giving you more than it's costing you.*

An example of this is if someone gets ill and the treatment doesn't seem to work. But by being ill, they are gaining rest and love and attention that might have been missing from their life. If that's a need that has been unmet for some time, there will be a natural resistance to feeling better, because they will fear they will lose the rest and love and attention.

Identifying and dealing with what the belief was doing for you means you won't need that belief anymore and you can more easily let it go.

We're going to cover secondary gain in more detail in Step Four, when we look at how it has been driving Imposter Syndrome for you. So, for now, I'm telling you about it so that it's on your radar and so that you know you haven't done anything wrong if you run the last two processes and find a 'sticky' belief!

Another common trap is resisting and fighting the beliefs. That's why we talked about the need to 'let go' of a belief, rather than 'getting rid' of it, so you're not rejecting a part of yourself – or going to war with your mind. If you get angry about that belief, then you're giving it your focus, energy and power, which makes it stronger.

The third trap is changing a belief and not thinking about which thoughts and actions you need to change. That's why we cover this in both of the methods: so that you can make the shifts to support that new belief. Changing a belief is instant. What takes the time and patience is practising it – and the new thoughts and habits that go with it. Often people clear a belief and think the job is done, but what turns that 'nice idea' into lifelong change is reminding yourself to keep playing with the new behaviours.

I'm curious: how might you support yourself with your new belief(s)? How might you remind yourself to take the new actions? This visualisation you did in the second half of the second strategy can easily be adapted to be something you do each morning before you get out of bed, imagining your new belief, the new thoughts and the new actions flowing through your day.

Taking A Pair Of Scissors To That Old Belief

As part of clearing old beliefs, it's really important to accept whatever effects they had on your life in the past and to forgive the 'old' version of you for any resentment you might be tempted to feel. There's no point in letting go of that belief, only to fill that space with guilt and regret. Honour the journey those beliefs triggered; the personal growth that happened.

To set yourself free from the 'energy of that old belief, it can be fun to imagine taking a pair of imaginary scissors to the ties it had to you, setting you and the belief free to go on your separate journeys. It's also important to take time to reflect on what you learned from running that old belief, so that history doesn't need to repeat itself. You might even find yourself reaching a place of gratitude.

When you release an old limiting belief,
also give yourself permission to move on.

A final tool I use with myself and my clients to clear stuck beliefs is a deep-dive version of EFT (Emotional Freedom Technique) that I have developed over the past few years, working with the physical body, rather than the cognitive mind, which we briefly discussed previously. It works incredibly well because it bypasses the thinking mind – which was partly responsible for the creation of the block – and clears it at a physical and energetic level. I'm also a hypnotherapist and used to use that for stuck beliefs, but I have found EFT more powerful because it can work in just a couple of minutes, doesn't require someone to go into trance, and is easy to teach them to do for themselves. My deep-dive process is something I only teach on workshops or in my one-to-one sessions, because it needs to be tailored to your individual needs. If you'd like to find out more, you can find resources in the Readers' Resource Vault.

You Are Not Broken. There Is Nothing To 'Fix'

Spending so much time and effort looking at your self-talk and clearing out your limiting beliefs can make you feel fabulous, when you're making progress. But if you're trudging through what can feel like a swamp, it can be easy to fall into the trap of feeling like you're broken and somehow 'unfixable'.

In case that has been happening to you (now or at any time in the past), I wanted to wrap up this section with a heartfelt message:

There's nothing 'wrong' with you, so there's nothing to 'fix'. You've simply been running some old habits and beliefs that have been stopping you from being *who you really are*.

Books, seminars, courses and therapeutic interventions can all help, when we want to make shifts. But the real work happens when we put down the book or get home from the workshop or therapy session. That's when the effort needs to start.

No one can wave a magic wand to take away the fact that creating change in your life requires two things:

1. Choice – a decision (which may need to be re-made every five minutes, at first!)
2. Action – a choice without action produces zero results

When we let go of the need to fix ourselves and stop seeing ourselves as broken or a 'project', it opens the door to treating ourselves more compassionately and those old patterns can melt away. This makes it easier to make those empowering choices about how to think, feel, behave and see ourselves, without judgement. It makes taking inspired action easier, too.

No matter what we learn from others, be they experts or a stranger in the street, insight or knowledge without action won't create the future we desire. That action doesn't need to be difficult, but it does need dedication.

Remember: with each and every breath we get to choose who we want to be, shifting our experience of life.

And I'm so proud of you for the progress you have made already. Whether you've completed each and every single exercise so far or are just picking the ones that resonate, you've taken action and changed your life.

Actually, you've 'unchanged' your life. You've been letting go of the self-talk and limiting beliefs you accidentally picked up along life's journey, so you can become more of who you really are. I'm so excited for you.

Exercise: Wrapping Up Step Three

What have you learned in this section?

Any surprises? Lightbulbs?

What are you going to be doing differently now?

And what's your next action?

Next, I invite you to revisit your answers from page 99 – your Big Why for ditching Imposter Syndrome, to get you ready to dive in with the rest of the techniques in this book. Because, with all the work you've done so far, now it's time to wave goodbye to Imposter Syndrome!

Step 4: Wave Goodbye To Imposter Syndrome

Which Masks Are You Wearing?

I was talking to the leader of a women's network in a multi-national firm recently about running a one-day workshop on Imposter Syndrome for their leaders. When I asked her one of my favourite questions – if she could wave a 'magic wand', what would she most like to change for these women – her answer was quick and clear:

"I want them to be able to take off their masks and to lead by being who they really are, not who they think they should be."

Most of us wear masks, but unlike Eleanor Rigby, we don't keep them in a jar by the door. We apply them invisibly and take them with us into our physical and virtual worlds:

- we pretend to feel brave when we're secretly feeling scared
- we behave in ways that feel out-of-kilter for us, because it's what we think others expect
- we modify everything from our appearance to our values, to try to fit in
- we turn down golden opportunities, pretending they weren't the right fit or timing
- we don't let our light shine, for fear of others' response

Those masks were chosen to protect us from our secret fears and hidden blocks. And we make subconscious micro-choices, from our earliest years, to shut down, play small, and be who we think others want us to be. We may find them useful on our journey towards success, but they come at a price: we are pretending; and hiding the real 'us' – playing a character in a film, denying the world the opportunity to see the light and genius and passion that you really are. The masks cause us to be inauthentic, as a method of self-preservation.

*But success from behind a mask isn't really succeeding. It's playing a role and denying yourself the chance to succeed **because** of who you are, not despite it.*

When I was seventeen and at Sixth Form College doing my A-levels, I used to love making my own clothes. I would adapt paper dress-making patterns to create clothes I really wanted to wear, choosing the brightest, boldest, most colourful fabrics. When I went travelling with my bestie around Europe that final summer before university, every photo showed me wearing combinations of clothes and hats that stood out in the crowd. I loved expressing myself through my choice of clothes and, looking back, it never once occurred to me to care about what anyone else thought.

Then I went to my first tutorial at university. As I was the only woman in the group, the young men around me stared and didn't know how to handle this strange creature that had bounced into their play-it-safe midst. I felt their judgement; their rejection; their unspoken fear, confusion and inability to understand me.

In that moment, I made an unconscious choice to conform; to change who I was and how I expressed myself; to fit in. By the end of my first month I had carefully hidden the real me under layers of jeans, baggy t-shirts and jumpers, donning the traditional uniform of the engineering student. Over time, I almost forgot that 'old me' was still there. There was an emotional shutdown, as well, as I became less bubbly and bouncy. I wore my baggy, boring clothes like an armour to protect me from rejection – from having to live outside of the tribe.

But the guys in my tutor group still never understood me, despite my new masks and armour. They didn't know how to talk to young women, and judged me, despite my efforts to be one of them. It took twenty years for me to realise that it had all been about their struggles with their insecurities and their hidden fears about hanging around with 'girls', rather than a personal attack on me or what I stood for. But by then the choice I had made was very much my 'new normal'.

Over the years, my deeply held need to express myself through my clothes would force its way back out to play, but was quickly shut down – this time by me. "Who am I, to wear such vibrant clothes?" or "What if they find out I'm a fraud and shouldn't be wearing this kind of thing?" Or I would tell myself I was too short or too fat or too old or too small-c conservative to dress like that. And I would shut down again, retreating to the safety of the jeans-and-jumpers uniform that everyone else was wearing.

I was doing what most other people do – changing how I showed myself to the world, in order to fit in; putting on those masks, that invisible armour which extended to more than just clothes, to be accepted; toning down my message, to avoid criticism.

And the crowd helped to reinforce this for me. If I stepped up with my message and stood for something, the then-new phenomenon of internet trolls would slap me right back down. In my corporate days, my boss would take me to one side 'for a chat'. I remember being sent on a training course to learn to be more patient because the men around me in the engineering team had complained to my boss that I thought too quickly and they couldn't keep up. So I stopped speaking up with ideas in meetings and pretended to be less clever than I was. My boss's boss criticised me for wearing Doc Marten shoes when I was walking around the factory, telling me I should be more feminine, despite the obvious safety reasons behind my footwear choice. I had ended up dressing like a man to blend in, to belong, and to protect myself from the industry-standard behaviours that created the #metoo movement. I taught myself that I had to pretend *not* to be who I really was, in order to stay safe and be accepted.

I wasn't being the *real* me. I was covering my inner diamond with layers of brown stuff, so it couldn't shine brightly enough to get me into 'trouble'. I was playing safe; playing small. I had changed the way I saw myself and matched my beliefs, thoughts and actions to that new, compromised version of me. I had morphed into being someone I wasn't. And it had been entirely my choice.

The past ten years have been a journey of actively clearing those masks. Without doing that, I wouldn't have been able to write this book or to co-lead a campaign that changed EU law or to be as visible as I am with the work I teach.

We – men and women – pick up our masks and our suits of armour from a young age, as ways of coping with life and protecting ourselves. The masks chosen by your inner seven-year-old aren't such a good fit by the time you're in your thirties, forties or beyond. Yet we keep wearing them, subconsciously reaching for them and we feel exposed without them

In the Imposter Syndrome Iceberg, we talked about how you need to go beyond mindset to clear Imposter Syndrome's patterns and effects. The work you have done in this book already on taming your Inner Critic and clearing out your limiting beliefs has laid strong foundations for this journey.

Looking at our masks and armour – and deciding which to keep – is the start of the identity level journey.

We pick up these masks from our earliest childhood and use them to feel safe, subconsciously choosing to hide a little part of ourselves from the world. This process can start when a teacher tells you off in front of the class for getting an answer wrong. You pick up a mask to stop you from speaking up, so you don't feel ashamed. It can happen if a parent shouts at you for being too boisterous, so you pick up a mask to hide the 'fun' part of yourself, conforming to the behaviour you mind-read that they wanted from you in that moment, forever. It can happen if a friend teases you for wearing new clothes that you love, so you pick up a mask to protect you from the dangers of rejection you think may come from expressing your individuality.

Over the years, these masks become second-nature to the extent that we don't realise we're wearing them anymore. We lose sight of who we *really* are and believe that the masks and armour reflect us, instead.

And those masks breed. They attract limiting beliefs, fears, excuses and thought habits to support and justify them. So a single choice when you were, say, five, can collect a hundred limiting beliefs and critical self-talk autopilot habits to keep it company. This is one of the reasons why mindset alone won't clear Imposter Syndrome for you – because you need to deal with the underlying identity-level mask that caused you to pick up those limiting beliefs and negative thought patterns. Otherwise you're only dealing with the surface-level symptoms and that deeper stuff will look for new beliefs and thoughts to fill those gaps.

There's even a current trend to intentionally pick up someone else's mask as an 'alter ego' to help us to be someone we're not, to feel more confident. To me, that's the ultimate self-rejecting sticky-plaster. I want to let my masks *go*, so I can show up in the world as who I *really* am, not have to remember to pretend to be 'Jennifer' in a Board meeting and 'Lucas' on stage.

And here's the bit where the masks bite you on the backside:

Remember the child who put on a mask to stop themselves from speaking up in class, for fear of shame and embarrassment if they got it wrong? Well, as an adult they struggle to speak up about their ideas in meetings and don't volunteer for opportunities to shine, which they secretly know they would love. They might develop coping strategies of becoming a people-pleaser and not saying what they really think, even if the situation they are in is causing them stress and pain.

The child who picked up the mask to hide the fun and playful part of themselves becomes the leader who believes that they have to work hard to succeed, who holds themselves – and their teams – to impossibly high standards, who beats themselves up if they let their standards drop. Even if they make it as a high achiever, they are unlikely to allow themselves to enjoy it. And this mask will also affect their personal relationships, as those around them feel they have to shut down in this way, too.

The child who was teased about its clothes, who shut down expressing its individuality, is more likely to become the adult who shies away from standing out and stepping up to lead. They might be able to do it, but it's more likely they'll do it in a traditional, conformist way that doesn't match who they really are. Leading would come at an inner emotional cost as the fear of rejection from that playground incident is amplified by decades of reinforcing the notion that blending in with the crowd is the only way to stay safe.

The biggest triggers for us picking up new masks or armour is shame. Shame is essentially 'guilt made personal' – we feel bad about something and, instead of remembering it was just a behaviour, something we did, we conflate that self-criticism as being about who we *are*. So we make a decision to hide that part of ourselves.

Our masks don't just come from things we think we got wrong. They can come from our fear of shining, too. So many of us were taught not to 'brag'; not to be big-headed; not to be boastful; to put the feelings of others first. We use masks to hide our gifts, as well as our flaws. We convince ourselves that allowing ourselves to shine and to use our gifts to their fullest somehow makes us a 'bad person' – which is an identity-level self-judgement.

I had a disturbing example of this with my sons recently. I was picking my teenager up from his Duke Of Edinburgh expedition, where he had hiked for two days and camped in a field after four solid days of end-of-year exams. He told us about how his team had got lost and how he had managed to navigate them back to the route, using the map – the first time ever – and how he felt proud of himself. He was exhausted and as I gingerly hugged him hello (pre-shower and de-mudding), I congratulated him on his achievement. It had been quite a week for him. But my seven-year-old son piped up with "Don't brag!"

A few well-directed questions revealed that a teacher at school had been drumming it into the children never to 'brag' about *any* of their achievements. It stemmed from Monday morning discussions when the children talked about what they had been doing at the weekend. My seven-year-old, with the level of analytical ability you have at that age, took this to mean that you should never, ever talk about anything you have done well – that you should actively hide and play down your achievements. I really hope that wasn't the teacher's intention and I'm very happy to have caught that one, before my son spent the rest of his life playing down his inner genius. But it shows how easily this mask-factory-block can be picked up.

Our masks get us pretending to be someone we're not, as well as hiding the genius of who we really are.

Our childhood masks increase the likelihood of Imposter Syndrome affecting us by creating the belief and thought framework that provides fertile ground for that gap between who we think we need to be to succeed and who we see ourselves as being in that context: the Imposter Syndrome Gap.

When we put on a mask, we are rejecting part of ourselves and denying who we really are. We are giving our unconscious mind the clear message that we are, in some way, not good enough. Then, because we're pretending and wearing that mask, we set up a fear of being 'found out', because we know we're acting a part.

It goes beyond Imposter Syndrome, too: rejecting part of ourselves is the trigger for many of the problems we experience in our wider relationships and experience of life. If you are genuinely comfortable in your own skin, equally at peace with the bits of being 'you' that maybe aren't so great and the bits that are your strengths, even your Inner Genius, this shifts how you react to the outside world and the actions you will take.

The more we can accept ourselves, the less likely it is that outside influences will trigger us into feeling bad. That's the nature of true resilience, as we'll discuss in Step Five. The more deeply connected you are with who you *really are* – the more you love and accept the *real* you – the more you take off your masks and set yourself free from the reasons why you put them on in the first place – the more you set yourself free from Imposter Syndrome. You become Imposter-Syndrome-proof.

When you have that confidence to be the *real* you, you'll find it easier to communicate your big vision message in a way that inspires others. You'll be more credible. You'll find it easier to connect with people. Your creativity won't be held back by limiting beliefs and fears. You'll find that passion and commitment to keep going, and you'll be able to celebrate the progress you're making, because you'll have trained your brain to spot it.

That confidence and congruence is contagious. When a leader makes this shift in themselves, those around them sense an unconscious permission to do the same. This can create transformational breakthroughs in how an organisation behaves, the outcomes achieved, and the happiness of the workforce and clients.

Taking off your masks and armour is a journey, not a destination. It's about looking at what you could do – or let go of – to be able to take off, say, one per cent more of a mask each day.

This is why I talk so much about how I don't want people to change their lives, I want them to *unchange* them. I want you to gently and safely let go of the masks, the armour and the coping strategies that no longer serve you, so you can become more of *who you really are.*

How To Spot A Mask

If you have any limiting beliefs, hidden excuses or secret fears from Step Three that were a bit 'sticky' – that resisted the processes we were using – then they are likely to be connected with a mask; one that has secondary gain supporting it.

Rather than 'pushing on through' or pretending that block isn't there, it's important to identify and clear that secondary gain.

As we've discussed, secondary gain comes up when you have a need to stay safe from a perceived threat, so it's not going to go without a fight, if you try to pretend it's not there. It's much better to find out what that hidden need is and to meet it in a healthier way.

Yes, you could use willpower and determination instead, but that sets up an inner conflict, as we've already discussed, and makes self-sabotage much more likely. And, frankly, if you've got willpower and determination going spare, I'd much prefer you to use it on taking inspired action towards your goals, once you've cleared out the blocks, rather than waste it on forcing your way past blocks that don't need to be there anymore.

Exercise: How To Spot Your Hidden Masks

Looking back at what you have learned from chatting with Glurg, which masks have you been wearing?

Where have you been perhaps pretending to be someone you're not?

And which masks have been allowing you to hide who you really are?

Picking one of them, what would you need to feel safe taking off that mask? What might you need to believe about yourself?

How will life feel, once you give yourself permission to take that mask off and leave it behind?

Which tiny actions could you take today, to start allowing yourself to become more of that version of you?

Letting go of out-of-date masks is an on-going process. This exercise helps you to experience how life might feel without one. And then you can use the limiting belief clearing work (see page 174) to let go of anything that had been keeping the mask stuck.

The rest of this section guides you through strategies to clear out the reasons why you needed those masks, so you can take them off and feel great about it. Before we get to some exercises to take off your masks – in a way that feels safe and inspiring – let's start with an aspect of putting on masks that is a business epidemic, even though it's the fastest way to hold yourself back from expressing who you really are.

Don't Forget Your Labels!

AKA the secret reason why most training courses don't work – and can even make things worse.

A modern epidemic in the business leadership world is our addiction to labelling ourselves. And when I talk about leadership, I'm not restricting my definition to those with 'CEO' on their business card. I strongly believe that everyone who inspires others to work with them to create a common vision is, in their own way, a leader – as we'll discuss in Step Five. This applies whether you're the CEO of a multinational company or just starting out on your career. We all need to show leadership in some way.

Thousands of books have been published on leadership, with models and archetypes and personality profiling, all to help us to lead, but there's a flaw I see in the approaches in so many of these:

> *Most of them are about what we need to
> **do**, to lead.*

As we covered in the Imposter Syndrome Iceberg model, that's just the surface-level symptom. Making changes at the behavioural level doesn't shift our beliefs or values or sense of identity.

> *If what we're **doing** is out of kilter with who
> we see ourselves as currently **being**, then
> we create inner conflict, self-doubt and
> eventually Imposter Syndrome.*

What tends to happen, instead, is that those models and archetypes and profiling systems give us permission to live inside new comfort zones. The labels we are given become the new boxes within which we limit our behaviours. I have lost count of the number of times someone has excitedly talked about the results they got on some leadership or team-building profiling test, proudly announcing "I am an [insert catchy profiling name here]!"

> *A personality test can only tell you about
> your behaviour. It can't tell you who you
> really are. Yet we allow it to change how we
> see ourselves.*

Whilst such tests can help us to become aware of some of the seemingly random things we do (we all love a good personality quiz!), at a deeply subconscious level many of us then fall into the trap of morphing our sense of who we *are* to fit the profiled category. If, say, someone is told they're 'an instigator', they will start to manifest more behaviour that matches that label.

But other behaviours they previously had that might have been useful fall away, because they don't match the label, so, for instance, they might become less collaborative, when that was previously one of their strengths. You hear them proudly announcing things they won't do any more – "Oh, I'm not going to the planning meeting this week, because I am an Instigator! You need Joe – he was an Implementer." And Joe stops speaking up about his brilliant ideas because Fred is the Instigator, so that's his realm.

The label has changed how they see themselves, so their beliefs, thoughts and actions line up to match.

Labels become the limits on our leadership.

Labels are like masks behind which we get to feel safe. They risk becoming switches that flick *on* the traits that are *permitted* by that label and that flick *off* those that *aren't*.

In the entrepreneurial world, I meet many business owners who have had their Myers-Briggs profile done. Often, one of the first things they will say to you is, "I'm an ENTJ!" I have even seen some printing this kind of thing on their business cards. They have their one-of-sixteen-boxes label and they subconsciously conform to it, not realising that each of these categorisations is, in fact, a context-dependent sliding scale and that humans are infinitely more complex than a model that had to be simplified in order to teach it and test it.

You see them switching off their intuition because the 'J' for 'judging' means they *are supposed to be* evidence-based in their decision-making. And they obey.

As we set about conforming to the label we were given, we forget that these models are based on external behaviours, but our behaviours are surface-level actions – symptoms and effects – not the causal level of who we really *are*.

In addition, our behaviours change, depending on what we're trying to do. In different environments and fulfilling different roles, we have different behavioural habits. To use the Myers-Briggs 'J' as an example, in the context of making financial decisions of my business, there's a major chunk of backing that decision with data, to support my intuition – a 'J'. When it comes to choosing whether or not to trust someone, however, my intuition has by far the larger say – a 'P'.

Someone might use lots of data for making a recommendation to a client on a major issue that is unfamiliar to them, but might act mainly on intuition for smaller problems that they have encountered before. So whether a person would get 'J' or 'P' in the test would depend on the contexts used in the questions.

It would be more accurate for someone to say, "I run an ENTJ preference in the context of leading my team in a corporate environment when we are working on positively-framed solutions to low-impact problems."

But that's not quite so catchy!

Whilst these profiling systems *can* be helpful in raising our awareness of our behavioural preferences, so we can choose whether or not we want to keep specific habits, we need to be careful not to let them influence our sense of who we really are, to become comfort zone boxes and limits on how we express ourselves. I'm not saying that these models are in anyway bad or flawed. But they can only assess our behaviours, not tell us who we are.

Leadership profiles are intended to give us insights, not instructions.

There's another problem with this kind of profiling and label-creating: most of us are living lives – exhibiting behaviours – that are an adapted version of who we really are. We have picked up strategies and 'coping mechanisms' from a very young age to handle what life throws at us. These commonly lead to us showing the world a partially shut-down and 'safe' version of who we really are. But all these models can test is that externally-visible behaviour. So the models aren't able to be accurate. They can't see to that deeper level. And the label you get given is the label that belongs to the constricted, adapted version of you; not the *real* you inside, because that can't be *questionnaired* into a box.

These labels can keep us stuck in the habits we secretly wish we could ditch. And they become a badge of honour or even virtual armour.

"Oh, I hate networking, because I'm an introvert[17]!"

---

[17] In this sense, the term 'introvert' doesn't mean shy – it's about where someone

Someone making this statement is much more likely to not enjoy a networking event because they will be telling themselves stories about how and why they hate them. This will shift their thoughts, emotions and physiology to make it harder for others to connect with them. And it becomes a self-fulfilling prophecy. But the person feels vindicated, because the results of some survey they did said they were an introvert and therefore would hate networking events and they have been proved right, because they just put up with two hours of chit-chat hell.

Looking back at what we covered in Step Two, all three Inner Critic triggers are there in that statement.

It's a generalisation – there's no hint that hating networking events is something that only happens sometimes or is an experience over which they have any choice.

It's a distortion because it is conflating a behaviour preference – running an introvert pattern – with their sense of identity.

It's a deletion because they are filtering out all previous experiences of networking that didn't fall into the 'hate' category and might even have been fun.

Yet this badge of honour that came from the label will limit how they behave, whether they enjoy themselves, how they filter the sensory perception of networking events, and how people experience meeting them. That label becomes a subconscious excuse to play it safe and to avoid connecting with others.

Great leadership doesn't need models and archetypes and strategies and labels. It needs people with the vision and the passion to inspire others towards achieving results that could never be achieved by a single person – people who have got out of their own way.

It's time to let go of our labels and to frisbee those masks into the recycling bin. And the very first step for that is understanding what – specifically – those masks were doing for us.

---

gets their energy from, based on the work of Carl Jung. Those with an introvert preference top up their batteries through quiet time. Those with an extrovert preference do so by being around other people. There's more on this and how it affects us at work in the Readers' Resources Vault.

Exercise: Which Labels Have You Been Relying On?

We're going to have another chat with Glurg. This time you're going to teach him how your 'labels' might have been getting in the way of you ditching Imposter Syndrome.

Start by telling Glurg about a specific example of when Imposter Syndrome has got in your way – just a couple of sentences.

Now complete the statement:

I can't ditch Imposter Syndrome in situations like that, because I am...

Which labels have you been giving yourself over this? How might they have been holding you back?

And what action could you take to let go of some of them today?

Secondary Gain: The Secret **** That Keeps You Stuck

Remember back in Step One we talked about why I don't care *how* you got Imposter Syndrome? How looking for causal events can actually keep us stuck? Well, the same goes for those masks and suits of armour.

Sometimes we will have a clear memory of the exact moment when we chose to put that mask on. And it can be important to do some inner work to clear the pain or fear that went with that experience. But if you don't have a clear, single memory, there's no need to go looking for one.

The hunt for 'why' can keep us stuck for years, subconsciously looking for an external event or person to blame for our current experiences. Even if you find that trigger event, unless you clear out the emotions that went with it, it can leave you stuck with Imposter Syndrome as a 'badge of honour' for having gone through the experience. It can cause us to give our power over today's life choices to some situation in our past that we can't change and to some person, who never asked for the responsibility of controlling what we achieve in life or who we allow ourselves to become.

I find that my clients get much better results if we let go of that search for an external trigger to justify Imposter Syndrome and instead look at clearing away the masks that have created the current problem. And the way we do that is to understand what those masks are *doing* for us.

Psychologists have a fancy term for this: secondary gain.

I like to think of it more along the lines of 'what is my crazy behaviour doing for me?'

And in fifteen years of working with leaders on the inside work that creates the outside world success, I have seen – countless times – that when mindset and attitude aren't enough, it is always because there is a secondary gain running under the surface. Clear that out and there's no need for the self-sabotage behaviours anymore and the masks become redundant.

Secondary gain crops up when you had a need that wasn't being met and your unconscious mind found an emergency solution. Its intention was to keep you safe from a perceived danger. That might be a physical danger, as for a colleague of mine who won't learn to drive because their Aunt was killed in a car accident, or a psychological or emotional one, such as not letting a potential life partner get close enough to commit.

Secondary gain sits at the 'what's important to us' level of the Imposter Syndrome Iceberg. It's in the foundation 'safety and security' level of Maslow's hierarchy of needs and the base chakra in yoga. Its job is to keep us safe, no matter what the cost.

Maslow's Hierarchy Of Needs

The secondary gain works hard to filter the options we perceive as being available for our behavioural choices. It rules out those that would not meet its need for safety in that specific context. And this is why it becomes the biggest barrier to change.

If you are running an unmet need to keep yourself safe from, say, public criticism, it doesn't matter what you do at the mindset and attitude level to persuade yourself to go on stage, it's all 'fluff' compared to the existential threat the bit of you running the secondary gain will see. It will do its best to keep you safe by sabotaging your actions on public speaking and, if you have the gritted teeth determination to push on through *despite* your subconscious fears, it will do its damnedest to make sure you hate every moment of the experience and play it safe with your message.

Your unconscious mind is trying to keep you safe and its emergency stop button is secondary gain.

We are rarely aware of the unmet needs that drive secondary gain, at a conscious level. And they get in the way of more than just our personal performance – those unmet needs form the basis of everything from family rows to international conflicts, as the work of Marshall Rosenberg shows us. He was an American psychologist who, back in the 1960s, gained a reputation as a mediator (even working with governments), using his method for Non-Violent Communication. In it he teaches people how to express what their *needs* are, rather than the effect-level *wants*, and to find common ground in those. Once that is established, everyone feels their *needs* are going to be met by the negotiation process and breakthroughs can happen. He got people 'talking to the unmet need' instead of 'talking to the drama' – which is what we've been working towards with the self-talk work you have done in Step Two and now here with secondary gain.

It's the same idea when that discussion is happening inside your head: if you try to push through what you *want* – e.g. speaking up with your great idea in a meeting – but that is at odds with what you *need* – e.g. staying safe from public criticism by not sharing your ideas, there's going to be a massive inner conflict.

But if you can spot that, *before* you self-sabotage, and find a way to meet that unmet need in a healthier way, the inner resistance disappears. That sets you free to take off that mask and enjoy whatever challenge it is you have set yourself.

How Can You Meet Those Needs In A Healthier Way?

As we've discussed, secondary gain comes up when you have a need to stay safe from a perceived threat, so it's not going to go without a fight, if you try to pretend it's not there. It's much better to find out what that hidden need is and to satisfy it in a way that empowers you, instead of keeping you stuck.

There's a simple (yet mind-warping) set of questions you can ask yourself to find out what secondary gain has triggered a particular mask.

The process is called 'Cartesian Co-Ordinates' because you ask yourself questions that form four directions in a grid. These questions are based on work by the French philosopher and mathematician René Descartes, back in the seventeenth century, as a way to bypass conscious thinking and open your mind to new possibilities and solutions. I have adapted Descartes' original questions to help you to use them to spot the secondary gain that is driving the show with your blocks – to help you get yourself unstuck.

The key to this method is letting answers bubble up, rather than trying to force them or edit them. And if one of the questions sends your brain into a spin, press 'pause' on that inner dialogue (ABC from page 127) and ask your body what the answer is.

Exercise: How To Spot Secondary Gain

Start by thinking about a project you have been resisting or an Imposter Syndrome based behaviour that has been hard to clear.

Start with the question from Step Three: I can't do that, because…

Write down at least five answers.

1.

2.

3.

4.

5.

As before, go through them and cross out any that your body tells you are genuinely nonsense.

Now, go through the list of those 'becauses' you are left with and pick one for this exercise.

Write it down.

For the purposes of illustration, I'm going to take the example of "I can't go on stage at the conference, because I hate public speaking."

… continues

Complete the grid in your workbook[18], answering each of these questions in turn:

What happens by having your [because goes here]?

What would happen if you didn't have your [because]?

What won't happen if you keep your [because]?

What won't happen if you don't keep your [because]?

In the context of "I hate public speaking", typical answers might be:

I get to avoid going on stage.

I'd have to go on stage and the audience might boo me.

I don't have to risk rejection and ridicule.

I won't be safe from public criticism.

Now, to wrap up the exercise, looking at your answers to all four questions, which elements produce the strongest physical response – you're looking for signs of tension or contraction in your body. Then use this information to answer the question:

What is [because] doing for me?

....

In our 'hating public speaking' example:

It keeps me safe from rejection, ridicule and criticism.

That's your secondary gain.

---

[18] Download it here: www.DitchingImposterSyndrome.com/vault/

Can you see how pushing on through and denying this unmet need might trigger the creative part of your unconscious brain to find ways to thwart your best efforts?

These secondary gain blocks were often created before we developed our adult cognitive functions – sometimes even at a pre-verbal age. So the best way to clear them is not, in fact, by reasoned thinking; there may not be 'reasoned thinking' cognitive processes in your brain to deal with. You'll get better results by getting back into your body, here and now, and clearing those blocks out at a physical level, which is what you have been doing with the belief-shifting exercises.

Now it's time to explore the *real* reason so many of us struggle with Imposter Syndrome – and it's the one habit you can kick that could set you free from it, forever.

It's Time To Stop Beating Yourself Up

When you strip away all of the stories, drama and fluff from Imposter Syndrome, it boils down to one thing:

Imposter Syndrome is triggered by our fear of being judged by others the way we judge ourselves.

Let's take our earlier discussions one level deeper and decode some of the language in the phrases we use to describe how we feel when Imposter Syndrome hits, in the context of self-judgement:

- **What if they find out I'm not good enough?** *I have already decided I'm not, and now I have to hide that truth from them.*
- **Who am I, to do that?** *If I do it, they'll find out I'm not qualified enough / too young / too old / getting ideas above my station.*
- **What if they realise they made a mistake in hiring me?** *I know they did, so I have to make extra sure they don't find out.*
- **I feel like a fraud.** *I'm not just not good enough, I'm faking it, too. I can't risk them finding out.*
- **I don't know as much as I should / as others in my field.** *I've already compared myself to them and I came up lacking.*

All of these examples start with us judging
ourselves and then feeling scared that
others may also discover what we have
decided must be a blindingly obvious truth.

So our self-talk around Imposter Syndrome isn't just about identity-level wording; it's about us judging ourselves at that deep identity level, finding ourselves lacking, and living in fear of the outside world finding out. In fact, this was one of the key differences thrown up by the 2019 Imposter Syndrome research study, when I compared people who struggled with it to people who didn't.

The Difference Between People With Imposter Syndrome And Those Without It

When I interviewed people who had less of an issue with Imposter Syndrome, they had three common traits:

1. They didn't let other people's opinions of them affect their choices.
2. They knew how to press 'pause' on their mind-story dramas, so they didn't get stuck in the mind-body-emotions cycle.
3. They had a strong ability to evaluate their performance and make changes, as necessary, without judging themselves over their past performance.

They didn't beat themselves up when things went wrong – they learned from such experiences. They didn't make their sense of success or failure contingent on second-guessing someone else's subjective opinion, they used data. They didn't let 'early warning system' fears drag them into the soap opera of emotions that can leave us in a crumpled heap on the floor. It's tough love time:

Others don't obsess about you anywhere
near as much as you worry they do.
And beating yourself up hasn't exactly
worked as a performance-improver, has it?

So how can you make that shift to stop beating yourself up so much? By letting go of judging yourself. I know it's easy to say. I'm going to share some how-to with you in the rest of this book, plus the work you have already done in Step Two and Step Three will really help.

*The single biggest key to setting yourself free from Imposter Syndrome is to shift from **judging** to **evaluating**, when you're looking at your performance.*

What's The Difference Between Judging And Evaluating?

Evaluating choices – showing discernment – is part of being an adult. We may still *want* that double chocolate ice cream sundae with extra whipped cream and marshmallows, but unlike the five-year-old version of us, we'll at least stop to consider whether it's a good idea, before we pick up the spoon.

Judging takes that same choice, but chooses to label it as right or wrong, good or bad, and ties that in with who or what is being judged, at an identity level, rather than simply seeing it as the behavioural choice. The ice cream sundae becomes a *bad* thing, rather than just a collection of ingredients. And we make it personal:

"Oh, I *am* awful for wanting that dessert!" This statement takes the behavioural choice and turns it into a judgement about who we are, and it will usually kick off a procession of beating-yourself-up thoughts.

*Judging happens when we mix up evaluating our **behaviour** with our sense of **identity**.*

It doesn't matter whether we are doing this in relation to ourselves or someone else, the problem is the same: we take an external behaviour – something someone has said or done – and tie it in to our assessment of who they *are*.

When we give feedback at this level, it sticks. It becomes hard to shift. It feels like part of *who we are*. Unchangeable. You now know, from the work you have already done in this book, that this isn't the case. But this is why self-judgement can be such a trigger for Imposter Syndrome.

If we can learn to accept ourselves, our strengths, not-so-strong bits, and all of the rest of the glorious chaos that makes us who we really are, and can feel comfortable in our own skin, then there's nothing to feed that Inner Critic of self-judgement. And we become naturally resilient when it comes to the moods and agendas of those around us (more on this in Step Five).

Judging is a dangerous habit, whether the conclusion is positive or negative, because it is hard-wiring our sense of identity with that feedback. It's one of the reasons why in schools and at home it is so vital to make sure we separate the child from his or her behaviour.

Judging = identity - about **who** *someone* **is**

*Evaluation = behaviour -***what** *someone* **does**

So I don't want anyone telling my kids they are 'good boys' any more than I want to hear them calling them 'bad boys'. Their behaviour doesn't make them good or bad as people. It is behaviour. It can be changed. And I don't want them building their sense of self on external behavioural feedback.

But I know how easy it can be to fall into this trap! The alternative is to give specific feedback on behaviour. For example, "You did really well with the spelling test to get them all right this week. I can see the effort you put in to learning those 'tion' endings." Or, if you need something as short as 'good boy / girl', you could try 'great work' or 'good effort'. The key is to keep the response about the behaviour, not the person.

How Can You Set Yourself Free From Judging?

It doesn't matter whether you're judging yourself or others. Your brain doesn't care who you're talking about with that identity-level feedback, it obeys and creates the neural pathways you'll need to run the 'oh, you're judging' script on autopilot, whenever needed. It will be running a pattern that fears if you're judging someone else, then they're likely to be judging you in return, even if there's clear evidence (such as great appraisals) that they're not.

The easiest way to stop judging yourself is also to stop judging others. That includes sharing gossip, which adds in the emotion of excitement to the neural pathways, making those 'judging' autopilots run even faster.

Exercise: How To Stop Judging

A simple way to do this in under sixty seconds is to adapt the ABC and the 1-to-3 processes we covered on page 127. There's a really simple change you can make to your language that can help to set you free from judging yourself and others:

Accept, Breathe, Choose...

then say:

Ok, and...

You can use it whenever you catch yourself thinking a judgemental thought.

The 'ok' is important not because you are agreeing with your previous thought, but because you don't want to beat yourself up over it (creating a negativity spiral and triggering your Sympathetic Nervous System's fight-flight-freeze response) or push it away (resisting it and thereby giving it all of your power).

The 'and' is important because a 'but' (our usual response) negates what came before it, potentially triggering an inner conflict and encouraging your Inner Critic to defend its previous statement.

Then you apply the 1-to-3 process: consciously choosing to think of three really positive things about yourself or the person you were judging – or three things you are grateful for about them or yourself.

So a rant about how unreasonably a co-worker might have been behaving could become:

"That was a judgemental thought. I accept that. I breathe in and out and let it go. And three things I appreciate about Fred are…"

The more you practise this, the more you will create new neural pathways that make it easier not to judge – or to compare yourself with – others. Remember: those autopilots use the same motorway.

This process means a self-judging thought will no longer have to lead you into a spiral of self-doubt and Imposter Syndrome. You're consciously choosing to turn that negativity into a cheerleader moment, whether it's for yourself or for whichever 'Fred' you were thinking about, at the same time as learning to recalibrate your internal evaluation system by retraining your Reticular Activating System to filter *in* sensory evidence of the things you are doing well.

And if you're resisting letting go of that judgement? If there's a part of you that really wants to *prove* and justify what a plonker 'Fred' is? Run it through the secondary gain process from page 198. Which secret unmet need is it meeting? What is holding on to that judgemental position *doing* for you? What do you need to release in yourself to let go of that attachment?

It's not about condoning awful behaviour. It's about no longer taking it personally and not judging others by tying that behaviour into their identity… and letting go of doing that to yourself, too.

And if judging others is something that comes up for you, it's worth bearing in mind that we tend to judge most in others what we are rejecting (or have already cleared) in ourselves. If we judge someone as, say, nit-picky, it might be because we know we also have that tendency, but have been working to clear it. Or – like the reformed smoker – we might have moved beyond it and feel the other person should, too.

Those we judge most are mirrors to our inner shadows. It takes guts to clear our shadows, rather than flinging that criticism outwards.

How Can You Shift From Judging To Evaluating, In The Longer-Term?

Remember: training yourself to *evaluate*, rather than *judge*, others teaches you to do the same for yourself. If you catch yourself judging – giving yourself or others feedback at the identity-level – shift back to talking about behaviours, instead.

Use the ABC process to give yourself a gap in your thoughts to be able to choose a more empowering self-talk dialogue.

Objectively check whether the feedback you are giving yourself is true – or just the projection of a hidden fear, distorting the facts.

And finally, treat the cycle as an exercise in self-compassion by asking yourself, "If I wanted to show support and compassion to the version of me I have just been judging, what could I say to myself to help them feel more positive again?"

This isn't white-washing or pretending; it's separating out evaluation of our performance from our sense of who we are, as a person, and checking we're telling ourselves the truth.

The Curse Of Comparisonitis

Another form of self-judgement is comparisonitis – comparing ourselves with others and deciding that they are better than we are. Did you spot the identity-level statement in there? The 2019 Imposter Syndrome Research Study showed that 77% of women and 60% of men who struggle with Imposter Syndrome regularly compare themselves to others and judge themselves to be lacking, even if the external feedback shows the opposite. These figures were even higher when I looked at just entrepreneurs, who tend to spend more time online and on social media, so have more opportunity to compare themselves with others.

Social media is full of glossy images of people looking their best, doing amazing things and wanting the world to validate and accept them, even if that's not our conscious intention when we share such posts. And the social media sites' algorithms mean that the images that show up in our feed are the most popular – so we're not just comparing our 6am-start bags-under-the-eyes grogginess with someone else's 'highlight reel'.

We compare our lives with the algorithm's
curated *list of the best bits of someone*
else's. It's easy to find ourselves lacking.

Despite what we might think about the world of internet trolls, our harshest critic is still the one inside us. That's why ditching Imposter Syndrome needs us to tame that Inner Critic, to know how to press 'pause' on its background ramblings, and to learn how to choose which thoughts to feed – hence Step Two of the process in this book!

Comparisonitis triggers the generalisations, distortions and deletions in our self-talk. We don't see the struggle and stress others went through, so we make assumptions about how easy it was for them. Imposter Syndrome gets us writing our own success off as luck, whilst we conclude that *they* must have *talent* to be achieving so much.

When we compare ourselves to others and judge ourselves to be lacking, it can cause us to give up on our dreams. Our confidence nose dives, we pour a swimming pool full of ice-cold water onto the fire of our ambitions and we grind to a halt on taking inspired action. We are subconsciously giving our power over what we will achieve and create to the person we compared ourselves to, despite the fact that they never asked for it.

You'll never achieve your dreams while
you're obsessing about what others are
doing.
The more you deal with your hidden inner
blocks and secret confidence-trashers, the
less you'll feel the need to compare
yourself with others;
and the less it will bother you, even if you
do.

Comparisonitis causes us to forget what we *can* do, dismissing our achievements with a single 'but'.

Each of us is on a unique journey, but it takes courage and perspective to see that. Comparing ourselves to others drains our energy and confidence. It can even cause us to secretly resent their success, feeling that life is somehow not 'fair', triggering the biochemical reactions of the emotion better known as 'jealousy' in the body, the self-talk thoughts, and the emotions that go with that mind-story.

It also makes us more likely to self-sabotage, because those judgemental mind-stories programme us to believe that success is 'bad' and will cause resentment and jealousy from others; that they'll no longer like us if we succeed. The stories we tell ourselves about others make us worry that others may say the same about us, if we allow ourselves to be successful. This can be a key factor for someone not applying for a promotion or opportunity they know they deserve, or from not 'owning' their achievements after a successful project and attributing them to the wider team.

When you are truly comfortable in your own skin, the need to compare yourself to others disappears.

The ability for others to unwittingly press the buttons you have cleared out disappears. And you reach a stage where secret jealousy and resentment no longer play a part in your 3 a.m. dialogue.

On those few occasions when it does, it's always possible to turn it into an opportunity to listen to your inner wisdom and make changes. Here's how:

Exercise: Turning Jealousy Around

Think back to a recent time when someone else's success has triggered you to feel jealousy. Ask yourself the following questions:

What is *real* in this? And what is my projection / mind-story drama?

What might I need to be doing, thinking or believing differently, so that this comparison won't bother me anymore?

What am I 'gaining' from these emotions? What do I get to avoid doing? Which aspect of myself to I get to avoid being?

... continues

What could I learn from the fact that jealous emotions are cropping up for me about this?

Reclaiming your confidence:

What am I doing well?

What do I feel grateful for in my life, at the moment?

What do I appreciate about myself?

The icing on the cake:

Go and do something that makes your heart sing – ideally involving movement – for ten minutes. Dance to your favourite music. Go for a walk. Do whatever you love doing, to fill your body with its happy-hormones and to let go of those icky emotions.

These ten minutes are a worthwhile investment, when you consider the risks of letting the feelings of jealousy or inadequacy get in your way for the rest of the day.

And a wonderful way to top this exercise up is with positive affirmations that actually work. In my research, I asked everyone how they had tried to ditch Imposter Syndrome and what had or hadn't worked. Not many people had tried much, but of those who had, the majority had tried working with positive affirmations and positive mental attitude, but found they made things even worse when they didn't work. We talked about why this is in page 84, where we discussed the Imposter Syndrome pantomime.

But there are ways to create positive affirmations that are uniquely tailored to your specific needs, so that they release you from judging yourself, connect you with your true, inner confidence, and help you to become more of who you really are. And that's the next step in our Ditching Imposter Syndrome journey.

How To Get Positive Affirmations To Work

We talked on page 84 about one key reason why positive affirmations may not produce the results we were hoping for – because they force you to 'flip flop' on a long-held belief, trying to turn a 'can't' into a 'can', so your unconscious mind's backfire effect kicks in to defend the status quo. But there's a second reason why positive affirmations can produce poor results. And that's the one we're going to deal with in this section, as you learn to create affirmations that work for you, to help you set yourself free from self-judgement.

Here's a little-known reason why generic positive affirmations so often don't work, no matter how many places you plaster them around your home and how many times a day you say them:

They are not tailored to you.

If your brain doesn't see them as relevant or believable and has no emotional connection with them, at a physiological level, they won't get you anything more the *'meh'* results.

And my research study showed that trying positive affirmations and experiencing no improvement made Imposter Syndrome worse, because they felt like a failure for trying to stop feeling like a fraud, but making no progress.

The other issue with most affirmations is that they can be so 'high level' and 'nebulous' that it is hard to connect with them on a physical, practical basis.

The idea behind positive affirmations (and why they *can* work wonderfully), is that they bypass your rational brain and go straight to your unconscious mind, where they are received as an instruction. They can create new neural pathways and edit the filters in your Reticular Activating System. But when they are too general or not relevant to your individual blocks, the process doesn't work – at least not as well.

If you're reciting "I am a creative being!" your unconscious mind has no idea what that means or how to create it for you. So it risks creating confusion, not change.

How To Create Mind-Blowingly Effective Positive Affirmations:

Go back to your 'because' exercise on page 169. This will have produced a list of 'what do I want instead?' statements for you. You're going to turn *these* into your positive affirmations, ideally starting with the words 'I am'. Start with the statements that you can see will produce the biggest breakthroughs for you – the ones you resonate with most strongly. There are five simple keys to creating powerful, positive affirmations from your 'what do I want instead' statements:

Remember: as with all of the exercises in this book, the next one has a sheet in the downloadable workbook with space for you to write down your answers. It can make a huge difference to the effectiveness of this process. You can get the workbook here, with some extra examples for this:

www.DitchingImposterSyndrome.com/vault/

Exercise: How To Create Positive Affirmations That Work

1. Turn your 'what do I want instead' into an 'I am' sentence.

Follow the usual rules for the statement about phrasing it positively and making it something that is within your control. You are giving yourself permission to *become* the person who *is* that statement.

2. Make it relevant.

By tying your positive affirmation in closely with your 'what do I want instead' statement, it is tuned to perfectly fit with what you need. Your brain will see it as relevant and will pay close attention.

3. Make it specific.

Your brain and body are more likely to connect with something specific than a fluffy high-level affirmation like 'I am filled with gratitude'. The more specific you can be, the more easily your unconscious mind will understand how to process and deliver this instruction.

4. Make it believable.

It needs to be something your mind can imagine is possible– *really* imagine, not just daydream. Otherwise the backfire effect will kick in and it will fight you, every step of the way. So don't pick "I'm the best xyz in the world" unless you genuinely believe it is possible. Ask your body, not your mind!

... continues

5. Emotional connection.

Pick an 'I am' statement that triggers anticipation or excitement or even slight nervousness (in a good way – remember 'eustress' from page138?) in your body. Having an emotional connection with your affirmation cranks up its power by a factor of thousands.

So, if one of your 'because' statements was about not being able to speak on stage because people might criticise you, you might have a 'what do I want instead' statement along the lines of:

"I am so confident in my message that I speak it with ease."

That becomes your affirmation – uniquely tailored to clear your blocks, aligned to your core values, and tuned to exactly what your unconscious mind and Inner Critic need you to be saying. If you put these specific affirmations on the mirror where you brush your teeth, on your phone's screensaver, and on the inside of the cupboard door where you hide the coffee pot, you'll have potent tools to set yourself free from out-of-date baggage like Imposter Syndrome, moving you towards becoming more of who you really are.

And a final ninja tip to get the most from your affirmations:

Don't **think** them. **Feel** them.

As you say them out loud – *meaning* them – allow the physical and emotional sensations of *becoming* that version of you to flood through your body and your mind. Imagine you are amplifying those physical and emotional feelings until you sense them washing through every cell of your body – and even expanding slightly beyond your physical skin, surrounding you with their glow. It might sound strange, but it feels amazing to walk through your day with your affirmations there as your cheerleaders.

You can create breakthroughs in as little as a week by doing this several times a day.

When you create your positive affirmations in this way, you'll feel the effect in your body, every time you say them. You'll sense the shift in your thoughts, as the affirmation rebalances your nervous system. You'll notice the changes in your actions. You will feel yourself shifting to become the person who believes the affirmation and who lives from that confident, empowered state of being.

And just imagine the impact these affirmations could have if you were to use a relevant one after you spot yourself running a self-judgement thought?

When you have got your affirmations and you can feel the difference they are making for you, there's a secret sauce that turns the work we have done together so far into what can feel like a magic wand. It can shift your inner state from chaos to calm, creative confidence in just a couple of minutes. And that's what we're going to play with next.

The Secret Sauce For Positive Affirmations

This process works really well for those times when Imposter Syndrome kicks in because you're about to stretch a comfort zone and grow. All this means is that your dreams have grown bigger than you believe you are – the gap between how you see yourself and who you think you need to be has opened up and Imposter Syndrome has popped up to fill that space.

You can use this two-minute strategy whenever those self-doubting dialogues kick off and it also makes an incredible way to start your day.

It works most effectively once you are comfortable with your affirmations and are anchored in to their effect on your body, your emotions and your mind. You don't have to be 'perfect' with them, but it really helps to be able to *feel* the shift they create for you.

Exercise: The Secret Sauce For Positive Affirmations

Start by choosing three of your positive affirmations to work with. Then run through this process, which takes under two minutes:

1. Start by standing up, to get the full effect of this process, though it will also work sitting down, if standing up isn't currently an option for you.

2. Take three deep, sighing breaths, to come back to the 'here and now', breathing in through your nose and out through your mouth with an 'ahhh'.

3. Softly close your eyes, if that's comfortable for you, making sure you can balance. Allow yourself to become aware of the physical sensations in your body, giving yourself permission to soften and let go of any areas of tension.

4. Choose one of your affirmations and say it out loud. Mean it. Say it with energy and intention. As you say it, experience it as a soft, warm, golden light at the centre of your chest, gently glowing and growing with each in-breath, spreading throughout your body.

With each out-breath allow yourself to let go of anything that needs to go to allow the affirmation to be your new truth – to create the new you. You don't need to consciously know what needs to be released with each out-breath; just have the intention of letting go each time you breathe out, creating the space for the affirmation to gently grow and wash through your body, aligning every cell with its message.

5. Do this for about ten breaths, until the physical sensations for that affirmation have reached what feels like a peak.

... continues

6. Move to your next affirmation and repeat the process.

7. Continue until you have done three affirmations in a row, feeling yourself becoming the person you need to *be* for those affirmations to really be true.

8. Now imagine there is a path in front of you, symbolising your day. See and sense that path being filled with the energy, the colours, the thoughts and the actions that are supported by your affirmations. Spend a few moments imagining yourself moving through the rest of your day from that place of grounded confidence, visualising the key events and tasks of your day.

9. Gently open your eyes and notice how you feel now. Notice how the way you are holding your body has changed. Notice the shifts in the physical sensations in your body. Notice how your thoughts have shifted.

How different might your day be if you allowed yourself to stay in this state for the rest of your day? What kinds of inspired actions might you take if you allowed yourself to feel this way, before you started?

What might change for you if you allowed yourself to do this for sixty seconds, three times a day?

Take some time now to make some notes about those shifts and to come up with some ideas for how you might remind yourself to play with this technique.

And next we're going to look at how to set yourself free from your past so you no longer need to drag it around behind you, like a heavy suitcase that steals the energy and joy from life as you lug it around, without even noticing.

Forgiveness Is The Key To Freedom

There's something about the look of immense relief on a client's or student's face when they finally let go of their past that moves me to tears.

Suddenly they start to glow, with a smile advertising agencies would scramble over each other to use on a billboard. It's clear that they have set themselves free from old baggage, which would have kept them trapped on the gerbil wheel of same-problem-different-actors, and that their experience of life has shifted forever.

If you make changes in your life but haven't released the old stories and habits that supported the no-longer-wanted behaviours, then you risk finding a new outlet for the needs those stories and habits were meeting. This is why we talked about secondary gain, earlier in this section, so you don't have to keep repeating history.

But sometimes there's a deeper block we need to let go of, which burns like acid in our hearts, causes us to grit our teeth, and can keep us stuck in patterns like Imposter Syndrome, no matter what we do to shift it.

And that block is lack of forgiveness and the resentment that creates.

You can't create a new future while you're still telling yesterday's stories. And that's where forgiveness comes in.

If we're secretly blaming someone or something for the pain we are experiencing and the masks we subconsciously chose to wear, we end up stuck with them.

We play the role of victim, often without realising it, needing someone to blame and resent for the life choices we didn't even notice we were making; someone to hold responsible for the regret we might feel. But it will never hurt them; it will only ever cause us pain.

"Resentment is like drinking poison and expecting your enemy to die."

This quote is sometimes attributed to Nelson Mandela and sometimes to Buddha. It's certainly a philosophy that Mandela lived and breathed after his release from Robben Island. He understood that holding grudges against those who had imprisoned him would taint the rest of his life. He chose to forgive.

Sometimes we're aware that we're holding a grudge (as is everyone who meets us), but often it's not conscious. And that grudge gives outside people or circumstances power over our present and future choices.

To release the grudge (or whatever we want to call that sense of blame and unfairness), we need to forgive. That might be someone, something or an event – which I call 'external forgiveness' – or ourselves – which is 'internal forgiveness'.

Forgiving Others

We all screw up sometimes. None of us is perfect. But when someone does something that causes us pain or triggers us shutting down, our natural instinct is to blame them.

When we blame someone else, we are effectively giving them power over how we respond to a situation and how it affects us, potentially for the rest of our lives. That's a Big Give. And chances are, they never asked for that responsibility.

To reclaim our power, we need to set that person free from our subconscious need to somehow change the past, or to have them admit they were wrong and apologise, or for them to change their behaviour. As Eleanor Roosevelt said:

"No one can make you feel inferior, without your consent."

You can replace the word 'inferior' with any adjective of your choosing. No one can *make* you happy or sad or confident or angry or excited. Those biochemical changes happen within you, triggered by your brain and delivered by your Autonomic Nervous System. So if someone 'makes' us feel, say, not good enough, they didn't. We did. They might have used extreme provocation, but at some level we consciously or unconsciously chose how to respond to their behaviour.

I'm not belittling how the behaviour of others can affect us. I have been on the receiving end of abuse that took me to the edge of a nervous breakdown. I know how powerful our subconscious reactions to others' behaviour can be. What that (eventually) taught me was that I played a role in the dance that we danced. The pain was caused by the self-talk stories I chose to feed and the fear-based-buttons I had, ready for the other person to press.

The first step towards forgiveness is compassion – for others and for yourself.

As we have discussed, happy people don't intentionally hurt others. People who are feeling good about themselves don't criticise and attack. When someone does something unkind, it's often because they are feeling bad about themselves and their life and they project that pain outwards, to get a release, to avoid dealing with the pain inside. Being able to feel compassion for them can help you to see that their behaviour wasn't about you – it was about *their* pain.

That's not in any way condoning behaviour that is completely unacceptable. It's about coming to a place of acceptance that it happened and giving yourself permission to let go of the pain, to move on. For traumatic events, you will most likely need professional support with this. But for the micro-grudges we carry with us each day about minor slights and people not behaving the way we wanted them to, forgiveness work can become as routine as brushing your teeth – and the effects are powerful.

> *Forgiveness is about setting yourself free from the pain of the past, not pretending that the behaviour was somehow ok. You are moving to a place of acceptance, rather than saying it was 'acceptable'.*

Often, the grudges we collect come from judging others, based on our standards and expectations about how they *should* behave. These expectations become filters through which we perceive the actions of others. They are based on our values – what's important to us – and our beliefs. These filters influence how we interpret people's actions. It's like putting a filter over a camera lens – it changes the image we capture. In the meditation world this is called 'projection' versus 'perception'.

Our perception is the unedited sensory data about what someone says or does. Our projection is our interpretation of it, based on our assumptions, our values and our beliefs. This is why it's so common for communication to be misunderstood – why two people can have the same discussion and take from it completely different meanings. And it's the source of the myriad of micro-grudges we carry around inside our heads and hearts. And those projections don't just stick with the person who triggered the initial issue. They get painted over any interaction that carries similar triggers.

When we expect people to behave in a certain way and they don't, it is often because they either didn't know about our expectations (we expect people to be mind-readers) or because they were in some way in pain. *Evaluating* in your head about whether or not someone's behaviour is acceptable is not a problem. It's when you make that evaluation *personal* on both sides that you end up in judgement-and-grudge-holding territory.

A person is not their behaviour.

When we stop projecting our assumptions about how people should behave onto others, it helps us to see their behaviour more objectively. We can start to come to a place of compassion for them – as a person, not necessarily justifying their behaviour.

It's important to forgive and let go, rather than keep pretending we're ok with something – often called a spiritual bypass, where we subconsciously use fake-compassion to move on, not having truly released the blocks or pain or resentment caused by a situation.

Exercise: Letting Go Of Past Grudges

Looking back over what you have learned about yourself and how you *do* Imposter Syndrome so far, there are likely to be out-of-date grudges keeping you stuck.

Choose one of these to work with for this exercise. If you sense there might be some of this holding you back from fully moving on from Imposter Syndrome, you can ask yourself the question:

"Who or what might I need to forgive, to feel fully free to create my own future?"

Let the answers bubble up, without judgement. They might surprise you.

And if there's a grudge you're secretly holding on to, you can do the secondary gain work on it to find out, "What is holding on to this grudge *doing* for me?"

And then make sure you get the support you need for that process.

Sometimes simply being aware that we need to forgive – externally or internally – can be enough to create that release. But sometimes, especially if there was trauma, we need support to move through to the other side. This is work I regularly do with clients, but it's beyond the scope of this book because the process is unique to each of them.

However, as a minimum recommendation, I would advise you to work through the secondary gain exercise from page 198, so you can identify what hanging on to the grudge is doing for you. Then I would combine this with the belief clearing exercises we covered in Step Three. But if what you need to clear is more than, say, a four out of ten, make sure you seek out a professional of your choice to support you on that journey.

Forgiving Yourself

Often, in my workshops and one-to-one work, people find it easier to forgive others than to forgive themselves. And when you've been clearing out the hidden blocks that have kept you stuck, dreaming big but playing small, for years, it's easy to beat yourself up, resenting the missed opportunities and regretting the choices you made. As you might have guessed by now, though, that's a great way to keep yourself trapped in that headspace.

Acknowledging the regrets and choosing to let them go is normally enough to clear this. Remember that your younger self made the best choices they could, based on what they believed about their options and the world. At some level, they made those choices to protect you. The fact that you might make different choices today is something to celebrate – you have grown and moved on.

You might want to imagine giving the younger you a hug, to let them know it's ok, that you don't hold anything against them, and to allow them to let go of the stress, worry and fear that caused them to shut down in whatever way they did.

In my client work, there are techniques I use that can help with this, if the issue is a biggie, but they are outside of the scope of this book, because they need to be tailored to the individual. For self-help, you can adapt the two techniques from the clearing limiting beliefs work on page 174, as well as the 'imaginary scissors' exercise on page 178.

It's really important to remember that this is about letting go, not fighting or getting rid. Your aim is to feel a sense of positive relief that sets you free from that old baggage.

The following two affirmations can help with accepting your past choices and forgiving yourself. They are:

I forgive myself for any past choices I might make differently now.

And:

I give myself permission to celebrate the person I have become.

Both of these hold the power to help you to let go, move towards a more positive future, and set yourself free from Imposter Syndrome.

Clearing out the grudges in your heart opens you up for the next stage of your Imposter Syndrome-ditching journey: retraining your Inner Critic to become your biggest cheerleader, with the power of gratitude.

The Power Of Gratitude

My research backed up what I have seen with my clients over the past fifteen years – that to clear Imposter Syndrome you need to make one vital shift that seems so insignificant that most people dismiss it. Yet it's the key to turning your Inner Critic into your biggest cheerleader.

In Step Two we talked about how our internal dialogue can affect our performance and you learned techniques to start to press 'pause' on negative self-talk and to choose which thoughts to feed. To clear Imposter Syndrome, you need to take this to the next level and the process to do that is deceptively simple: you're going to reprogramme your Reticular Activating System.

By now, you've learned the strategies for clearing out limiting beliefs, hidden blocks and secret fears. You've worked on letting go of judgement and taking off your accidental masks. So you're a different person to the one who started reading this book. And that means you've already started retraining your RAS to spot the external evidence that supports your new beliefs and values as the now-more-you version of you.

This will already be having a positive effect on your self-talk and the actions you're taking. The next step in this process is using the power of gratitude to turn your Inner Critic into your biggest cheerleader.

When asked what they had done to clear Imposter Syndrome, respondents in the research study found one of the most effective techniques was to consciously become aware of the things they *could* do and *had* achieved, rather than focusing on what had gone wrong. They said this was a turning point for them. They would keep lists of successes, a 'brag file' as one respondent termed it, of positive feedback and reviews, and a semi-secret folder in their email for storing messages that contained encouragement or praise. They would review these when they wanted to stretch a comfort zone, as a way of preventing Imposter Syndrome from arising.

But I don't want you to have to wait until you're feeling scared that 'feeling like a fraud' might come back for you. I'd rather you did one simple thing each day that can help you to build *true* confidence, to feel grounded, to retrain your RAS to become that virtual cheerleader, and to help you to inspire those around you to feel more positive, too. It's one simple thing:

Saying 'thank you' more often than you complain. And starting with the small stuff.

We all know how easy it is to fall into the 'complaining train' trap in our self-talk. Complaining about today doesn't make tomorrow any better. It reinforces the neural pathways and Reticular Activating System filters to focus on what is going wrong in life. That gets us on that slippery slope to stress, anxiety and depression.

I was discussing this with my Masterminders recently and one of my members objected to the idea, asking why on earth she should celebrate anything before she had completed the hugely complex project she was working on. My answer? That you're *much* more likely to actually complete that project and to enjoy the journey if you celebrate your wins at each and every step along the way.

We started this process when we talked about celebrating your micro-wins in Step Two. Now we're going to build on it to understand how powerful gratitude can be as a preventative for Imposter Syndrome. It's about choosing to focus your energy on what's going well, rather than what is dragging you down.

When we're stuck in the midst of stress, worry and feeling depressed, it's easy for our self-talk to feed the mind-stories about how awful everything is and how nothing will change.

Gratitude doesn't just reprogramme your brain, it retrains the cells in your body to want and accept more positive emotions, helping to reduce the addiction to the stress and fear-based chemical reactions they might be running. There's more on this in the Readers' Resource Vault.

And when you're ready to shift the way you experience life to retune that inner radio station to a more positive vibe, gratitude is one of the easiest ways to do it.

I write a lot about gratitude and there are practical resources for you in the Readers' Resources Vault. For now, here is how to get started:

The Four Keys To Gratitude Success

1. **Little and often**

   Stop to practise gratitude at several points during your day. It can be great to do it before you get out of bed in the morning, last thing at night, or when you notice your stress-gremlins coming out to play.

2. **Get specific**

   The more specific you can be on what you feel grateful for, the more potent it will feel. Feeling grateful for, say, 'life', doesn't trigger the same physiological and emotional response as feeling grateful for the beauty of a flower that you saw on your walk to the office.

3. **Don't think it, feel it**

   Gratitude isn't a cognitive activity. It's something you want to experience in your body, to fire off those biochemical reactions that cut your stress levels and trigger your happy-hormones. Allowing yourself to feel each thing you feel grateful for, and consciously giving that feeling permission to grow, cranking up the invisible dial, can shift you from grumpy to great in under sixty seconds.

4. **Write it down**

   Writing your gratitude down makes it feel more real. And it provides an incredible perspective-shifting resource for those days when grey clouds take over. Just as people who write down their goals are more likely to achieve them, so people who write down their gratitude make faster progress towards turning their Inner Critic into their virtual cheerleader.

How Does Gratitude Help With Imposter Syndrome?

- Daily gratitude helps to shift your brain's focus from what's going wrong to what's going well, changing your RAS filters.
- It can boost your confidence by reducing self-judgement.
- It can help you to recalibrate your internal referencing system, so you spot your strengths and feel more confident about sharing them.
- It gives you a healthy form of resilience, rather than the 'bounce-back' version most advocate (more in Step Five).
- And it can help you to feel safer in taking inspired action towards your big vision dreams.

Exercise: What Are You Feeling Grateful For, Right Now?

Write down three things you're feeling grateful for, right now. Make them specific. Then allow yourself to *feel* each one.

1.

2.

3.

What has shifted in your body? Your thoughts? Your emotions?

Revisiting The Old Imposter Syndrome Blocks

Now you know what you know and you've shifted what you have shifted, let's revisit the most classic blocks and behaviours that accompany Imposter Syndrome. In my research, respondents talked about their self-talk when Imposter Syndrome strikes and the kinds of actions that followed.

These fell into five main categories and we're going to cover each, in turn, to look at how the work you have done so far can make them irrelevant, no longer needing to be part of your future. The statements in each section are direct quotes from the research study.

1. I'm a fraud

- What if they find out I'm faking it?
- What if they find me out?
- What if they figure out I don't belong here?
- I feel like a fraud.
- I have to fake it to make it.

This is where the inner-critic-taming, limiting-belief-ditching and releasing self-judgement strategies in this book really come into play.

When you reprogramme your Reticular Activating System to filter *in* evidence of what you are doing well and you have cleared out the limiting beliefs that caused you to judge yourself, you'll begin to see that you aren't a fraud or a fake – that you *do* belong.

If you spot any of these thoughts trying to creep back in, remember that they're generalisations (see page 135). The way to strip generalisations of their power is to make the thoughts more specific. For example:

"How, specifically, do I feel like a fraud?"

"What is it, specifically, I'm scared of that means they might find me out?"

Then ask yourself: "Is it *really* true? What objective evidence do I have to support this mind-story?"

And you can wrap it up with the magic question: "What do I want, instead?" and start taking action towards that.

As your inner confidence grows, you'll no longer feel like you're faking it. As you retrain your brain to spot the things you excel at, you'll realise you're not a fraud and there's no one waiting to 'find you out'.

And as you start to set yourself free from harsh self-judgement and spend less time comparing yourself with others, you'll be accepting that you *do* belong.

So you'll no longer need to wear the masks that made you feel like a fraud.

2. I'm not good enough

- I don't know as much as I should.
- They must have made a mistake, choosing me.
- I'm not as good as others in my field.
- What if they find out I'm not good enough?
- I lack confidence and doubt myself.
- I compare myself to others.
- I get stuck in negative thinking / Inner Critic.
- I turn into a perfectionist.

This is a generalisation, where sometimes a single trigger can cause us to write ourselves off as a person. This pattern is the territory of Step Two and taming your Inner Critic. That's where you learned how to press 'pause' on your negative self-talk. And it's about clearing out your limiting beliefs, plus all of the strategies in Step Four. It's a daily process as you build strong foundations for your confidence and start to connect more deeply with your innate gifts - the inner genius that only you can bring to the table.

Forgiving yourself and having compassion for yourself are the keys to releasing this old pattern. Remember: you get to decide what 'good enough' means – you get to set the standards, and perfectionism doesn't help with this one. There is no such thing as positive perfectionism, as we discussed on page 36.

The absolute key to turning this around is removing the identity-level judgement that is actually about your behaviour. Even if there is some truth that – for certain things – there's room for improvement, that's about your skills and behaviours, not you as a person. "I *am* good enough, even if my behaviours or skills could improve."

3. It was luck / it won't last

- I only got here through hard work (not ability) or luck.
- I put my success down to luck.
- I'm on a winning streak, it's bound to end soon.
- I'm waiting for my 'Icarus moment' when it all falls apart.

These self-talk stories come up when we believe that we don't really deserve our success; that it is somehow dependent on the whim of others.

The more you can 'own' your genius and believe in yourself, the more you can let go of judging yourself, the less likely these stories are to come up.

And, actually, the fact that you 'got here' and you're 'winning' and have 'success' is brilliant. It means you *can* do it! There's no reason why your luck should end any time, ever. Because it wasn't down to luck. It was down to you.

As for your luck running out, unless you're psychic, why bother worrying about a future you don't even want? How about spending that energy on consciously creating the future you *do* want, instead?

So if this one is coming up for you, revisit the work on celebrating micro-wins from the last chapter, the self-judgement work from earlier in this section, and do the limiting beliefs exercises on the self-talk phrase, as we covered in Step Three.

4. Playing small & not 'owning' your inner genius

- I don't speak up with my ideas.
- I avoid opportunities I know I could handle.
- I don't put myself out there.
- I keep quiet when I know I have the answers / don't speak up with my ideas.
- I turn down opportunities I secretly want.
- I don't put myself forward for promotions or awards.
- I don't take credit for my success or say it was a team effort.
- I discount my rates without being asked or don't ask for a pay rise I know I have earned.

When you know what you want and are excited about that vision, it helps you to overcome any fears about speaking up. Your message becomes bigger than your fears. Playing small is always fear-based. And it's a linear scale – not an on-off switch. You can choose, each day, to speak up, say, one per cent more. Do that for three months and you're at double where you were yesterday.

Doing the grounding work and confidence-building work from Steps Two and Three will really help you with this. Then simply take a deep breath and do it! Speak your truth, with courage and compassion.

5. Not taking action on your dreams

- I self-sabotage.
- I procrastinate.
- I don't take action on my goals.
- I don't complete important projects.

Secondary gain. Every. Single. Time.

These behaviours are surface level symptoms with underlying causes. They come from the Four Ps of Imposter Syndrome. At some level, the behaviour is doing something for you – allowing you to avoid some perceived risk or threat of pain. You don't clear these by 'pushing on through', as we discussed earlier. It's about looking at the unmet need that these behaviours address and finding a healthier way to meet it.

The work on secondary gain in Step Four guides you through exactly how to do this.

Exercise: What Has Shifted So Far?

Thinking back to before you started reading this book, how did your self-talk, limiting beliefs and Imposter Syndrome get in your way?

Looking back over what we have covered so far in Steps One to Four, what has stood out for you? Which changes are you making? Any insights? Lightbulbs? Surprises?

And what are you now doing differently, as a result of the work you have done throughout this book and the blocks you have cleared?

What's the next action you're going to take to further set yourself free from Imposter Syndrome?

To complete Step Four, it's time to look at the four keys to making change last. And the great news is that you've already done all four of them by this stage of the book.

How To Make Change Last

I've been well-known in my tribe for my repeated efforts to give up coffee. I used to be a 5-mug-a-day girl – and we were talking *real* coffee. The 'giving up' thing started back in 2008 when I was studying to become a meditation teacher. Caffeine and calm didn't mix, according to my meditation master. And, deep down, I knew he was right.

During the 5-day retreats for each module of the training, I would dutifully give up coffee and often even tea. After the first few days of headaches and irritability, I'd be resentfully ok, though struggling with exhaustion. I could even keep it going for a month, once I got home. But the moment I had a single sip, I was back on the caffeine.

It wasn't that I lacked willpower. I had done more than the '21 days' psychologists tell us it takes to break a habit. There was another reason why ditching coffee seemed so impossible for me: I didn't actually want to.

I'm often asked how long it takes to change a habit. Psychologists argue about whether it's twenty-one days or twenty-eight. The world of yoga will argue it's forty-two days or one hundred thousand repetitions. But what do I answer?

How long does it take to change a habit?
It's instant.
Every. Single. Time.

As soon as you have genuinely committed to that change.

But if you haven't really committed, then it won't happen.

As Jim Rohn said: "If you really want to do something, you'll find a way. If you don't, you'll find an excuse."

If we really want to do something, we'll find the time or resources or headspace. If we don't, we won't. It's why so many of my online programmes come with a bonus workshop on how to 'magically' make more time – because "I don't have enough time" is the single biggest excuse I hear when people tell me they can't make the changes they want to in their life or business – yet it's rarely the whole truth.

There's a three-lettered word that will change your world – and make ditching old or creating new habits easy. But few of us get there.

And that word is YES. We talked about this on page 170 when I introduced you to my favourite Italian word – *basta!* – *enough!*

As soon as you have committed and made the choice to do or change something, you'll find the way and the resources. Sometimes it takes what I call a 'basta-moment'. You don't have to wait until you hit a rock bottom to turn things around. You can choose to have a basta-moment at any time, to start turning things around.

Changes made with the energy of "this stops now – I'm changing!" actually work. Those made with 'maybe-energy' rarely do. When you're in the 'maybe-zone', then both outcomes are still possible, and you create an inner conflict where your unconscious mind tries to deliver on both at once, with the one that's already programmed in your brain as a habit is more likely to win.

To change a habit, we need to get to the point where we are more committed to our dreams than to our excuses.

Once you have said YES and made the choice to change, all you need to do is to allow that new habit to grow; making it part of your daily rhythm and building those neural pathway motorways that we talked about on page 21, so it becomes your new autopilot.

Changing the habit is instant. All that takes the time is remembering that you have changed it! Practise it intentionally, mindfully, with positive emotions and those neural pathways will form even more quickly.

So, here are the four keys to creating change.

The Four Keys To Creating Change

To maximise your chances of the changes you want to make with this book working, there are four key steps you can go through.

1. **Get super-clear about your Big Why for making your change.**
    We covered this already in Step One. What will this change do for me? How does it move me towards my big vision or my dream goals and outcomes?

2. **Use your imagination to create the new neural pathways.**
    Remember we said that your body can't tell the difference between a mind-story fear and legitimate fear? Well you can use this to your advantage, when you want to change your life!

    Imagine you've made that change – that you can step into the shoes of the 'you' who has done it. Gently close your eyes (assuming that's safe for you right now!) Allow all of your senses to experience how it will feel to have made that change; to be living the life of the version of you who lives and breathes that.

    Notice which thoughts you're thinking. Experience which actions you're taking. See what you can see when you have made that change. Hear what you can hear. Become aware of the physical sensations and how you're holding your body. Spend a few minutes on this and allow yourself to become fully aware of the physical experience of having made that change.

    Do this three times a day for sixty seconds and you'll rewire your brain and create that habit in a way that's fast, fun and forever.

3. **The missing link – take action**
    But there's one step that most people miss out when they are visualising their future. When you're doing step 2, you can be firing off the cascade of positive biochemical reactions in your body that reward you for having achieved something. But you haven't actually done it yet!

    Life is lived in your body, not in your mind, so this final step makes your change become reality.

You do this by actually taking action towards your change. Pre-empt where you might fall off the wagon and deal with those pitfalls. Maybe you're forgetful, so set a reminder on your phone. Perhaps you're lazy (many of us are!), so get yourself an accountability buddy. Perhaps it's a time-thing? Get the actions for this change into your diary. Make it your top priority for the next three weeks.

4. Celebrate your successes.
We're great at beating ourselves up. Instead, if you celebrate every tiny success, those micro-wins, you're triggering the reward centres in your brain to notice the new behaviour and they will set your filters to want to bring you more of that. Paying too much attention to when it goes wrong reinforces the old neural pathways.

Yes, if you slip up, by all means take some time to learn from it, to figure out how it happened and to make sure it can't happen again, but don't go down that Inner Critic spiral into giving up.

And if you need someone to buddy with to celebrate those successes, sort that at the start of your habit changing journey! Make sure you've got the support that you need.

You Can Do This!

> *"If you can imagine it, you can achieve it. If you can dream it, you can become it."*
> *William Arthur Ward*

Think about the times when you've been brilliant at making changes: what made it work? What support did you get? What might get in your way? And what might you do to make sure that doesn't happen? Play to your strengths on this to make it as easy as possible for yourself.

And if your 'yes' to change is just a whisper, perhaps due to past experiences or the fear of the future or failure, here's a technique you can use to crank up your commitment to a change.

Exercise: What If Your 'Yes' Is Just A Whisper?

Pause for a moment and close your eyes. Become aware of your breathing in your body.

Take three deep sighing breaths – in through your nose and out through your mouth – allowing yourself to come back here now.

Become aware of where in your body that 'yes' is – even if that feels like a strange thing to do.

On a scale of one to ten, where one is 'not at all' and ten is 'hell yeah!', how would you currently rate that 'yes'?

Imagine you are sending your breath to that area of your body. Let it rest there for a few moments. There's no judgement. Just acceptance.

Then, with each in-breath, allow your 'yes' to gently grow. With each out-breath, imagine you're breathing out and letting go of any mind-story fears around that 'yes'. Continue this for about a minute.

Now how big does that 'yes' feel on your one to ten scale?

And as a final tweak, imagine there's a dial at that yes-point. Notice the arrow pointing to the number you just said. And gently turn that dial up a couple more notches. How does that feel?

Now do the visualisation from step two of the exercise you just did on page 229 and notice what has shifted!

When you're ready to release the practice, allow your breath to deepen slightly, move your body, have a stretch and perhaps a yawn, then open your eyes with a smile on your face.

Wherever level your 'yes' is up to right now, that's perfect. You've made progress on ditching Imposter Syndrome. You've looked at how you *do* it, discovered how to tame your Inner Critic's drama-stories, started clearing out your hidden blocks and limiting beliefs, learned how to spot and release secondary gain, and so much more. The next step on your Ditching Imposter Syndrome journey is about becoming the leader you were born to be, however you 'lead' in life.

Step 5: Becoming The Leader You Were Born To Be

People sometimes ask me why my Ditching Imposter Syndrome process doesn't stop at Step Four, once you have the tools to clear out Imposter Syndrome. And I get it: most of the time we focus on what we want to change and stop there. But, the way I see it, that takes you from the pain-point to feeling ok. I want to help you get to great – and beyond.

A life lived in 'ok-ness' is not a life lived to its full extent; it's not one where we get to make the difference we are *truly* here to make. There's nothing wrong with that, but it's likely to collect regrets at a faster rate than memories.

So I take those who work with me on Imposter Syndrome to Step Five, to reconnect with their inner genius (we have full access to it when we're young) and to take the next step towards becoming the leader they were born to be.

As we've already discussed, I don't believe that leadership is tied to the job you do. It's not the preserve of CEOs. It's a way of living that inspires others to co-create a better version of the world.

'Leader' isn't a job title. It's an attitude.

I believe that each of us is born with the innate ability to lead, in whatever way we choose, whatever our official 'job' is, but that the fears and blocks we have covered in this book have caused us to shut that ability down. Sometimes that's a partial shutdown. Sometimes it's a shutdown that triggers wearing masks and pretending to lead in a way that doesn't fit with who we really are. Sometimes it's about running away from standing up to be seen and speaking up with our ideas and dreams.

By the end of Step Five, you'll have your practical action plan for becoming more of who you really are, connecting with your inner genius, being *healthily* resilient, and stepping up to make a bigger difference in your world.

Unmasking Your Inner Leadership Genius

I had been a self-help junkie since my early twenties, devouring books and courses, trying to change myself, my habits, my thoughts and my results. But so many of them left me feeling disappointed, even more of a failure. I changed, but I still didn't feel the way I had hoped for about myself.

Then, one day, I had a real lightbulb moment. I had been sitting in a meditation practice as part of my Meditation Teacher Training in 2008 and I saw the proverbial light. I realised I had spent decades trying to change myself. What I actually needed to do was to *unchange* myself – to release the layers that were hiding my inner light; to let go of the coping strategies and masks that I mistakenly thought were keeping me safe.

I learned that my inner journey was about becoming *even more* of who I *really was inside*, rather than the 'sanitised' version I had been allowing the world to see.

When I work with leaders of women's networks in businesses and ask them what, if they could wave a magic wand, they would change for their members, they often give me long lists of practical, symptom-level changes they would love to see. When I ask them what the women would need to change about themselves, to allow all of this to happen, there's a near-unanimous type of answer:

*"I wish they could **be who they really are** and be able to lead with the whole of themselves, not trying to fit into stereotypes and expectations."*

They wish their members could find the confidence to be who they *really* are.

This book has given you the step by step how-to for that – to tame your Inner Critic and start clearing your limiting beliefs, hidden excuses and secret fears. Then you did the work on Imposter Syndrome, at that deeper level which goes beyond mindset. You looked at your masks, what they were doing for you, and learned how to let them go, without the world falling apart.

You have been clearing out those blocks that are like layers of muck which, over the years, obscure the bright shining light of who you really are.

I hope you can feel the difference already.

The rest of what we're going to do together here will build on that, creating deeper-acting shifts that allow you to become more of the *real* you, to become the leader you were born to be.

When I first started talking with clients about this book, one of them asked me a question when I told them what the book's subtitle was going to be.

"So you think everyone is *born* to be a leader? That leaders are *born* and not *made*?"

And it's a great question.

Yes, I believe that each of us has deep inside us the ability to care deeply about something and to lead others on a journey to help us to make the changes we are here to make in the world. It doesn't mean each of us should become Prime Minister or a CEO. There are many different ways to lead. A parent is a leader for their children. A friend is a leader for their tribe on some aspect of life. A teacher is a leader in their classroom. A colleague will lead some aspect of a project for the team.

I strongly believe that we need to let go of our concept of leadership as being something reserved for those with an approved status or background or rank or salary. When each of us takes action to make a difference on those things we care about, we become leaders.

We each have the ability to lead, in a way that fits with who we really are. And, yes, our leadership abilities (surface level behaviours) can be learned, honed and taught. But that desire to lead, to make a difference in some way, comes from deep within. That can't be created in a training course. So in that sense, leaders are *born* and not *made*.

But most people will never lead, because it can be scary. In current times, with internet trolls and public ridicule the reward for a simple faux pas, it's much easier to play safe, stay quiet, and keep doing what we've always been doing. All too often we see those who lead us being ripped to shreds on social media or being role models we would never want to emulate, as values like integrity and courage and collaboration are sacrificed on the altar of ego and power.

So we leave leadership to those who hunger for it or whose careers land them in the 'corner office'.

Yet imagine a world where each of us is more able to share our message with courage and compassion, to take inspired action towards making the difference we are *really* here to make, instead of reaching our last moments and wishing we had done it all differently.

And imagine a business where everyone felt safe to speak up with their great ideas, were fully accepted for who they really are, and had the certainty that they wouldn't be criticised for being human and fallible. Can you imagine the educated risks that could be taken and the breakthroughs these might lead to?

There are two core types of leadership and they are a choice – often driven by culture. I see the difference between these two as the single biggest cause of the 'glass ceiling' and lack of gender diversity at Board level in business. In too many companies, one of these types of leadership is acceptable up to around Director level, but then only the other will do.

At the deepest level, there are two primary emotions that drive all other emotions: love and fear. All human emotions can be arranged in those two categories. And the same goes for leadership styles.

When we lead from fear, people are scared to make mistakes, they take fewer risks, they feel more stressed. Negative self-talk and self-judgement increase, affecting personal and team performance. We have already talked at length in this book about how fear negatively affects creativity, problem solving and our ability to concentrate. Success revolves around achieving results whilst avoiding threatened negative consequences. The typical fear-led management style is criticising, often shifting into bullying. Coercion, public chastisement and fear of failure are the core themes.

The other style of leadership is leading from love. This creates an atmosphere where everyone feels included and valued, where they know their voice will be heard and that they matter, where they know that their manager has their back and is on their side, to inspire them to achieve results they never knew they were capable of. Teams led in this way tend to produce better results through collaboration, improved personal and team performance, increased creativity, and lower stress levels. Managers who lead in this way aim to inspire people to achieve goals, rather than having to resort to fear and threats.

Of course, it's not black and white. There is a sliding scale between these two core drivers for leadership. And just as someone can become overly critical in a fear-based leadership model, so they can become overly compassionate in the love-led team, avoiding those more challenging conversations, through fear of upsetting people. Both of these extremes are a sign that the leader is not comfortable in their own skin.

One of the trends I have seen with my work is that women (I'm generalising) tend to prefer a more compassionate and inclusive style of leadership, leading from their hearts in a head-based world. They want to lead with the *whole* of who they are, not just their minds. Men tend to prefer the less ambiguous action-led style of leadership, where there is less acceptance of emotions and more focus on results, which can easily cause people to shut down and can tip into fear-based leadership.

Many women thrive in corporations with heart-led leadership, until they reach a certain level, when the culture changes. Many larger companies have a level of management above which compassion is no longer an acceptable focus, where competition – though not publicly visible – is pronounced, and the way these women used to lead no longer fits the company culture. This triggers the fear response for these women. They are left with a choice: to change who they are showing themselves to be and lead in a more masculine style, or leave. And that's what many of them do.

This dramatic shift in culture at the most senior levels, along with the sudden disappearance of a nurturing boss, because the CEO is too busy, is a key aspect of the glass ceilings that mean we see so few women on company boards. This is something I regularly write about and you can find resources and references in the Readers' Resource Vault[19].

When people are stressed, scared and feeling like they might get 'found out', they pick up the masks that protect them; the behaviours that keep them safe, be it micro-managing or doing 'whatever it takes' to make sure their team doesn't mess up.

Even the best leadership training in the world is not going to produce a change in outward behaviour and leadership style unless it addresses and clears the leader's hidden fears. At best, it will be a sticky plaster that allows them to develop more coping mechanisms until the next time it 'all goes wrong', when they will revert to type.

Leadership requires us to look in the mirror and to clear out as much of our inner baggage as possible, so that we don't project it on to others. With leadership comes responsibility for the well-being and choices of others.

It's why – and I'll say it again:

*Changing the world isn't so much about
what you do, as about who you allow
yourself to become.*

It's all about allowing yourself to become the real you. To get you

---

started on the next stage of that journey, it's time to look at the two most powerful words you have most likely already used today that hold the power to set you free to become who you really are or to keep you stuck where you no longer want to be.

The Power Of "I Am"

We talked earlier about how Imposter Syndrome strikes when there is a gap between who you see yourself as being, and who you think you need to be, in order to achieve or create something. In that space Imposter Syndrome lurks.

But there are two incredibly important words we use, daily, without even noticing, which keep us stuck in that gap. They have the power to boost your confidence or trash your self-worth. Instantly. They dive right in at the 'identity' level of the Imposter Syndrome Iceberg.

Each time we use them, we tell ourselves and the world who we feel we are. These two words talk directly to your unconscious mind, which treats them as instructions, to be obeyed without questioning; without us realising we're doing it. And no amount of positive self-talk will bypass this response.

Those two words are:

"I am..."

As soon as you use the words 'I am', you lock in whatever comes after it as part of your identity, as you give yourself a label. And this can widen the Imposter Syndrome Gap.

'I am' statements create a physiological response in your body as it, too, obeys.

"I am tired!" fires off the biochemical reactions to support that instruction. "I am full of energy!" does this, too, with very different effects.

So "I am a fraud" has the potential to reinforce your fear of being found out, your beliefs about not being as good as you think you should be, your self-talk about needing to avoid 'them' realising they made a mistake in choosing you for whatever you're working on, and this fires off the stress-cycle that trashes our performance.

What can you do if your 'I am' self-talk is holding you back?

The longer-term solution is to deal with the subconscious fears, beliefs and triggers that caused a particular 'I am' statement to become an autopilot response in your brain. That's what Step Three was all about. But if you need an emergency quick fix, the good old ABC works wonders.

- **Accept** – that you said an 'I am' statement that could keep you stuck.
- **Breathe** – in through the nose and out with a sigh, letting go of the stress response or the secret need to beat yourself up.
- **Choose** – to think a thought that opens up possibilities for you, rather than keeping you in a box.

The key here is to choose a thought that allows you to expand and grow, rather than creating a new box to hold you back at some point in the future, just as you covered in Step Four when we talked about how to choose positive affirmations that actually work. I don't want you to ditch 'I am', but I do want you to use this power phrase consciously.

Use this space to write down some of your most common 'I am" statements – and decide which you want to keep, and which it's time to let go of:

Want More? It's Time To Get Your Verb On!

When you use 'I am' followed by a noun or adjective, you freeze time. A throwaway self-talk thought becomes an unchanging identity-level statement. If ABC hasn't been enough to unfreeze that for you, then it's time to rephrase it to bring movement back into the frozenness, putting the possibility of change back into your language.

Putting my engineering hat on, it's like the difference between static and dynamic friction. When you start a car engine from cold, it causes much more damage to the engine's components than driving does. There are two factors at play here. The first is that the oil you need to lubricate the parts that rub against each other is mainly in the sump – the 'bucket' below the engine where that oil is stored when the car hasn't been used for a while. So it's like having a massage on dry skin. It rubs harder. Once the engine is running, the oil is more evenly distributed and flows to protect those surfaces.

The second factor is the difference between static and dynamic friction. To get something moving from a standstill position takes more energy (effort) than to keep something going, once it's moving. It's a bit like how it can take a while to get our joints moving when we wake up in the morning. But once we're up and at it, we don't notice them anymore.

It's the same with the self-talk we use.

'I am' statements are harder to shift using the techniques from Step Two than verb-based statements. 'I am' is like that cold-start engine with its static friction and no oil. Verb-based statements are like the well-oiled engine that's happily humming its way along the road.

Verbs imply movement and action to our subconscious mind, so they're a great way of getting you unstuck.

Let's look at a practical example:

Imagine you're telling yourself a story about being worn out at the end of a busy day. Your self-talk might include phrases like, "I'm utterly exhausted" or "I'm so worn out." Try saying them out loud a few times and notice the response in your body.

Chances are, it obeys.

And it feels permanent. In that moment, that identity-level instruction is being obeyed by every cell in your body. Those biochemical reactions feed your self-talk and emotions, and so the cycle continues.

To turn this around, switch to a different verb.

You're not going to 'Pollyanna' this and pretend you're feeling vibrant with boundless energy when you're slumped over yet another emergency coffee. You're going to practise honouring how you feel, whilst tweaking your self-talk to make that 'I am' statement less permanent.

How about, "I *feel* utterly exhausted, or "I *feel* so worn out"?

Try those on for size and notice the different shift in your body. Can you sense that your body becomes aware that this is a transient state? That it's not forever? That it might change?

Now let's play with the classic "I'm not good enough" statement. How about, "I notice that I'm *thinking* thoughts about not being good enough."

Can you feel the difference?

You can do the same with self-talk about your behaviour. When you talk about it to yourself in terms of *verbs*, rather than *I am* statements, it's no longer identity-level feedback; it's hanging around towards the top of the Imposter Syndrome Iceberg with your actions. It's no longer a personal attack.

Don't Be A Flip Flop

The key to playing with your 'I am' statements is not to try to do a U-turn with them, flipping from 'am' to 'am not', as we discussed on page 86.

I decided to study mechanical engineering when I was fifteen, partly because I thought that studying German and Russian would mean I had to become a teacher (and I had spent a decade watching what a rough deal kids gave them) and partly because I wanted to know how car engines worked. I had been helping my then boyfriend to build a kit car and that's when I discovered that a car engine's row of cylinders fire off in a certain order – 1, 3, 4 then 2, rather than 1, 2, 3, then 4. When I asked my physics teacher why this was, he couldn't tell me.

I picked mechanical engineering so I could find out. After five years, it had never been covered on my degree and my lecturers didn't have any direct experience with engines. So they couldn't tell me either. It wasn't until I was working as an engineer in an engine manufacturing plant that someone told me the truth – and it was really obvious, once I knew it.

Each time a cylinder fires in a car engine, there's a small explosion. That is the first stage of how the power from the fuel is converted into movement for the car. That explosion is like a massive punch on the engine and it causes the components to distort – albeit tiny amounts – thousands of times a minute. By having the first cylinder fire and then the third, followed by the fourth and back to the second, you create a flowing wave of that distortion, a bit like an infinity sign. If you went from cylinder four straight to cylinder one it would be like bending a plastic school ruler hard from both ends – you'd risk it snapping in the middle as you flipped the stress in the engine from one side to the other. And it would make the whole engine rock back and forth like a seesaw. It would cause structural damage and be extremely unpleasant to drive.

It's the same with 'I am' statements. If you flip an 'I am not good enough' into an 'I am good enough', it sets up an inner conflict, because part of you has invested decades (most likely) in thoughts, beliefs, fears, values, behaviours and identity-level stuff to support the 'not' version. We're back to the Imposter Syndrome pantomime from page 84.

Instead, you want to create a flowing wave that takes you from the 'not' through 'maybe' into 'probably' and finishing with 'yes'. But even then, you don't want to be choosing 'I am' statements that might leave you stuck again in the future. That's replacing one frozen-in-time statement with another. Instead, you could choose phrases like:

I'm not good enough => ~~I am good enough~~ => Each day I learn to value my strengths more

I am exhausted => ~~I am bouncing with energy~~ => Each day I take actions to build my energy levels in healthy ways

I am rubbish at => ~~I am great at~~ => Each day I improve at...

Have a play with your Imposter Syndrome 'I am' statements and notice what shifts. Use your 'I am' with care!

'I am' isn't always bad. If you add this into your affirmation work from Step Four, it becomes a powerful tool to create identity-level shifts. The key is to make sure the 'I am' statements you choose will never limit the way you can experience life, as you grow and stretch your comfort zones.

And once you've experimented with this, it's time to decide who you *really* want to *be*.

Who Will I Allow Myself To Become Today?

We're great at talking about 'to do' lists, but when did you last think about your 'to be' list?

Motivational speakers sometimes joke that we are human *beings*, not human *doings*. It's clear which of those society values more. But, when you line up with who you *really* are, as a human *being*, the *doing* becomes much easier and more effective.

Imagine if, each morning, instead of turning straight to your 'to do' list you spent sixty seconds lining up with who you want to *be* that day?

I'm not talking about impersonating someone else. I'm talking about which aspects of who you really are would most help you with that day's tasks.

Some days you might want to line up with the version of you that's super-efficient; other days you might need to connect with your inner creativity; or perhaps you need to be a collaborator in the morning and a decision-maker in the afternoon. When we consciously choose to connect with these aspects of ourselves, bringing those elements of our inner genius out to play, we increase our productivity and fine-tune our performance in ways that time management seminars could never teach.

We all have inner genius, even at those times when we tell ourselves we are stupid. The problem comes when we lose touch with our inner gifts or when we compartmentalise them or when we use masks to hide them.

Your inner genius isn't about your capabilities or things you could learn on a training course. It's about your hidden superpowers. And when we know how to 'own' our superpowers, genuinely connecting with the way we love to do things, there's much less space for self-doubt and Imposter Syndrome.

A classic example of this is a mother returning to work after maternity leave. Clients often tell me that after a year or more out of the office they feel they have lost some of their skills and are worried about going back into the workplace, especially if they have more than one child and will be juggling childcare and school events with running their home and their career.

But we forget about the skills that the year of maternity leave developed for us. Many of us become master negotiators (getting the toddler to eat broccoli), have incredible productivity (it's amazing how much you can get done in the thirty minutes that the kids are asleep), have developed impressive prioritisation techniques (you have ten minutes and twenty things to do – it's a great way to focus on what makes the biggest difference) and we have often developed the patience of the proverbial saint.

That time out of the office has changed who we are, allowing us to connect with aspects of our inner genius that perhaps weren't there before. When we bring those elements of 'us' back into the office, it transforms the way we work.

> *Your inner genius is rarely found inside your comfort zones.*

Often events that stretch us allow us to connect with hidden aspects of our inner genius. So the more you stretch yourself (I'm talking 10% here, not to breaking point), the more you will discover your superpowers. If you stay stuck inside your comfort zones, those superpowers can shrivel and die.

A superpower is part of who you really are, rather than a learned skill. Once you have connected with it, you practise and develop it, but in essence it's an identity-level thing. And we all have them.

I have one that's totally random and is often the butt of family jokes: I have an innate talent for knowing exactly how much food will fit in a dish. I never measure anything while I'm cooking, but somehow every time I make something like lasagne, there's the perfect amount of the various sauces to fill the dish to exactly the right level. No matter which dish I use.

I have another superpower that is more useful in my work context – the ability to design a transformational course in under an hour, when I'm in flow and feeling inspired. And my favourite superpower is the ability to spot someone's hidden block intuitively – the one that has been keeping them stuck for *so* long – and to know how they can easily release it.

Our superpowers can be things we take for granted, because they feel so easy to us, and we assume that everyone else finds them easy, too. But they don't. They're part of our unique set of gifts that allow us to achieve our goals and to inspire others towards theirs. And ignoring our superpowers – writing them off as things anyone can do *because* we find them easy – is one of the warning signs of Imposter Syndrome, which is why it's so important to identify them and to accept that they are special.

Exercise: Connecting With Your Inner Genius & Superpowers

Your inner genius or superpowers are things you can take for granted. Consciously connecting with them can really help with tackling Imposter Syndrome. So here are three self-mentoring questions that can help you to spot them.

1. Think about the things you find really easy, which – being objective – others don't. These might be jobs others love to give you to do. It might be work that gets you feeling inspired. It might be things that others are always asking you about, which you do without thinking. Write down at least five things, below:

2. Now think about things you love doing – that make your heart sing. Write down at least five.

3. Finally, think about those times when you're really 'in flow', when time seems to disappear. Write down five examples, below.

Going through the items you have written down, what are the common threads? What is it you find easy that others don't? What do you enjoy that others often struggle with? These are clues to your inner genius – your superpowers – make some notes, now.

The Great Thing About Superpowers

Here's the fabulous trick that most people miss when it comes to their inner genius and superpowers: they forget that they are transferable.

So the mum returning from maternity leave forgets that the negotiating she has been doing with her kids will also help her to negotiate with her team, back at work.

We compartmentalise our inner genius.

That's why it's such a useful process to decide, each morning, who you need to *be* that day to get the most from your day. And you can map your inner genius across into different contexts in life.

Using Positive Affirmations To Rocket-Charge Your Superpowers

Use the process from page 210 to choose your affirmations, then make sure they are 'expandable' – you don't want them to become new 'boxes' to limit who you can become and how you can express your inner genius. So you'll want to include phrases like 'even more', which include a sense of the potential to expand and grow. It can really help to start with 'I am' plus a present tense continuous verb, rather than just 'I am', as you used previously, and remember to be specific.

For example:

Every time I meet with my manager, I am showing him more of my expertise in problem solving.

Whenever I present to the Board, I am becoming more confident in answering their questions in a way that helps them to trust me.

Today, I am becoming an even better negotiator.

What If There's A Superpower You Need, But Don't Have?

Start by looking for examples of where you *do* demonstrate this in life, even if it's just on a small scale. Then clear out any hidden blocks that might get in the way of you becoming more of that (Step Three) and wrap it up with the affirmation work from Step Four and this step. Use the finished affirmation as your mantra each morning, really allowing yourself to *feel* yourself *becoming* that version of you. Apply the secret sauce from page 213 and notice how that superpower grows within you, until you can easily connect with that aspect of your inner genius.

So, you might be an expert at organising your family, under pressure, but at work your 'to do' list expands like an oil spill, threatening to overwhelm the entire office. Start by looking at how you 'do' your superpower at home and which elements of this you could bring into the workplace. And remember to address any secondary gain, if you find yourself resisting this!

Exercise: Using Your Superpowers To Clear Imposter Syndrome

Go back to the various discussions you have been having with Glurg and look at a specific situation where Imposter Syndrome came up for you.

Explain to Glurg which superpower would have helped you to get through that, without Imposter Syndrome coming out to play. Which superpower do you choose:

Think of a situation where you *do* exhibit that superpower. Describe to Glurg how you do it – how you *become* the person with that superpower.

Now imagine you're watching the previous Imposter Syndrome scenario on a movie screen. Except this time the 'you' acting out that situation is living and breathing having that superpower. How has the scenario changed?

How might you start to build this superpower into your daily life, in a way that is positive and supports you?

Flow Not Force

Back when I was a kid, I remember a group of us getting obsessed with graphology – the study of handwriting and what it says about your personality. As early teen girls, anything that helped us to understand ourselves was devoured, from teen magazine quizzes to palm reading. But the handwriting thing really stuck with me.

It could be neat and careful or loopy and flamboyant. It might be light and airy or created with such force that it nearly tore the paper.

This teenage lunchtime-filler brought up an insight that stays with me, even today: how you mow the lawn. That was how the long-forgotten book described it. When you look at your handwriting, is it slanting forwards, sloping backwards, or upright? The analogy was of pushing a lawnmower, leaning forwards, being pulled by it by leaning backwards, or walking with your back straight, because the lawn mower is self-propelling.

Even now, it's one of the things I subconsciously check with handwriting.

The theory went that someone who has forward-slanting handwriting is pushing and forcing their way towards their goals, potentially living half a step in the future, and on the fast-track to burnout. Those with backward-sloping handwriting were supposed to be laid back, letting life pull them, and less likely to take the inspired action that is sometimes required to succeed. Those with upright handwriting were considered to be balanced and in flow.

Nowadays, I have no idea whether those handwriting assumptions were correct. But the behaviours they describe are a great way to look at how we create our lives and our attitude towards goals and leadership.

It comes down to force versus flow.

The push-the-lawnmower and the pull-the-lawnmower profiles are both giving away their power. The push-person is trying to control and force circumstances, believing that hard work and long hours are the path to success. The pulled-by-the-lawnmower person is going with the 'what will be will be' motto and is allowing life to 'happen *to* them', giving their power to some unseen force of destiny.

The middle way is the one I want to talk about in this section.

Don't force it. Allow life to flow.

When we're forcing life to happen, we're pushing; we feel a strong need to be in control, even of the things that are patently beyond our control.

252 • DITCHING IMPOSTER SYNDROME

You can tell when you're in this space because you'll be using phrases like 'have to' and 'must' (remember 'shoulditis' from page 141?). If you've been running a perfectionist pattern, this need to be in control can turn you into a micro-manager, constantly worrying about someone in the team messing up.

When we're in 'forcing' mode, we're effectively using our own energy to make things happen, sending ourselves into that fight-flight-freeze stress response, and shutting down our inner creativity.

Goals become small-scale wars which we have to 'slay' or 'crush' or 'annihilate'. Someone thinking this way about their goals is likely to clench their jaw, tense their body, and prepare to fight their goals with gritted determination. 'Failure' to 'slaughter' the goals is unthinkable.

Ironically, this is the hardest way to achieve goals. This ultra-masculine, testosterone-fuelled form of leadership is a fear-based way of leading. After the initial excitement and adrenalin rush, the stress response leaves you less likely to perform at your best and the fear of failure makes people less likely to take creative risks. Yet it's surprisingly widespread, even in milder forms.

The magic happens when you get in flow.

We all know that feeling of being 'in the zone'. Runners get it, when time seems to disappear and it's just them and the road. Musicians get it, when they produce music they didn't consciously know they could. Writers get it, when words pour out onto the keyboard and they look back at them, with no idea how they wrote that piece. Even in the workplace we get it – when a meeting runs brilliantly, when a proposal flows, when we're lost in doing something we love.

When you're in flow, you're connected with your inner genius. You're leading with the whole of your Being, not just your head.

And when we approach projects looking for the 'flow' and not the 'force', we can create breakthroughs. Fast. Plus, it's much more fun.

This is leading from love, not fear.

It's not about always choosing the 'easy option'. It's about lining up with your outcome and *allowing* progress to happen, rather than feeling you have to *make it* happen. And 'flow' isn't about being passive and allowing life to happen *to* you. Instead, it's the ultimate 'getting out of your own way'.

When we set the intention to *allow* a project to *flow*, we create an environment where everyone can contribute, where creativity can flourish, and where we can take the shortest, fastest path to the group's outcome.

There's another aspect of the force-vs-flow dance that's important to discuss: how we handle our personal blocks – our fears, secret excuses and limiting beliefs.

Are you the kind of person who obliterates a block – blowing it out of the water? Do you force your way through, acting as though it isn't there? Do you swerve to avoid it?

All of these are 'force' actions. And there are times where you have to pick one of these, to reach your destination. It can be exhausting, hugely stressful, and can lead to physical and mental health issues.

Most of the time the 'flow' option will give you much better results – with a more enjoyable journey:

Flowing is about acknowledging the block, dealing with it, so that it no longer affects you, then flowing right on down that road towards your goal. The huge bonus with this is that the block won't ever be there in future, to get in your way again. That's exactly what the previous sections of this book teach you to do.

> *Ironically, flowing takes more courage than forcing. It requires you to trust your inner genius, to trust those around you, to become the **conduit** for the change you want to see, rather than the **creator** of it.*

When we 'force' and 'push', most people will feel a tension in the area of their solar plexus – above your stomach, a few inches down from your sternum. In the worlds of meditation and yoga, this solar plexus area (manipura) is the energy centre that is responsible for your personal power and your sense of control. When this area is tense, the energy can't flow through it. So we end up using our *own* internal power source to create change. When it is open and relaxed, you become a conduit for that energy. And – engineer-approved woo-woo[20] alert – when I work with leaders who are standing in their power and leading with flow, not force, that energy centre is vibrant and active. It helps them to inspire others with their vision and to create growth and breakthroughs, with ease and grace.

The solar plexus area is also the seat of our courage and personal strength. So closing it down, by pushing and forcing, creates the need for more pushing and forcing, which can quickly result in bullying.

---

[20] Engineer-approved-woo-woo is what my clients often call my blend of demystified ancient wisdom and engineer's common sense.

Flowing leadership involves two main components, once you have a clear and achievable goal:

1. Taking inspired actions – the ones that lead to breakthroughs, not 'busyness' and burnout.
2. Allowing the success to flow, by clearing out your inner blocks – getting yourself out of the way.

Success isn't a straight line.

I prefer to think of it as a game of allowing life to flow through me and pulling out the tent peg I had bashed in to keep me stuck, like that baby elephant from back on page 160. Trying to stick rigidly to the 'straight line' path means we soon end up trying too hard to compensate for when 'life' knocks us off-course.

Our out-of-date beliefs are like the solitary tent peg that holds back the elephant. We push and pull and try to force our way past those blocks, but soon realise that this hurts, so we stop. But as we learn and grow and change who we are, over the decades, those old blocks hang around – tiny tent pegs with a massive effect. They might have been created when we were seven, but they're still effective at keeping us stuck, even when we're forty-seven.

And the more we recite our self-talk mantras of "I can't do that, because…", the more we are bashing those tent pegs even more deeply into the ground. As we long to sail the ocean, we feel tethered to the ground like Gulliver in Lilliput. Those tent pegs become our adult equivalent of a child's security blanket. We could pull them up and set ourselves free from them in moments. But we don't.

Limiting beliefs are like tent pegs you bash into the ground, which stop you from heading towards your dreams and goals.

And that's why so many people end up forcing, rather than flowing – they don't know how to clear those old tent pegs, so they pull against them and push on through with hustle and deadlines and workaholism and super-stress.

If, instead, we could learn to pull up the tent pegs, as we did in Step Three, we could then focus on flowing through life, free from whatever was holding us back.

Sue found exactly this when she was promoted to lead a team of twelve. She went from having just two junior members of staff working for her to leading people who had been senior to her, when she started at the company.

After the initial excitement, she soon found that the team had their own ways of working, which were inefficient and caused problems with timing and quality on the delivery of client work.

Sue spent many sleepless nights, wondering how best to approach this problem, totally convinced that there was no way the team would take directions from her – the first woman to ever lead that function in the business. And she found it hard. Within weeks she was dreading going into the office and her team was starting to talk behind her back about her being irritable and snappy.

Sue and I had a couple of sessions together and soon unpicked two limiting beliefs that were causing her to 'push' and 'force' project success. The first was the super-common belief that great results have to be hard work. The second was that people didn't like change.

Once we cleared these and Sue got 'out of her own way', she was able to have positive, honest discussions with the team, who told her they had long wanted to improve the processes, but hadn't felt able to ask their old boss. Work started to flow and be fun again.

Courageous Alignment

As I've said before, changing the world isn't so much about what you do, as about who you allow yourself to become.

And the essence of this is Courageous Alignment.

By 'alignment' I mean *allowing* yourself to *become* the person who achieves the goal. This is the key ingredient for being in flow – for becoming a true leader. Courageous alignment is where your outside actions and inside world are lined up.

If you try to achieve a goal whilst *not* seeing yourself as being the kind of person who succeeds in whatever it is, you'll end up either self-sabotaging or forcing. Both lead to pain and are the hardest ways to succeed.

One of the most powerful things you can do when you start a new project or role is to ask yourself:

*"Who do I need to allow myself to **become**, to ensure the success of this?"*

Then focus on what you need to *let go of* to become that version of you, because that 'you' is already there, waiting for you, or you wouldn't be inspired to take on that mission. There's rarely anything that needs to be 'added in', apart from any project-specific skills.

Great leadership is about becoming who you really are and allowing the world to see that version of you. For me, that's true authenticity and vulnerability. It's not about woe-is-me sympathy stories. It's about Courageous Alignment – when you take off your masks and your armour and show up 100%, without self-judgement, taking the inspired actions that will create results.

Vulnerability isn't about washing your dirty laundry in public. It's about showing you're human - fallible - with hopes and fears and dreams. But, above all, it's about showing you care.

Courageous alignment is about becoming the person who achieves a goal and taking action from *that* version of you, not the version who feels scared and not good enough, who has to hide behind masks and deny their inner genius, in order to feel safe.

The best way to understand this is to experience it.

Exercise: Courageous Alignment

Think about a comfort zone you want to stretch – one that excites you but about which Imposter Syndrome has been having a chat with you.

Ask yourself: "Who do I need to allow myself to *become*, to *allow* this project to be a success? Write some notes in your workbook – without editing or judgement!

Now, softly closing your eyes, imagine you are stepping into *being* that version of you. Choose one of those qualities at a time, starting at your heart and allowing that quality to flow throughout your body, then the next one, and the next one.

As you breathe in, allow each quality in turn to fill every cell in your body. As you breathe out, let go of any blocks or resistance.

When you have done this for three qualities, allow yourself to rest in that experience for a few moments. Notice what you notice.

How does your body feel?

What kinds of thoughts are you thinking?

What can you hear, in your mind's ear?

What can you see, in your mind's eye?

As you experience being that version of you, what kinds of actions are you taking?

How do you feel about the project?

And finally, what advice would you give to the 'you', right here, right now?

There's no need to wait until some future point to allow yourself to become that more whole version of you. If you can imagine it now, if you can *allow* yourself to experience it, right here, right now. Surely there's no point in going back to the 'old' version of you and waiting, is there?

You have all of the tools you need to release those blocks, to connect with your inner genius, and to take the next steps towards becoming the leader you were born to be. Today. Here. Now. With each and every breath.

The Power Of Your Breath

Obviously you are breathing or reading this book wouldn't be your priority just now. But few of us understand the power of our breath.

In yoga and meditation, the breath is our prana – life force. The study of breathing is called Pranayama. When we connect with our breath, consciously, it can give us clarity or courage or calm. And it's a ninja-level element to bring into your leadership journey.

Not only can your breath help you to align with becoming the leader you were born to be, as you experienced in the previous exercise, it can help you to intentionally release limiting beliefs. It can also help you to feel more confident or to calm your stress response or to shift your mood or even to energise the room, when you are presenting. Your breath has the power to shape your emotional state, to release hidden blocks and to create change in your life.

You will see in later in this step how it can help you to reclaim your personal power and to have more patience with people who are annoying you. First, I invite you to play with how conscious breathing can help you to step into Courageous Alignment more easily. This exercise builds on the classic yoga mountain pose (Tadasana), which is the foundation for the modern 'power pose', then adds in using your breath to increase your confidence in a way that feels natural and doesn't require pretending or 'faking it'.

Exercise: Breathing For Confident, Courageous Alignment

Take a 'snapshot' before you begin: noticing how your body feels, where there is tension, which emotions you are experiencing, and the kinds of thoughts you are thinking.

- Standing with your feet about hip width apart, take three deep, sighing breaths: in through your nose and out through your mouth with an 'ahhh'.

- Gently rock your body from side to side and front to back (tiny movements) to become aware of your feet on the floor. This is easiest without shoes, if that's an option for you.

- Slightly soften your knees, so they aren't locked. Tilt your pelvis slightly to and fro, until you feel its natural balance point. Allow your spine to slightly lengthen, lifting your sternum and relaxing your shoulders. Tuck your chin slightly down and allow your face to relax.

- Imagine your feet are firmly planted on the earth beneath you, growing roots. You might see these roots or feel them growing or just get a sense of them reaching deep into the earth, so you feel strong and anchored.

- As you breathe in, imagine you are breathing in from the roots into the soles of your feet, up through your legs, your torso, your shoulders, neck and into your head. As you breathe out, let the breath travel back down into the earth.

- With your next in-breath, breathe a sense of calm and confidence from the centre of the earth. Feel the energy of the mountain pose filling your body, from your feet, through your legs, your pelvis and hips, your torso, up through your shoulders and neck and into your head.

- When you breathe out, consciously let go of any blocks to your confidence with your out-breath.

- Continue this at a pace that feels comfortable for you for a few minutes, allowing that sense of calm, courage and confidence to gently wash through every cell in your body.

Prepare to release this exercise by taking another 'snapshot'. What has shifted for you?

This breathing technique works most effectively if you have practised it regularly; then it can shift your inner emotional state in seconds, with the corresponding positive effect on your self-talk, your confidence and your performance. Think about it as 'power pose without pretending'!

If these techniques resonate with you, you can find out more about Pranayama in the Readers' Resource Vault. And there are also details there of my training 'Pranayama for Business Leaders'.

Moving out of forcing into flowing is key for another important trait for leaders: resilience. And it's time to find out what that *really* is – and how the traditional definition of it can actually make Imposter Syndrome worse.

The Resilience Myth

When we're looking at being more of who we really are, resilience is one of the biggest masks we can wear. We often get it back-to-front and it can actually trigger Imposter Syndrome.

The mainstream understanding of 'resilience' is the ability to bounce back from adversity, to pick yourself up after knocks, to be thick-skinned in the face of conflict and to be able to cope with stress, radical change and trauma. People talk about being able to 'carry on regardless'. It's such a buzz-word that it's now being taught in schools, workplaces and in countless books.

But what if we have resilience wrong?

In my first ever graduate job interview, I was locked in a room (that's how it felt!) with the company's Chief Engineer and HR Director. I had already had to admit, in response to a question about how planes stayed in the air, that I was at least partly convinced it was magic, but I knew which questions to ask to find out the physics behind it, if they really wanted to know.

They didn't seem to mind too much, until the Chief Engineer asked the deadly catch-you-out question. He asked which subjects I enjoyed in maths, as part of my mechanical engineering degree. I have always had a love of patterns and problem solving and the first answer that came to mind was 'Laplace transforms' – fiendishly difficult equations that could take multiple blackboards to solve and definitely earned you a pint in the student union bar if you got the right answer.

The twitch of a smile warned me I should have chosen more wisely.

He gestured towards the HR Director, told me she had no engineering background, and asked me to explain to her why Laplace Transforms were useful.

My Inner Critic threatened to start screaming like the crowds in the first five minutes of the Harrods sale, until a voice inside me said, 'you've got this – just talk'.

I desperately looked around me for inspiration and my gaze fell on the table on which the HR director was resting her notebook. That was it!

I explained that Laplace Transforms are useful as a way of predicting whether hitting something in a certain way will cause it to wobble and come back to rest or to shake itself to bits. You can use it for everything from kicking a table leg to see if it will take the blow, to whether a storm will cause a skyscraper to self-destruct. Sometimes things need to move so they won't shatter when knocked.

I got the job. And it taught me a valuable lesson.

Twenty years later, training to become a meditation teacher, it took me a while to realise that it was ok to get knocked off-balance – life didn't have to be a perfect 'flatline' of acceptance and inner peace. In the meditation world, we talk about how our inner emotional state is like a pendulum. When life knocks us, that pendulum is going to swing. The more often you meditate, the less it will swing and the sooner it will come back to equilibrium, because we haven't dived into the mind-story fears and drama-stories that trigger the biochemical responses in the body that create our emotions, which feed the drama-stories...

Studying meditation taught me that it is ok to have that inner peace pendulum swing; what is important is how easily it comes back to its equilibrium, restoring your sense of inner groundedness and calm.

In the business world, resilience is often seen as the ability to keep going, no matter what is going on around you, bouncing back from adversity and to 'tough it out' when things are hard.

CEOs tell me that resilience is an essential trait in their team members.

What they mean by this is that people shouldn't get 'phased' or freaked out by the challenges and changes the job will entail. But most people are dealing with this at the 'effect' end of things – once the negativity has become a mind-story-drama, rather than preventing the need for resilience in the first place.

262 • DITCHING IMPOSTER SYNDROME

Resilience is seen as the ability to endure or bounce back from adversity. But that first requires an employee to suffer, which should be unnecessary.

There are two ways that the need for resilience can be triggered at work:

1. External stress triggers and environmental factors
2. Mind-story dramas that trigger our internal stress response

One could argue that a decent employer would reduce external stress triggers, such as having to work long hours, unreasonable deadlines, lack of flexibility to fit work and family in, the fear of losing your job, difficult working conditions, fear of change, or treating staff badly. In these cases, resilience is surely the 'tail wagging the dog'? No CEO has the right to demand staff be resilient to working in a toxic negativity environment.

But there's the second side: much of the stress and pain people feel in their jobs comes from the stories they are telling themselves about them – as we discussed at the beginning of this book. We need to take responsibility for how our self-talk is affecting our experience of the outside world. In this situation, resilience needs to be about preventing ourselves from creating that internal stress experience, rather than bouncing back from it afterwards, or pushing on through those worries and fears, as most people do. That leads to mental health issues and poor performance.

In my work, I don't see the value in 'after-the-event' resilience. I teach people 'preventative resilience'.

There is much we can do to prevent workplace stress, but it does require cultural changes. Insisting that staff be resilient to it seems pretty negative. Work becomes about surviving, not thriving. In this context, resilience is about coming back to being ok *after* you have gone through the pain and the drama. It's about how quickly you can put on the masks and armour after you have been through something that was a challenge. It is about how we deal with the after-effects of day-to-day stress and conflict.

Modern resilience isn't about preventing the stress, whatever is going on. It's about how quickly you can bounce back, once you have been through the mill.

Modern 'resilience' is like grabbing that inner pendulum with both hands and **forcing** *it to be still.*

Most of the time we're not talking about resilience to the awful stuff that can happen, like losing a loved one or getting a horrible medical diagnosis or being on the receiving end of hard-core public trolling. Personally, I don't believe that focusing on minimising the time to 'bounce back' is appropriate for such circumstances. In business, we're talking about resilience to losing a contract or being yelled at in a meeting or being criticised or missing out on a promotion or exhaustion from working crazily long hours or from a colleague winding you up.

All of this risks falling under the 'gritted teeth determination' version of resilience; pushing on through the pain and pretending you're fine. That's about 'forcing', not 'flowing'.

Can you sense, from what we have covered so far in this book, how all of this can make Imposter Syndrome worse?

There's a concept in materials science, a key part of my engineering degree, which talks about how much you can stretch or bend something, before it breaks. If you deform something within its 'elastic limit', it will go back to the same shape it was before you did whatever you're doing to it. But if you take a material past its 'elastic limit', then it will never return to its former shape. Imagine bending a plastic school ruler – it's that point where it stays part-bent or even snaps.

This 'keep going whatever the cost' is the human equivalent of taking someone beyond their elastic limit – beyond the point at which they can genuinely bounce back and be ok – into their 'plastic region' where materials deform until they snap. It can even trigger Complex PTSD and the hypervigilance issues we talked about on page 112.

And when it comes to being trolled or having someone wind you up, the problem with being resilient to this is that it often takes the form of being thick-skinned, which is like wearing armour to keep others out, to protect ourselves. That's like living in Shutdown Central. It stops us from connecting with those who are being kind and helpful, in order to protect ourselves from those who know how to touch our secret 'raw nerves'.

True resilience is about taming your Inner Critic so that it doesn't go crazy when someone presses your buttons. It's about learning how not to worry so much; how not to take things personally, without getting to passive-aggressive 'not caring'. It's about clearing out your inner blocks, so that there are fewer buttons to press. It's about knowing how to press 'pause' on those mind-story fears and drama-stories, so that we don't go through the fight-flight-freeze response fifty times a day. It's about being in flow, not forcing. It's about knowing how to ride those waves.

That's the essence of what you have been doing in this book.

It's not about pushing down powerful emotions and pretending that everything is ok, numbing the pain with your favourite addiction, having to take something to help you sleep, and then getting up tomorrow to do it all over again.

True resilience is not about forcing or pretending. It's not about putting a happy face on it. It's not about pushing yourself to stay positive when inside you're crying.

It's about knowing when your batteries need topping up. It's about being human. It's about knowing that, deep down, you're ok. And that other people's stuff isn't really about you. It's about feeling safe to show up without your masks or armour. It's ok to show you're human – that you have emotions – that you have a life outside work. You can do all of this and still be professional. There's a long continuum between 'automaton' and 'gibbering wreck' and your unique version of *true* resilience lies somewhere on that scale.

> *We can't always control what happens in life, but we can always choose how to respond.*

In life, brown-stuff happens. Two people can experience the same thing but have completely different responses. One may wobble – for a moment – take that deep breath that brings them back to equilibrium and then head towards a solution. Another may feel out-of-control, get stuck in their mind-story dramas, turn that super-sized molehill into a mountain and then spend days, weeks or months having to 'push on through' and put a brave face on things, to be able to cope.

Remember the 'gain' we talked about on page 118 with my TV aerial? The earlier in the stress-trigger-process you can press 'pause' on your autopilot stress reactions and negative self-talk stories, the less of an effect the stressor will have on you. And the pendulum of your inner peace will come back to its calm point more quickly. Then you are truly resilient.

Courageous alignment is the essence of true resilience.

True resilience is about reclaiming your personal power to consciously choose how you respond to life. The more aligned you are with who you *really* are, the easier this will be. The less you are judging yourself – and others – the more naturally resilient you will become. As we mentioned earlier, no one can make you feel inferior, without your consent.

In this statement, Eleanor Roosevelt is reminding us that no one can *make us* do or think or feel anything; at some level, it is always our choice. We always have the power to choose how to respond. Yes, there are people in life who may deliberately provoke us to feel bad or sad or angry, but the power to choose which thoughts to feed is always our own.

So if you're telling yourself the mind-story of 'he *made* me so angry!', he didn't. He said or did things that pushed your 'angry button' triggers and you either went through your well-rehearsed autopilot response or you consciously chose to get angry. But he didn't physically get inside your head and trigger the Autonomic Nervous System responses that create anger.

When you are grounded in who you really are, accepting yourself fully, clearing out your inner blocks and taming your self-judging Inner Critic, you'll notice that pendulum doesn't need to swing as crazily before it returns to its calm point. And it never needs to shake so hard that it shatters. You develop a longer fuse. Stuff doesn't stress you as much anymore. People don't get to you anymore. You have fewer buttons to press. True resilience becomes your 'new normal'.

The whole 'it's not personal' thing is a big topic. You are not responsible for other people's emotions and they are not responsible for yours. To dive into this more deeply, I've got an interview for you with my friend Joel Young, whose big mission is to help people to set themselves free from the pain of taking things personally. You can find it in the Readers' Resource Vault.

One of the best ways to train your inner pendulum to return to its equilibrium point is daily meditation. It's much easier to tame your inner self-talk and press pause on your mind's drama-stories if you have fewer thoughts – either positive or negative – and therefore less of an Inner Critic to tame.

I'm not talking about meditation apps, though they're a great start.

These tend to be more about being mindful and are often 'guided visualisations', rather than true 'meditation'. When you meditate, you connect much more deeply with who you really are, gain insights into those habit-blocks that have been keeping you stuck, learn the difference between projection and perception (see page 137), and connect with your sense of inner peace much more easily. The Readers' Resource Vault has extra resources for you, if you're interested in exploring this.

Exercise: Becoming The Leader You Were Born To Be

Take a piece of paper and draw two columns on it. At the top of the first column write 'ways I am not being me'. At the top of the second column write 'ways I show the world who I am'.

Think back over the past week about things you have said and done and write them down in whichever column they belong in.

Now go through each item and ask yourself how you *feel* about having made that choice. Are there any in the 'not being me' column that you would like to change in the future? What internal resources would you need to be able to do that? What would you need to believe about yourself and the world to let your light shine more brightly in those situations? Make an appointment in your diary to run those insights through the limiting belief tools in Step Three.

The more you can clear out those hidden blocks, allowing yourself to become the person who doesn't have those fears or limiting beliefs, who doesn't need to pretend any more, the more easily you can be the *real* you and – at a subconscious level – give those around you permission to do the same.

Next look at those in the 'ways I show the world who I am' column. Are there any of these that you could crank up a few notches? Any other areas of your life where you could apply these? Take a few moments now to visualise how that might feel, becoming aware of how you would hold your body, the thoughts you would be thinking, what you would be seeing and hearing, how your body would feel. Sense the relief and expansion this brings. And know that if you can imagine it, you can create it; starting right now.

Each and every breath you take is an opportunity to make a fresh start.

... continues

Now look at your life story. Each of us is a leader in some way, even if it's not on our business cards as a job title. As you flick through the photo album of your life so far, what in your story means you can be an inspirational leader? Where have you shown courage? Where have you achieved something you had thought was impossible?

Write those things down. Keep them with you. Let them be your talismans of courage, confidence and commitment to take off the masks you never intended to wear and to be more of who you really are, each day.

You don't have to be perfect at this. But if you aimed to feel 1% more comfortable each day for the next three months, imagine how different you will feel by the end of that period!

When I work with my clients, I talk about this being *real* self-care. It's a buzzword these days, particularly in entrepreneurial circles, where we're finally understanding that there needs to be balance between hard work and looking after ourselves. But:

Self-care isn't just about fragrant baths and expensive massages. It's about accepting yourself for who you really are and letting that version of you shine out to the world, a little bit more each day, with love, not judgement.

Yoga can also be immensely powerful for building natural, healthy resilience. I've got simple postures to help waiting for you in the Reader Resource Vault[21], including the 'flowing tree', for when you need to be flexible in your response to triggers, and the 'peace posture', for letting go at the end of a stressful day.

---

[21] www.DitchingImposterSyndrome.com/vault/

Influencing Authentically

There's an exercise I love to do on workshops where you sit back-to-back with a partner and talk about your day. One talks, the other listens. But they're not listening to their partner's words. They're listening to their *mood*. Once people are tuned in to each other, I add in another layer: the same conversation, still talking about their day, but this time whilst *thinking* about a food they either love or hate. Soggy, over-cooked Brussel sprouts come up surprisingly often in the latter category. And their partner has to identify which category it was.

It always amazes people how easily they can tell.

For those who are keen to stretch these skills, I add in another layer. This time, same conversation, but instead of thinking about food, they set the intention to inspire a particular emotion in their listener – either positive or negative. So it might be joy, hope or fun – or it might be jealousy, worry or mild fear. At a deeply unconscious level, it changes the words we use, our tone of voice, our body language and many other 'tells' that give away our intention and emotions.

To inspire an emotion in others, we first need to create it in ourselves. Intentionally.

When you're tuned in to it, this is really easy to spot. Humans are built with inner radars for this stuff. It's how you know that someone is, say, sad, even if they're denying it. It's a sixth sense. But we rarely listen with such conscious attention in daily life.

When we're speaking, we are rarely aware of our internal mood and how it might affect others. When we're happy, we want everyone around us to be happy. When we're down, we unconsciously try to drag everyone else there to join us. And our audience obeys.

On stage, a high-energy, positive speaker will lift the mood of the crowd. A low-energy speaker who is secretly doubting themselves will drag down the mood and leave the next person on stage with a tough challenge to get people back up again.

People can sense our emotions – triggered by the frequency of our inner radio station (see Step Two) – and that influences how they receive our message. It triggers their inner filters and has a major impact on the quality of the conversation.

If a leader's inner dialogue is constantly about 'what if they find out I'm a fraud?' and other fear-based self-talk messages, then that is the 'energy' with which they will be speaking. If their self-talk is coming from a place of confidence, hope and grounded self-assuredness, that will shine through.

The snag is that we rarely use our emotions intentionally when we're speaking, on stage, on the phone or in meetings. The more we push down emotions that make us feel bad, the more we feeding them, subconsciously, the more they will cloud how others receive our message, and the more they will drag down those around us.

Knowing how to connect with others at that deeply positive, emotional level, to inspire them to listen to your message, is the third key to influencing authentically. The first is Courageous Alignment and the second is harnessing the power of your breath to stay grounded and present in this moment, both of which you have just covered. And this third key has a name: intention.

Leading With Intention

Imagine if you prepared for a meeting with someone and, instead of stressing about what you want to *say*, your focus were about how you want them to *feel* at the end of the discussion and what action you want them to take. When we set *that* as our intention and get lined up with that internal state, the words flow and come to us in the right way at the right time.

For example, I was working with a client who had been promoted and was going to be working abroad for a few years. He had built strong relationships with his current team and was concerned about how they might take the news. He had been lying awake at night for a week, worrying about how to explain to them what was happening – what to say.

When we shifted from the *what* to the *who* – who he was going to *be* in that meeting – and he set the intention for how he wanted them to *feel* at the end, he set himself free from worrying about the words. He decided he wanted them to feel safe that the change they were about to go through would be ok. He wanted them to feel inspired to keep performing as well (if not better) with their new manager. And he wanted them to feel happy about what they had all created together. With this as his intention, he wrote down five things he wanted to tell them, lined himself up with that internal state, then took them with him on that inner journey.

He proved to them and to himself that leadership is not so much about what you do and say, but more about who you allow yourself to be. In that moment, he *became* the leader who inspired those three emotional states in his team.

There's a block that gets in the way of us doing this, though...

Our current obsession with leadership models and profiling can help us to gain insights into our behaviours, but it can also over-complicate how we go about leading. When you feel constantly on the look-out for which profile you or someone else is running, you end up stuck in your analytical thinking mind, disconnected from your innate people skills and your intuition. It's as though you have tattooed each person's label onto their forehead and you feel you have to interact with them through that filter.

The very labels we want to avoid, because they keep us stuck in a model's particular 'box', become those through which we process the actions of others.

In my client's case, he was stressing about how Fred was a 'type twelve', so would need to have the information presented in such-and-such a way, whereas Joanna was a 'type seven', so she would need it *this* way. The analysis risked driving him to communication-paralysis and his message failing to inspire.

> *"Happiness is when what you think, what you say and what you do are in harmony."*
> *Gandhi*

I'd take the liberty of adding in an extra on this: they need to be lined up with who you *are* – Courageous Alignment.

The more we can take off our masks, clearing out the hidden blocks that stop our inner diamond from shining, the easier that is. And the easier it becomes to lead and influence authentically, instead of hiding behind our armour; from love, not fear.

Instead of worrying about leadership models and strategies, imagine how much easier your role would be if, before each piece of communication:

- you were to ask yourself what your intention was behind it
- how you wanted the person to *feel* after receiving it
- whether it was coming from a place of love or fear

How might these simple questions shift your experience of leading? How might it affect your team's performance and well-being? And how might it change the results you co-create?

That's the power of leading with intention.

Setting Your Day's Intention

Exercise: Morning Meditation

When you wake up in the morning, before you reach for your phone, sit up in bed and take three deep, sighing breaths – in through your nose and out through your mouth with an 'ahhh' sound. Softly close your eyes.

Become aware of your body. Notice your points of contact with the bed beneath you. And tune in to your breathing, letting your focus rest on it for a few breaths.

When you're ready, ask yourself: "Who will I allow myself to be today?" Give that a name – one or two words. Imagine you can sense this in your chest area, gently expanding with each breath. Breathe in that essence of you. Breathe out as you let go of any blocks that might get in your way.

Continue this for about ten breaths, allowing this essence of you to gently expand throughout your body.

Now ask yourself: "How do I want others to experience me today?" That's your day's intention.

Repeat the process above, this time with your intention expanding effortlessly from your chest area to fill your body – and beyond.

Finally choose one of your mantras to support you through your day and imagine yourself walking through your day, saying your mantra at key points, so that you know you have all the resources you need inside of you to succeed.

As you prepare to release your practice and start your day, take three deep, meaningful breaths with the intention of energising yourself and truly waking up your body, before you open your eyes and put your feet on the floor, fully grounded, right here, right now.

Consciously Creating Your Future:
Mission Vs Goals

One of the most common challenges I see my clients facing is one you might not expect, yet it affects the majority of us: they don't know what they want.

They might be seen as rising stars in their organisation, on the fast-track to senior positions, but they've been so busy in the 'doing' that they have lost their clarity over why they are doing it, or what they want it to lead to. They end up going through the motions and creating their life by accident.

As we discussed in Step One, knowing *why* you want to do something helps to connect you with your inner motivation – the energy to take inspired action and the energy to keep going, even if you're not in the mood. When it comes to your career, though, or even life in general, not knowing what you want can lead to 'busyness', overwhelm, stress, anxiety, listlessness and even depression as the daily grind seems pointless, other than for your salary cheque.

The final thing we're going to do in Step Five is to get you consciously creating your future. You're going to weave in the work about who you really are to help you to decide what you want to create – your big vision. This can change over time and it's a strategy I use for everything from business planning through to course structure design.

I talk about your big vision, rather than goals, because a vision or mission is more powerful than even the biggest goal. A mission or vision is about something you want to become or something you want the world to become. It evokes an emotional response and therefore hits your motivational triggers. Whereas a goal is something you do, so it creates a more cognitive response. Some projects are a combination of both. But if you want to get the most from this section, aim for the *becoming*, rather than the *doing*.

*A vision is about **becoming**. A goal is about **doing**. That's why a vision gets people more excited than a goal. A vision is the **why** behind a goal's **what**.*

Exercise: Consciously Creating Your Future

Start by reviewing your answers to the superpowers exercise on page 247. Write below up to three of your favourites:

Now imagine you can step into a hula hoop on the floor that deeply connects you with one of your superpowers. As you stand in that hula hoop, that superpower washes through each cell in your body. It spreads out around you, washing through everything you think and say and do.

Repeat this with your remaining superpowers.

Now imagine you can travel forward in time to your eightieth birthday party. Your friends and family are surrounding you with love and laughter and you have just blown out the candles on your amazing cake.

In a quiet moment at the party, you think back across those years since you stepped into the hula hoops of your superpowers. You notice the things you achieved and who you allowed yourself to become. You can see how those superpowers are part of your inner genius and how taking off your masks allowed you to do all of this more fully.

What does the 80-year-old you most celebrate about what you created and who you have become? What difference have you been able to make in the world? What did you *stand for*? Let the answers bubble up and make notes in your workbook.

The 80-year-old you wants to give you sign posts along the path, so you know you're on track. They will do this with key achievements and accomplishments. How will you know that you're making progress towards your big vision?

And if the 80-year-old you could give you one insight or piece of advice about the difference you are here to make in the world, what would they love to tell you?

Come back here now and take a moment to make notes on what actions you will take, as a result of what you have now learned.

Leading From Your Heart In A Head-Based World

As we wrap up this section on becoming the leader you were born to be, I'd love to share with you my big vision for the world of leadership: leading from your heart in a head-based world. And, no, it's not woo-woo or spiritual nonsense.

The days of all business leaders having to run the masculine version of a hard-hitting CEO are gone. The businesses getting the best results are those that realise that taking care of the wellbeing of their employees isn't just a box to be ticked, but a value around which to grow their entire business. It's time to lose our fear of the F-word – feelings – and to stop worrying that unless everyone behaves like an automaton the business will fall apart. The opposite is true.

When I talk to business leaders about leading from their heart in a head-based world, they sometimes assume it's about being fluffy and should be reserved for the person in HR who is responsible for employee wellbeing – often a junior role. They tell me they don't want to get overly emotional or into navel-gazing; that leading from your heart is illogical and will cost them business contracts and money; that they don't want to have to have a box of tissues on every desk.

Firstly, none of that is the case, as we'll explore now. And secondly, the days of near-autocratic leadership where the employee is a semi-machine, supposed to be devoid of emotions, are dying. The businesses that are flourishing, even in a tough economy, are those that realise business is about *relationships*, as well as KPIs[22]. They are the ones that realise their teams perform at their best when they are happy, feeling they get to make a difference, where everyone is valued and supported to do what they do best.

None of this comes from the old head-based leadership models. We can't *think* our way to those levels of success and impact. There has to be a *feeling* element, too.

The thinking mind, as we've seen with the Imposter Syndrome Iceberg, is a long way towards the 'effect' end of the scale. When we lead (and live) only from the thinking mind, we end up dealing with sticky plaster solutions to mindset issues and fire-fighting problems.

---

[22] KPI – Key Performance Indicator

When you put our focus into being more of who you really are and leading from your heart, your mind can come along for the ride. No one is asking you to munch lentils and wave joss sticks or swap your suit for a kaftan (though all of these are options!) Then you get to lead with the *whole* of who we are, not just your logical thoughts.

You will never 'think' your way into a breakthrough.

Have you ever had the experience of being, say, in the shower and having a breakthrough on how to solve a problem that has been bugging you? Or being out on a walk and coming up with a brilliant idea? Or chatting with someone and the two of you suddenly realising how to create a fantastic new product or service?

The thinking mind, with its logical, rational preferences, is good for problem solving. But there's more to growing a thriving business than logically solving problems. When we restrict ourselves to mind-level working and leadership, we're missing out on the inner genius that seems to come from nowhere and creates breakthrough ideas, challenging long-held assumptions and expanding possibilities.

To be open to doing this, we need to be working at a level beyond the cognitive mind.

And we need to be working from a place of love, not fear. Remember all of the ways that stress-stories can trash performance? I had a great example of this as I was writing this section of the book. My seven-year-old son had been set some maths homework on a maths website. He normally loves this, because the exercises are games, complete with music, and it feels fun. But last night's homework was different. It was 'against the clock' and every few seconds you would lose five points, if you hadn't solved the next part of the maths puzzle.

The instructions were vague and it took him a little while to work out what was required. The constant time pressure and threat of 'failure' meant he soon couldn't think straight and he 'lost', even though the questions were the kind he'd normally answer quickly and easily. The addition of stress made it impossible for him to solve them. It took him into his fear-zone and it took us an hour to calm down his tears at 'failing' his homework.

People do not deliver their best performance when they are scared or stressed – it's a neuroscience thing, as we've already discussed. Yet so many businesses are run this way. Unreasonable deadlines, fire-fighting, internal politics, quotas, targets and threats of repercussions if these are missed are counter-productive. It is leadership through fear.

Shifting this to be leading from your heart – from a place of love – helps people to feel inspired, safe, more confident, valued, more courageous, more able to speak up with ideas, accepted, calmer, more grounded, and able to give their best performance.

You don't have to throw away your business targets to lead from your heart.
It's not about ditching metrics. It's about shifting the way we inspire people to work towards them.

When you lead from your heart in a head-based world:

- you'll notice you cut stress levels and sickness time
- you'll find that the more intentional communication reduces conflict and improves team performance and morale
- people will be more likely to speak their truth, with compassion, leading to better ideas and more productive meetings
- people will have more self-awareness and will be able to make the most of their strengths
- confidence will increase and Imposter Syndrome will decrease, as people get to be more of who they really are, instead of wearing masks
- commitment to the company's goals will be stronger and people will work smarter, as less time is lost to the Four Ps of Imposter Syndrome – perfection, procrastination, paralysis and people-pleasing

Leading with compassion – from the heart – means that people will raise potential issues sooner, while they're still easier to handle. It's not about diving into woe-is-us sympathy. It's not about indulging everyone's self-talk drama-stories. It's about everyone seeing each other as valid human beings with hopes and dreams and worries and fears, all of which play a vital role in achieving objectives.

I'm curious, with the work you have been doing in this book, what are your thoughts now on leading from your heart in a head-based world? I'd love to hear from you. Details of how to get in touch are in the Readers' Resource Vault.

Exercise: Leading From Your Heart In A Head-Based World

What do you notice is working about leadership in your current environment?

How does your current leadership style or that of those you work with affect you in a positive way?

What, if anything, about your leadership style and behaviour perhaps gets in the way of people working at their own 'inner genius' level?

What does 'leading from your heart in a head-based world' mean to you?

Are there times that leading solely from your 'head' gets in the way of your own or your team's results?

How could you incorporate more of leading from your heart in a head-based world into your working life?

Who Are You Now?

And finally, as we reach the end of Step Five – the final of your five steps to ditching Imposter Syndrome, it's really important to notice the changes you have made in your world as a result of the work you have done in these five steps.

It always amazes me how much progress we can make, without realising. And I don't want that for you, because one of the secrets to staying motivated on this journey is celebrating the changes you *have* made, rather than grumbling about those you haven't.

There will have been exercises that created breakthroughs for you, some of which you resisted (hint: they often hold the secret gems!), and actions you're getting ready to take.

When you can see the progress you have made and have written down your next actions, they are much more likely to happen. And the exercise on the next two pages will also help you to identify what future support you might need, to keep you on track.

So let's wrap up Step Five by reviewing the incredible progress you have made so far and celebrating your successes.

Exercise: Celebrating Your Successes

It's party time! You've made your way through nearly 300 pages of this book. It's time to honour the progress you have made. Allow the answers to the questions below to bubble up, without analysis and without judgement.

What has changed for you with your self-talk and your relationship with your Inner Critic?

Are there any bits of Ditching Imposter Syndrome that you have loved? Which have really resonated with you? Lightbulbs? Insights?

Are there any bits you have avoided? What did avoiding them do for you?

Are there any bits you want to go back and revisit? When will you do that?

What are you going to be doing, saying or thinking differently, as a result of the strategies you have covered?

How are you feeling now about your life? Your career or business? How is that different to from before you started reading this book?

Which shifts have you taken towards your 'Big Why' for ditching Imposter Syndrome (from Step One)?

How has your Big Why changed, for the next stage of your journey?

... continues

And if you could zoom forward in time, five or ten years from now, what advice and encouragement might you give yourself?

Your Action Plan:

Thinking about the very next step on your journey, what actions are you going to take next?

What might derail you?

What support can you put in place, to make sure that doesn't happen?

And finally, how will you make sure you are noticing and celebrating the progress you are making?

I'd love to hear some of your answers on this. If you want a cheerleading happy dance, you can get in touch with me to share your breakthroughs. My current contact details are in the Readers' Resource Vault at www.DitchingImposterSyndrome.com/vault/

I would be honoured to get to celebrate with you why you are hopefully glad that you have read this book!

But this doesn't have to be the end of our journey together. To complete our time together for now, here are some potential 'next steps' on your Imposter Syndrome ditching and leadership journey.

What's Next?

Congratulations! I'm so proud of you for getting to the end of this book. And I can't wait to hear about the shifts you've created already.

As for 'what's next', I would suggest you start by letting these changes settle, so you can get used to the 'new you', before embarking on any other change work. If you got stuck on any of the areas we have covered, you might want to revisit them in a couple of weeks or get yourself some coaching or mentoring, to work through them. There's no point in leaving those blocks hanging around, once you know you want to ditch them.

And if there were any aspects of the work you found yourself resisting, it's worth putting time in your diary to revisit them in a couple of weeks' time – they usually hold surprising gems.

When you're ready for the next step, it would be incredible if you could dive in more deeply on the topics from Step Five – becoming the leader you were born to be. The world is desperate for leaders who are being who they really are, who are passionate about making a positive difference.

Which of the Step Five topic areas resonated with you? Was it Courageous Alignment? Influencing authentically? True resilience? Leading from your heart in a head-based world? Something else?

You will find articles, videos and training, to inspire you with this in the Readers' Resource Vault, including how to connect with your intuition – an essential leadership superpower.

If you're not sure which 'next step' is the right one for you, you can run it through the 'eightieth birthday test' from page 274, to try it on for size, first. Remember: this journey is about who you *allow* yourself to *become*, rather than learning skills or strategies.

Turning the process around, you could imagine who you want yourself to become in, say, five or ten years' time, then walk back in time to work out what you would need to practice and also to let go of between now and then, to allow that version of you to thrive.

Above all, please give yourself a massive congratulatory hug for the journey you have taken through this book. And thank you so much for allowing me to walk by your side as your guide.

Want To Work With Clare?

I have spent the past fifteen years leading workshops, mentoring business leaders and entrepreneurs, and advising forward-thinking businesses on how to support their teams to thrive, creating breakthroughs, not burnout. If you want to work together, here are some options:

Do-It-Yourself

- You might like to read one of my other books (details of some over the page) or listen to my podcast (see Readers' Vault).
- You could take one of my online courses or masterclasses, to deep-dive on topics discussed in this book.

Done-With-You

- You could join one of my group programmes or Masterminds, which can be accessed online from anywhere in the world.
- You could join me for a face-to-face workshop or retreat.

Bespoke

- I have over fifteen years of experience as a professional trainer and can design bespoke programmes to meet your company's needs, including helping you to objectively identify what those needs are.
- I also offer consultancy in leadership, team performance, productivity and innovation.
- I have a handful of places each year for one-to-one mentoring.

Find out which of these might be the best fit for you:

www.DitchingImposterSyndrome.com/vault/ for online and group programmes.
www.ClareJosa.com for workshops, mentoring or bespoke work.

Also By Clare Josa

Dare to Dream Bigger

If you're running your own business, on a mission to change the world, but need to get out of your own way, this book has been described by readers as the 'mentor on their bedside table'.

In Dare to Dream Bigger, Clare guides you through the Seven Cs of Business Breakthroughs, along with the deeper-than-mindset work you need to do to make your business the success you deserve it to be.

Dubbed 'the inside work MBA' by fans, it's essential reading for anyone who is hungry to step out of their comfort zone and take the next big leap in their entrepreneurial journey.

ISBN: 978-1-908854-79-7

Novel:

You Take Yourself With You

If you enjoy drama, intrigue, exploring human nature and conflict - with a generous dollop of humour - then you'll love Clare Josa's compelling debut novel about hope against the odds.

Frequently described by reviewers as 'unputdownable' it's a page-turner that will keep you gripped, but won't give you nightmares!

ISBN: 978-1908854889

Acknowledgements

It takes a village to write a book – or at least that's how it feels. An author can't do it on their own and I certainly wouldn't want to! Huge thank yous go to:

The past fifteen years of clients and students, without whom the methods and insights in this book would not exist. Thank you so much for everything you have taught me.

Lorna Fergusson, my fabulous editor at Fiction Fire: thank you for your innate gift to spot where the structure needed shifting and for helping to make this book better than I could have on my own. Without your encouragement, clarity and humour, this book would not make as much sense as it hopefully now does!

To Jacquie O'Neill: thank you for being such a fabulous designer and intuitively creating a cover I adore, but which I could never have imagined.

To my 2019 Author Masterminders: while I was ostensibly helping you to write your book, you have helped me to write mine, more than you can imagine. Through teaching, we learn. Your enthusiasm, encouragement and questions have inspired me and kept me going, when I was ready to procrastinate. Thank you all so much and I can't wait to read your books!

To my fabulous beta-readers: thank you so much for reading the work-in-progress manuscript and giving me the 'beginner's eyes' feedback I needed to make sure everything makes sense. I'm so grateful to you for taking the time to help me.

To my boys – who have far-too-often had late dinners and a zombie-brained mother: thank you so much for your unconditional support and for understanding how the writing process can take over. I hope that you never need to read this book.

And to my husband Peter, the world's most wonderfully pedantic proof-reader: thank you for believing in me even when my belief in myself wavered. I couldn't have done this without you.

Exercises

Download your companion workbook here:
www.DitchingImposterSyndrome.com/vault/

Index Of Key Terms

Made in the USA
Las Vegas, NV
14 June 2022

50240393R00173